SECOND EDITION

ENGAGING
WRITING 2

Essential Skills for Academic Writing

Mary Fitzpatrick

College of Marin

PEARSON
Longman

Engaging Writing 2: Essential Skills for Academic Writing, Second Edition

Pearson Education, 10 Bank Street, White Plains, NY 10606 USA

Staff credits: The people who made up the *Engaging Writing 2* team, representing editorial, production, design, and manufacturing, are Pietro Alongi, Rhea Banker, Aerin Csigay, Gina DiLillo, Oliva Fernandez, Nancy Flaggman, Gosia Jaros-White, Amy McCormick, Linda Moser, Mary Perrotta Rich, Debbie Sistino, Jennifer Stem, Paula Van Ells, and Patricia Wosczyk.

Cover image: Colin Anderson/Getty Images
Text composition: Rainbow Graphics
Text font: New Aster
Photo credits: see page xxii
Text credits: see page xxii

Library of Congress Cataloging-in-Publication Data

Fitzpatrick, Mary, 1953–
   Engaging writing. 1 : essential skills for academic writing / Mary Fitzpatrick. — 2nd ed.
           p. cm. — (Engaging writing 1 Essential skills for academic writing.)
   ISBN 0-13-608518-0 — ISBN 0-13-248354-8 1. English language—Rhetoric. 2. Report writing. I. Title.
   PE1408.F467 2010
   808'.042076—dc22

                                                                 2010022162

ISBN-13: 978-0-13-248354-4
ISBN-10: 0-13-248354-8

PEARSON LONGMAN ON THE WEB

Pearsonlongman.com offers online resources for teachers and students. Access our Companion Websites, our online catalog, and our local offices around the world.

Visit us at **www.pearsonlongman.com**.

Printed in the United States of America
1 2 3 4 5 6 7 8 9 10—V011—15 14 13 12 11 10

Contents

PART I   **WRITING PARAGRAPHS AND ESSAYS**   1

CHAPTER 1   **Role Models: Writing an Expository Paragraph**   3

This chapter focuses on role models and why they are important to us. Students will review paragraph structure as they write about their own role models or those of a particular social group. In the chapter-opening reading, a second-generation Filipina-American reveals the importance of role models to minority youth.

CHAPTER 2 Culture, Identity, and Homeland: Writing a Division
Paragraph and Essay

*This chapter focuses on culture and ethnic identity. Students will use
logical division to write an expository paragraph about their ethnic
identity, their country, a celebration, or a person's life, and then they will
learn how to expand that paragraph to an essay. In the chapter-opening
reading, a native of New Orleans describes several parts of his unique
ethnic identity.*

CHAPTER 4 Marriage and Family: Writing a Comparison/Contrast Essay   113

This chapter looks at family structure and how it is changing around the world. Students will work on comparison/contrast essays on topics such as married life and single life, the lives of men and women, and changes in courtship and marriage across generations. In the chapter-opening reading, a former member of the Japanese Prime Minister's Gender Equality Council explains how the lives of Japanese women and their families have changed over the past seventy-five years.

This chapter focuses on young people's transition from school to work and the role of education. Students will write an argumentative essay on a topic such as the cost of a college education, the teaching of ethics in schools, and the need to eliminate discrimination in the educational environment. The chapter-opening readings present opposing views on the policy debate about whether high schools should encourage all students to plan for college.

To the Instructor

Engaging Writing 1 and *2* teach students the concepts and skills of academic writing, from paragraphs to essays. These books grew out of the need for materials with thematic lessons, ample modeling, and instruction that is fully integrated with the students' writing process. *Engaging Writing 1* and *2* are comprehensive and user-friendly texts that fully support the needs of intermediate (level 1) and high-intermediate-to-low-advanced (level 2) ESL learners. *Engaging Writing 1* focuses on paragraph writing and introduces the essay in its final chapter; *Engaging Writing 2* begins with a one-chapter review of the paragraph and then concentrates on the essay.

Those familiar with *Engaging Writing* (2005) or *Engaging Writing 1* will recognize in *Engaging Writing 2* the same solid pedagogical features.

- **A well-crafted instructional sequence with clear applications** allows for progressive skill building and varied learning experiences.

- **An emphasis on process** gives students a solid foundation for future academic writing tasks.

- **Multiple realistic models** familiarize students with rhetorical principles and help them set goals for their writing assignments.

- **An appealing and appropriate range of themes and topics** sustains students' interest and acquaints them with academic content.

- **A student-centered, communicative approach** supports engagement and learning for all students.

- **Critical thinking** is demonstrated and encouraged throughout the chapters in pre- and post-reading activities, presentation of the mode, prewriting demonstrations, and revising and editing instruction and tasks.

- **Academic vocabulary** is highlighted, with words from the Academic Word List (Coxhead, 2000) identified in the vocabulary exercises and the glossing of the chapter-opening readings.

- **A complete appendix** provides readily accessible instruction and exercises in grammar and mechanics.

- **Peer review forms** offer a review of the rhetorical instruction of each chapter and provide an opportunity for students to have an audience for their writing.

- **A teacher's manual** offers suggestions for using the text as well as an answer key, and will be available online @ www.pearsonlongman.com/engagingwriting.

New to the Second Edition

Those familiar with *Engaging Writing* (2005) will notice some changes to the second edition, *Engaging Writing 2*.

- *Engaging Writing 2* has two parts: Part I contains the familiar thematically oriented and process-based writing instruction, and Part II teaches the use of source material in writing.

- Part I begins with a new Chapter 1, which reviews paragraph writing and prepares students for Chapter 2, which shows how to expand a paragraph to an essay. Part I has been trimmed to five chapters, a number that can be easily managed in one term. Chapters 2 through 5 teach logical division, cause and effect, comparison/contrast, and argumentative essays, and all have been updated with fresh models and exercises.

- Part II expands upon the paraphrasing and summarizing work that appeared in the first edition. In an easy-to-follow sequence of explanation and practice, Part II informs students about the need for academic honesty and shows them how to quote, paraphrase, summarize, and cite as well as incorporate source material in an essay.

Flexibility

Engaging Writing 2 is designed to give instructors not only a total writing program but also maximum flexibility in meeting the instructional needs of students of diverse abilities, learning styles, and backgrounds. Instructors may select portions of *Engaging Writing 2* to suit their course goals and term length.

- Students needing to review paragraph writing may start with Chapter 1 of Part I, while those ready to expand a paragraph to an essay can begin with Chapter 2. Chapters 2 through 5, which are best done in sequence, present the modes of logical division, cause and effect, comparison/contrast, and argument. Instructors may select those parts of each chapter that best suit their instructional needs. More advanced students will find topics not generally covered in texts of this level, such as the use of concessions and qualifiers in arguments.

- Instructors of academically bound students will want to devote time to Part II, which teaches the use of source material in writing. Part II may be studied concurrently with Part I—for students and instructors alike, working on portions of Part II between the Part I chapters offers an agreeable change of pace. Instructors who intend to have their classes complete all of Part II should begin Part II upon completing Chapter 1 of Part I.

- Appendix IA and IB, which provide grammar and mechanics review, are intended to be used as a reference. Students will find notes within the Part I chapters where specific topics in the Appendix may help them with their writing assignments. In addition, when instructors note gaps in an individual student's knowledge, they may assign portions of the appendix to that student.

Engaging Writing 2 provides a natural sequence to *Engaging Writing 1*. It both builds on the concepts and skills presented in *Engaging Writing 1* and gives students the solid foundation in process, rhetoric, language skills, and the appropriate use of sources that college writing demands. This second edition, with the new Part II, offers instructors greater flexibility to integrate instruction in essay writing and in the use of sources, and, at the same time, it offers students a more complete understanding of what it means to use others' writing in their own texts.

How a Chapter Works

Engaging Writing 2 fully integrates instruction with the students' writing process. Each part of a Part I chapter is designed to meet the students' needs at a specific stage as they prewrite, draft, revise, and complete an assignment.

■ READING FOR WRITING

Before You Read   This informal exercise or activity opens each chapter, giving cues about ideas and issues that run through the reading.

Reading   Students encounter a variety of texts and topics. Each opening reading introduces students to the general theme and the rhetorical focus of the chapter.

Understanding the Reading   The follow-up discussion questions not only promote students' deeper involvement with the content and issues of the reading but also require them to use a full range of critical-thinking skills and to take note of the strategies professional writers use.

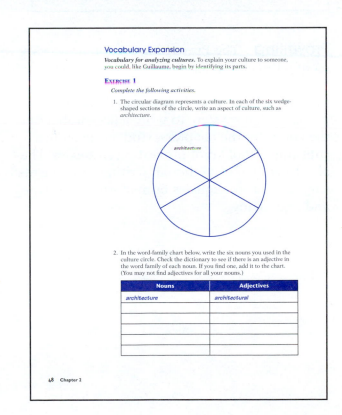

Vocabulary Expansion   Students learn and practice selected vocabulary related to the chapter theme. As they proceed through the text, they learn about broad features of the lexicon, such as word families, and specific features, such as participial adjectives and words that function as more than one part of speech. Short exercises encourage dictionary usage and serve as a warm-up to the chapter writing assignment.

■ WRITING

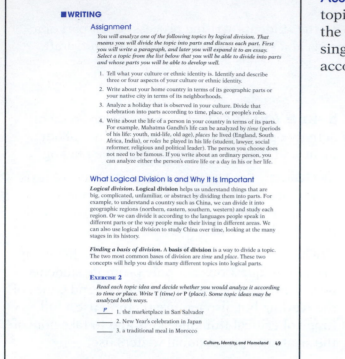

Assignment Students choose one of several topics related to the chapter theme. While all the topics in a chapter require the use of a single rhetorical mode, they vary enough to accommodate multiple interests and ability levels.

Prewriting The Prewriting section provides techniques and tips to help students come up with and organize their ideas and material. In each chapter, a "case study" shows students how to prepare, step-by-step, to write a first draft. Over the course of the chapters, students acquire a substantial tool kit of prewriting strategies. They also learn that even though writing assignments vary, every task requires brainstorming, focusing, and organizing.

■ REVISING

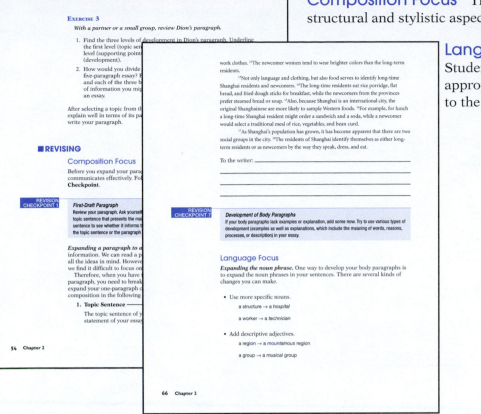

Exercise 3

With a partner or a small group, review Dion's paragraph.

1. Find the three levels of development in Dion's paragraph. Underline the first level (topic sen... level (supporting point... (development).

2. How would you divide... five-paragraph essay? F... and each of the three b... of information you mig... an essay.

After selecting a topic from t... explain well in terms of its pa... write your paragraph.

■ REVISING

Composition Focus

Before you expand your para... communicates effectively. Fo... **Checkpoint.**

REVISION CHECKPOINT 1

First-Draft Paragraph
Review your paragraph. Ask yoursel... topic sentence that presents the ma... sentence to see whether it informs t... the topic sentence or the paragraph...

Expanding a paragraph to a...
information. We can read a p...
all the ideas in mind. Howeve...
we find it difficult to focus on...
Therefore, when you have...
paragraph, you need to break...
expand your one-paragraph c...
composition in the following...

1. **Topic Sentence** ———
   The topic sentence of y...
   statement of your essay...

54 Chapter 2

work clothes. [12]The newcomer women tend to wear brighter colors than the long-term residents.

[13]Not only language and clothing, but also food serves to identify long-time Shanghai residents and newcomers. [14]The long-time residents eat rice porridge, flat bread, and fried dough sticks for breakfast, while the newcomers from the provinces prefer steamed bread or soup. [15]Also, because Shanghai is an international city, the original Shanghainese are more likely to sample Western foods. [16]For example, for lunch a long-time Shanghai resident might order a sandwich and a soda, while a newcomer would select a traditional meal of rice, vegetables, and bean curd.

[17]As Shanghai's population has grown, it has become apparent that there are two social groups in the city. [18]The residents of Shanghai identify themselves as either long-term residents or as newcomers by the way they speak, dress, and eat.

To the writer: _____

_____

_____

REVISION CHECKPOINT 7

Development of Body Paragraphs
If your body paragraphs lack examples or explanation, add some now. Try to use various types of development (examples as well as explanations, which include the meaning of words, reasons, processes, or description) in your essay.

Language Focus

Expanding the noun phrase. One way to develop your body paragraphs is to expand the noun phrases in your sentences. There are several kinds of changes you can make.

- Use more specific nouns.

    a structure → a *hospital*

    a worker → a *technician*

- Add descriptive adjectives.

    a region → a *mountainous* region

    a group → a *musical* group

66 Chapter 2

Appendix II: Peer Review

Peer Review Form

■ **CHAPTER 1—***Role Models*   **EXPOSITORY PARAGRAPH**

WRITER: _____   READER: _____

Read a classmate's paragraph and answer each of these questions.

1. Does the paragraph have three levels?   ❏ yes ❏ no

2. Is the main idea stated in the topic sentence?   ❏ yes ❏ no

   Write the controlling idea of the topic sentence. _____

3. Does the paragraph contain supporting points that are clearly presented in sentences?   ❏ yes ❏ no

4. Did the writer use examples, explanation, or quotations to develop the supporting points?   ❏ yes ❏ no

   Are the examples and explanation specific enough?   ❏ yes ❏ no

   If you would like more detailed examples, write questions to guide the writer.

   _____

5. Did the writer use transitions when necessary to mark the supporting points and examples?   ❏ yes ❏ no

   If yes, write down two transitions the writer used.

6. Does the paragraph contain sentences with subordinating conjunctions? ❏ yes ❏ no

   If yes, write down two subordinating conjunctions the writer used. _____

   _____

7. Does the paragraph have a concluding sentence?   ❏ yes ❏ no

296 Appendix II

Composition Focus This section teaches the structural and stylistic aspects of the chapter mode.

Language Focus
Students learn sentence skills appropriate to their level and to the chapter mode.

■ PEER REVIEW AND FINAL DRAFT
Students exchange papers with their classmates and fill out the assignment's Peer Review Form, which is located in Appendix II. This activity not only reviews the main teaching points of the chapter but also reminds students that they are writing for an audience. After receiving feedback from their peers, students make final changes and proofread before handing their papers in to their instructors.

About the Author and Reviewers

About the Author

Mary Fitzpatrick teaches ESL at the College of Marin in California. She has also taught with the San Francisco Community College District, the Academy of Art University in San Francisco, and Santa Rosa Junior College. Her particular interest is teaching writing to English language learners.

Reviewers

Pearson Longman is grateful to the following individuals who have helped to shape *Engaging Writing 2*:

Carolyn Baughan-Roper, Illinois State University, Normal, IL; **Leslie Biaggi**, Miami-Dade College, Miami, FL; **Joyce Cain**, University of California–Irvine, Irvine, CA; **Sharon Cavusgil**, Georgia State University, Atlanta, GA; **Evelina Dimitrova-Galaczi**, American Language Program and Teachers College, Columbia University, New York, NY; **Anthony Halderman**, Cuesta College, San Luis Obispo, CA; **Janet Harclerode**, Santa Monica College, Santa Monica, CA; **Melanie Holland**, Mt. Hood Community College, Gresham, OR; **Steve Horowitz**, Central Washington University, Ellensburg, WA; **Greg Jewell**, Drexel University, Philadelphia, PA; **Gwendolyn Kane**, Rutgers University, Piscataway, NJ; **Vivian Leskes**, Holyoke Community College, Holyoke, MA; **Thomas Leverett**, Southern Illinois University, Carbondale, IL; **Craig Machado**, Norwalk Community College, Norwalk, CT; **Judy Marasco**, Santa Monica College, Santa Monica, CA; **Molly McGrath**, Hunter College, New York, NY; **Jennifer Murphy**, Georgia State University, Atlanta, GA; **Myo Kyaw Myint**, Mission College, Santa Clara, CA; **David Ross**, Houston Community College, Houston, TX; **Alice Savage**, North Harris Community College, Houston, TX; **Mille Stoff**, Miami-Dade Community College, Miami, FL; **Steven Storla**, Houston Community College, Houston, TX; **Elizabeth Wiegandt**, Miami-Dade Community College, Kendall Campus, Miami, FL.

Acknowledgments

I want to express my thanks to all the people at Pearson Longman who helped to make this book possible including Debbie Sistino, Mary Perrotta Rich, and Malgorzata Jaros-White.

Credits

Text Credits

Page 4: *"Kapwa—Our Shared Identity—and the Influence of Role Models."* Judy Patacsil. Used by permission of the author.

Page 44: "To Be an American, Black, Catholic, and Creole." Dr. Alfred J. Guillaume, Jr. Used by permission of the author.

Page 75: "Global Economic Disparity," *Global Connections: Canadian and World Issues*. Bruce Clark and John Wallace, copyright © 2003, pp. 200-206, Pearson Education. Reprinted with permission of Pearson Canada Inc.

Page 114: "Lifestyle Changes in Japan." Sumiko Iwao. Used by permission of the author.

Page 152: "Should the Purpose of a High School Education Be to Send All Students to College?" "Yes" adapted from "College for All?," *Change*, January/February 2008; "No" adapted from multiple sources.

Page 193: "Serendipity in Science." M. Hayden. Adapted from *Serendipity: Accidental Discoveries in Science* by Royston M. Roberts.

Page 221: "The Rainforest in Your Cup" adapted from Curtis Runyan, "The Rainforest in Your Cup," *World Resources Institute*, January 2004.

Page 224: "The Ecological Capital of Brazil" adapted from *Environmental Science: Earth as a Living Planet*, Fourth Edition, by Daniel Botkin and Edward Keller. Copyright John Wiley and Sons, Inc. Reproduced with permission from John Wiley and Sons, Inc.

Page 225: "The Death of the World's Coral Reefs" by Joshua Reichert from Editorials in *The San Francisco Chronicle*, July 20, 2001. Used by permission of the author.

Photo Credits

Page xxiii, Shutterstock.com; **p. xxiv,** Shutterstock.com; **p. 3,** (top left) Eric Fougere/VIP Images/Corbis, (top right) Russ Elliot/AdMedia/Newscom, (bottom left) AP Images/Kennell Krista/SIPA, (bottom right) Shutterstock.com; **p. 43,** (top left) Adam Jones/Danitadelimont.com/Newscom, (top right) Shutterstock.com, (bottom left) Shutterstock.com, (bottom right) Shutterstock.com; **p. 73,** (top left) Robert Fried/Alamy, (top right) Dinodia Images/Alamy, (bottom left) Kevin R. Morris/Corbis, (bottom right) Marco Cristofori/Alamy; **p. 113,** (top left) Shutterstock.com, (top right) Shutterstock.com, (bottom left) Shutterstock.com, (bottom right) Shutterstock.com; **p. 151,** (top left) Shutterstock.com, (top right) Shutterstock.com, (bottom left) Shutterstock.com, (bottom right) Shutterstock.com.

About *Engaging Writing 2*

Welcome! You are about to begin a new writing class. As you use this book, you will read about new topics, explore ideas, and do a lot of writing. Your writing will improve as you proceed step by step toward writing for academic success. Let's get started by talking about what the title of this book means. Look at the dictionary definition of the verb *engage*.

> **en•gage** /ɪnˈgeɪdʒ/ *v* to attract and keep someone's attention

With a partner or a small group, discuss the following questions.

1. When you talk to people, how do you engage them?

   _____

   _____

   _____

   _____

2. When you write a composition, how do you engage readers?

   _____

   _____

   _____

   _____

To **engage** (or to be engaged) means to be very interested, to be active, to be a part of something, or to make something a part of your life.

When you talk to people, you can smile, make eye contact, ask them if they understand, and watch their faces for signs of interest. When you write, however, you don't have as many ways to be sure that you are engaging your readers.

As a writer, you have to think about the people who will read what you have written. You have to guess what they need to know. You need to be clear and organized so they can follow you. You need to explain things to them and give them examples so that they can experience the things you have seen and heard.

Now look at the dictionary definition of *engage* followed by the preposition *in*.

> **engage in** *v* to take part or become involved in an activity

As you use the chapters of this book, you will engage in reading, discussion, thinking, writing, revising, and editing. Learning to write well takes a lot of effort and engagement. To begin, look at the writing assignment below.

Assignment

As you proceed through the chapters of *Engaging Writing 2* and write your compositions, your teacher and classmates will be your audience. That is, they will be the readers of the papers you write. Write a letter introducing yourself to your teacher and classmates. Tell them about yourself—where you are from originally, where the members of your family live, what your interests are, why you are studying writing, what goals you have for the future, and anything else you can think of that will help them get to know you.

PART I

Writing Paragraphs and Essays

In this first section of *Engaging Writing 2*, you will develop your writing skills. You will start by reviewing paragraph writing and then learn how to expand a paragraph to an essay. As you proceed through Part I, you will write essays of various types—logical division, cause and effect, comparison/contrast, and argument. At the same time, you will master the writing process and improve your sentence skills as well.

In Part II you will develop further academic writing skills. You do not need to finish Part I before you study Part II; in fact, you may begin and work through Part II while you are doing Part I.

Role Models

Writing an Expository Paragraph

In this chapter you will read and write about role models. A role model is a person who serves as an example for other people. In the eyes of those who admire them, role models have special qualities that make them attractive, memorable, and worthy of imitation.

This chapter will help you

- organize ideas from general to specific and put specific details into logical groups.
- develop a prewriting outline.
- write a paragraph with a topic sentence, major supporting points, and specific support.
- add background information to your paragraph.
- use transitions to introduce major supporting points and examples.
- use subordinating conjunctions to join clauses.

Before You Read

Think about the following questions for a few minutes. Take some notes, and then share your ideas with a partner.

1. Have you had people you admired at different times in your life?

2. Did you consider any of these people role models? That is, did you want to be like them?

3. Has any role model had a positive influence on you?

Reading

KAPWA—OUR SHARED IDENTITY— AND THE INFLUENCE OF ROLE MODELS
by Nene Judy Patacsil

1 I am a second-generation Filipina American born and raised in San Diego, California. My name "Nene Judy Patacsil" was given to me by my immigrant parents. The name "Nene" in Filipino refers to the youngest daughter. "Nene" was added to Judy (after the American actress Judy Garland) because of the family tradition to have eight letters in first and last names. My name reflects *kapwa*, which in Filipino means shared identity. Having a shared Filipino and an American name also reflects who I am.

2 My father was twenty-one when he first immigrated to the U.S. in 1928. He came to pursue a graduate degree, but the harsh realities of racism and the Great Depression halted that dream. He stayed, however, and worked menial jobs until Japan bombed Pearl Harbor and the Philippines. He joined the U.S. Army to fight in World War II and met my mother in the Philippines during the war. Since my father was a U.S. citizen, my parents decided that there would be better opportunities for the family in the U.S. They crossed an ocean of dreams and made various sacrifices to start a new life in a new country.

3 I grew up in southeast San Diego. This was one of the primary areas in southern California in the 1950s and 1960s where people of color could purchase property due to **red-lining** and discrimination. The neighborhood was culturally diverse, somewhat impoverished, and consisted of African Americans, Latino Americans, and a small group of Filipino Americans. I had friends from various ethnic groups and races, and this influenced me to have a strong commitment to diversity.

4 The first generation of Filipino Americans at that time, including my parents, attempted to remain close-knit within their own ethnic group. They formed Filipino American organizations such as the Filipino Women's Club, the Ilocano Friendship Club, and the House of Philippines. They

red-line: *to refuse home mortgages to areas considered to be high risk; in effect, a discriminatory practice*

spoke their Filipino dialects including Ilocano and Tagalog. They celebrated events such as José Rizal Day, in honor of the national hero of the Philippines, and Philippine Independence Day, and worked to maintain their cultural connection to the homeland. For their children, they emphasized maintaining Filipino cultural values, such as respect for elders, close family relationships, and an internalized sense of debt called *utang na loob*, which means reciprocal obligation. This describes the permanent sense of gratitude and indebtedness that children feel towards their parents for the gift of life. Although my parents spoke a Filipino dialect to each other, due to fear of discrimination in the U.S., they often avoided the Filipino language in our home and spoke only English to their children.

5   Growing up, I received double messages about my Filipino culture. My parents tried to show us that the Filipino culture was important. Yet we knew our culture was not recognized as such by **mainstream** America. Filipinos and even other ethnic groups were seldom seen in the media. I saw that my parents, like other first-generation Filipino American immigrants, were not recognized as Americans. Instead, they were seen as foreigners regardless of their citizenship even though many of them, like my father, fought for the United States during World War II. As a teenager, I wanted to find role models to look up to that mainstream Americans would also admire. I watched as my siblings struggled with who they were, each of them identifying either with the Filipino culture of the Philippines or the White, Black, or Latino cultures of the United States. There was no clear image or role showing what a Filipino American of our generation was to be.

6   As a child, I had identified more with the Black, or African American, culture, thinking that the African American group represented America, at least for people of color. I identified with their struggle and with their hopes and dreams for empowerment and recognition. However, I soon began to realize that America did not really accept African Americans, nor did it readily accept other people of color as Americans. I came to the realization that being American meant being white.

7   I also struggled throughout adolescence, trying to find that role of being Filipina American, and so I chose a best friend who was biracial Filipino and white, someone who I thought represented who I was, a person who was Filipina and also American. I became involved in the Filipino American student organizations in high school and community college. It was there that I finally made connections with Filipino American role models, which helped with my **identity resolution**. These role models were sons and daughters of first-generation early immigrants who had experienced their own struggles of **acculturation** and ethnic identity resolution through the 1950s and 1960s. Though their numbers were few, some of them were active in the community and asserted an American identity that included pride in being brown and

(continued)

mainstream: *refers to the majority or dominant group*

✳**identity resolution:** *the process of finding solutions to questions about one's own identity, usually during adolescence*

acculturation: *the process of adapting to a new culture*

Filipino. They learned the history, the struggles, and the contributions of Filipino Americans in this nation. They reached out to youth and young adults and served as role models. They helped me transfer to a university and pursue my education, the dream my parents had for each of their five children. Although all of my siblings attended colleges or universities, I was the only one to fulfill that dream of completing a Bachelor's, Master's, and doctoral degree. My siblings had the ability and opportunity to do the same, but for some reason they did not complete their education. They had few Filipino American peers in college. There seemed to be even fewer Filipino American role models who had finished college and who could encourage them or pave a path for them to follow.

8   The limited number of Filipino Americans who did finish their college education made efforts to be role models. They worked as counselors with ethnic outreach programs such as the Educational Opportunity Program (EOP), peer-counseling programs, and grant-funded programs that focused on uplifting the Filipino American community, and sometimes they did so as volunteers. They set a path for me to follow and contributed to my journey of ethnic identity resolution. I often wonder what would have happened if I had not had access to some of those role models. I ask myself if I would have attended college. Although I had the grades to attend college in high school, my counselor did not encourage me to apply. I also wonder if I would have learned to take pride in my heritage and sought to learn more about who I am as a Filipina American, if it had not been for my own experience and exposure to the few Filipino American role models I met.

9   A role model is a special person who shows others how to perform behaviors, provides a reference point, and serves as a reinforcer (Kemper, 1968). Role models may provide positive lessons about how to act as well as negative lessons that discourage undesirable behaviors (Gipson & Cordova, 1999). I have seen how interactions between youth in the Filipino American community and older members provide a sense of **validation** for youth. This validation can lead to the formation of positive ethnic identity. This is demonstrated in the youth taking classes in Filipino language or Filipino martial arts, and making informed decisions to avoid getting involved with gangs.

10   Role models have been an area of interest for me for many reasons. I found that my role models significantly impacted who I am today, what I decided to do professionally, and my commitment to the community. Looking back, I realize now the first role models who helped me understand my culture were my parents. My parents and other active members in the community helped me with identity resolution and contributed to my developing pride in who I am as a Filipina American. In community college I met a Filipino Studies instructor who also helped motivate me and inspired me to transfer to San Diego State University and continue my education. Professionally and personally, I have a strong commitment to the community, as I hope to do for others what my parents and active community members did for me. I work in

✳**validation:** *respect or social acceptance*

the field of education and I am very active in giving back to the community. I do so with the hope of coming full circle and serving as a role model to others.

Gipson, D. & Cordova, D. (1999). Women's and men's role models: The importance of exemplars. In A. Murrell, F. Crosby, & R. Ely (Eds.), *Mentoring Dilemmas: Developmental relationships within multicultural organizations.* Mahwah, N.J.: Lawrence Erlbaum Associates, Publishers.

Kemper, T. (1968). Reference groups, socialization and achievement. *American Sociological Review, 33,* 31-45.

ABOUT the AUTHOR Judy Patacsil is a counselor and professor at San Diego Miramar College. She teaches Filipino studies and psychology and also is a licensed psychotherapist.

Understanding the Reading

With a partner or a small group, discuss the following.

1. How does Patacsil's first name, "Nene Judy," reflect her identity?

2. How did Patacsil's parents try to help their children form identities as Filipino Americans?

3. As a child, what negative messages did Patacsil receive about her identity as a Filipina American?

4. What kind of role models did Patacsil look to as a child? What kind of role models did she look to as a high school and community-college student? Why did it take her so long to find these role models?

5. Do you think role models are more important in minority communities than in majority communities? Why or why not?

6. In academic writing, authors often present a general idea and follow it with examples. Notice these three sentences from the end of paragraph 9:

   > I have seen how interactions between youth in the Filipino American community and older members provide a sense of validation for youth. This validation can lead to the formation of positive ethnic identity. [This is demonstrated in the youth taking classes in Filipino language or Filipino martial arts, and making informed decisions to avoid getting involved with gangs.]

   examples

   Locate two more examples in the reading, and write "example" in the margin. Then find the general point each one illustrates and underline it. Share your findings with your teacher and classmates.

7. *Source notes:* The names and dates in parentheses refer to authors' published works. [For example, "(Kemper, 1968)" in paragraph 9 refers to an article by Kemper.] When we use an author's words or report on his or her research, we need to identify the source. Sources are usually listed at the end of the reading. How many sources are listed for this reading?

Vocabulary Expansion

Dictionary use and word families. As you write, you will discover that you need to expand your vocabulary. When you consult your dictionary, you will find that the dictionary can give you the meaning of not just one word, but of related groups of words, or word families. Look at these three word families. Notice that in two of the three examples the word endings for nouns and adjectives are different.

respect (noun) a feeling that someone deserves special consideration because of his or her qualities or achievements

respected (adjective) relating to someone who deserves special consideration because of his or her qualities or achievements

model (noun) someone or something that provides an example which people want to copy

model (adjective) relating to someone or something with good qualities that people want to copy

profession (noun) a job that needs a high level of education and training

professional (adjective) relating to a job that needs education and training

For more on nouns, see Appendix IA, page 262, and for more on adjectives, see Appendix IA, page 235.

In this book, words that belong to the **Academic Word List** (a list of the 570 most common word families found in college texts) are identified with a star (✳) symbol.

EXERCISE 1

A. *Use your dictionary to complete the word-family chart below and on the following page.*

		Nouns	Adjectives
1.		accomplishment	*accomplished*
2.		ambition	
3. ✳		commitment	
4.		compassion	
5.		confidence	
6. ✳		cooperation	
7.		courage	

	Nouns	Adjectives
8.	determination	
9. ✳	devotion	
10.	diligence	
11.	discipline	
12.	dynamism	
13. ✳	focus	
14.	frugality	
15.		generous
16.		imaginative
17.		ingenious
18. ✳		innovative
19.		level-headed
20.		modest
21.		passionate
22.		persistent
23.		practical
24. ✳		resourceful
25.		sincere
26.		supportive
27.		trustworthy
28.		unselfish

B. *Some word endings often appear on nouns. From the words in this chart, identify four endings for nouns:*

_____, _____, _____, _____.

Some word endings often appear on adjectives. From the words in this chart, identify four endings for adjectives:

_____, _____, _____, _____.

 For more on word endings (suffixes), see Appendix IA, page 287.

C. *Choose an appropriate word and word form from the chart in Exercise 1A to complete each example. (You may find more than one possible answer.) If the word you choose is a noun, write (n.) after the sentence, and if it is an adjective, write (adj.).*

1. My father said, "It is true that I have been successful in business, but I attribute my success to the love and support of my family." He taught us by example to be __*modest*__. (*adj.*)

2. "I always keep my word. That way, I keep my friends," says Joe. He is a _____ person. (   )

3. Uncle Rigoberto, who is a police officer, said, "Everyone is frightened sometimes, but we would never accomplish anything without mastering fear." I admire his _____. (   )

4. Benjamin Franklin said, "If you [want to] be wealthy, think of saving as well as getting." Franklin encouraged _____. (   )

5. My aerobics teacher Helen is very _____. As she exercises, she continually smiles and talks, motivating the class by saying, "Hey, everybody, you're doing great. Let's work a little harder now." (   )

6. My older sister went to the local tailor and asked him to teach her to make clothes in exchange for cleaning his shop. Then she bought a sewing machine and made some clothes on her own. She sold the clothes to pay tuition for college. I admire my older sister's _____. (   )

7. My great uncle stressed the value of _____. He always said, "Things that are worthwhile don't come easily. It takes about twenty years to become really successful at anything." (   )

8. Mrs. Jones taught us _____. She often said, "If you believe you are going to be something, you will eventually become that." (   )

9. Oscar is a very _____ person. He studies from 9:00 P.M. to midnight and then gets up at 4:00 A.M. and studies until 7:00. Then he goes to work. (   )

10. Jun always said, "I keep my eye on my goal and never look back." I respect him for his _____. (   )

11. I was inspired by Hana's _____. She did volunteer work in a free medical clinic, made sandwiches for the homeless, and visited elderly people during her free time. (   )

12. Papa is a _____ man. He figured out how to charge the car battery by connecting it to the household electricity. Papa says, "Any problem can be solved. It just takes a little creativity." (   )

■ WRITING

Assignment

Choose one of the following topics and write a three-level paragraph containing examples. Use correct paragraph form as shown on page 13.

1. Introduce and explain a role model you have now or one that you had during an earlier time in your life. Discuss two or three *characteristics*, or qualities, of this role model, and develop each characteristic with examples.

2. Explain a kind of role model chosen by a social group, society, or culture. Discuss two or three characteristics of this kind of role model, and support each characteristic with examples.

    One example of a kind of role model is the type of person who grew up poor and became wealthy through planning and hard work. For example, Andrew Carnegie is someone who went from "rags to riches," so people in the United States looked up to him, especially during the early twentieth century.

These assignments ask you to discuss characteristics of role models. That means that you cannot just describe a role model or tell the story of a role model. You will need to identify two or three qualities of a role model or a kind of role model, and organize the paragraph around them.

What Expository Writing Is and Why an Expository Paragraph Has Three Levels

The assignments on page 11 ask you to *explain*. Writing that explains is called **expository writing**. In expository writing, you need to do two things: provide specific information, and organize that information. First, collect specific details or examples to illustrate your topic. Second, once you have collected your examples, organize them in logical groups. Each group will be about one characteristic of the topic. Because you will be grouping details and connecting the groups to the more general characteristics, readers will then be able to see how your details support your ideas.

To help readers follow your thinking, your expository paragraph will have three levels: 1) a **main point** presented in a topic sentence, 2) major **supporting points,** which identify the characteristics of the topic, and, finally, 3) **specific support (examples, explanations,** or **quotations)**.

THE TOPIC SENTENCE

Supporting Points

Specific examples

The Topic Sentence (Level 1)

We usually make our main point in one sentence at or near the beginning of a paragraph, which is called a **topic sentence**. It is usually the most general sentence in a paragraph. Its purpose is to help the reader focus on the topic and to prepare the reader for the supporting points that follow. Look at this topic sentence and supporting sentences.

> TOPIC SENTENCE (LEVEL 1):
>
> My father is my role model because he is kind, generous, and trustworthy.
>
> MAJOR SUPPORTING POINTS (LEVEL 2):
>
> My father shows kindness to everyone, but especially to his children.
>
> Generosity is another of my father's qualities.
>
> Everyone who knows my father has found him to be a trustworthy man.

The Major Supporting Points (Level 2)

The supporting points are more specific than the topic sentence but more general than the details or examples. The supporting points must be clearly stated in the paragraph because they connect the topic sentence and the examples. The topic sentence and the supporting points are marked in this paragraph.

Uncle Wei

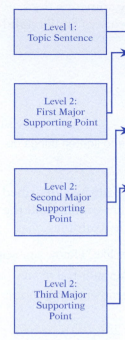

Level 1:
Topic Sentence

Level 2:
First Major
Supporting Point

Level 2:
Second Major
Supporting
Point

Level 2:
Third Major
Supporting
Point

[1]My role model is my Uncle Wei, who is a tax accountant, because he is very careful, honest, and funny. [2]First, Uncle Wei takes great care with everything he does. [3]I remember one night around midnight I found Uncle Wei working at his desk. [4]I asked him what kept him up so late. [5]He said he suspected there was an error in a tax return and he would search for it until he found it—even if it meant staying up all night. [6]Second, Uncle Wei prides himself on being very honest. [7]If a client's finances are in bad shape, he tells him or her so directly. [8]And if someone wants Uncle Wei to make false statements on a tax return, he refuses to comply and stops doing business with that person. [9]Finally, Uncle Wei is also a joker. [10]Taxes put people in a grumpy mood, so Uncle Wei tries to lighten things up with little jokes like "I know you would like to pay your taxes with a smile, but I'm afraid the government wants real money," or "I hear the coming year will be the one when the government lowers taxes . . . it always is." [11]Everyone who knows Uncle Wei appreciates his care, honesty, and sense of humor, and I hope to be like him some day.

Specific Support (Level 3)

If your paragraph has a topic sentence and supporting points, but no specific support, your readers may say, "Why is that important?" or "I don't think that's true." Readers do not see the importance or truth in what they read without specific support, or development. To convince readers, a paragraph needs a well-developed third level. Here are three ways you can develop the third level of your paragraph.

1. **Examples** are descriptions of situations or events that support general ideas. You can use examples to help readers understand and remember your major supporting points.

   SUPPORTING POINT:

   Uncle Wei takes great care with everything he does.

   EXAMPLE:

   I remember one night around midnight I found Uncle Wei working at his desk. I asked him what kept him up so late. He said he suspected there was an error in a tax return and he would search for it until he found it—even if it meant staying up all night.

2. **Explanations** tell what something means or why someone does something. You can use explanations to add to readers' understanding of your major supporting points.

SUPPORTING POINT:

Uncle Wei is also a joker.

EXPLANATION:

Taxes put people in a grumpy mood, so Uncle Wei tries to lighten things up with little jokes . . .

3. **Quotations** are someone's actual words. They are always identified by quotation marks. Use quotations to help readers understand the major supporting points and to add interest to the examples.

> . . . Uncle Wei tries to lighten things up with little jokes like "I know you would like to pay your taxes with a smile, but the government wants real money," or "I hear the coming year will be the one when the government lowers taxes . . . it always is."

TIP
The topic sentence may not be the first sentence in a paragraph, but it will be near the beginning. The last sentence in each of these paragraphs is a concluding sentence, which is not part of the specific support.

EXERCISE 2

Read the paragraphs. Underline the topic sentences, put a double line under the major supporting points, and put brackets [ ] around the specific support. In the margin next to the paragraph, identify the kind of support as "example," "explanation," or "quotation." The first part of the first paragraph has been done for you.

1.   **Se Ri Pak**

explanation
and quotation

¹My role model is Se Ri Pak, the South Korean golfer, because she has two great qualities. ²First, during her fourteen-year career in professional golf, Pak has shown that she is determined to be the best. [³Although she has had some low points in her career, she has never given up. ⁴Pak said, "There have been some ups and downs, sometimes an unlucky bounce here and there, but it makes me work harder."] ⁵Second, Pak is a person with initiative. ⁶ That means she makes decisions and takes action without waiting for others to act. ⁷In one tournament, Pak had hit her ball into a pond. ⁸Instead of taking the penalty, she removed her shoes and socks, waded into the water, hit the ball out of the pond, and went on to win the championship. ⁹I admire Pak's determination and initiative a great deal and would like to be like her as I work toward my athletic goals.

Stewart, Mark. *Se Ri Pak: Driven to Win.* Brookfield, Connecticut: Millbrook Press, 2000.

"Se Ri Pak Looking for Fifth Major Win at U.S. Women's Open." *The Morning Call* 29 June 2009.
  1 Aug 2009 <http://www.mcall.com/sports/golf/all-s-pak.69411599jun29,0,7567614.story>.

2.

Muhammad Yunus

[1]My role model is Muhammad Yunus, an economist who started a banking system for the poor. [2]I admire Yunus because he is compassionate and he is a practical problem-solver. [3]First, Yunus, who was an economics professor in Bangladesh, was sensitive to the problems of poor people. [4]He said, "What good were all my complex theories when people were dying of starvation on the sidewalks and porches across from my lecture hall?" [5]Yunus studied village life and discovered that if poor people could borrow tiny sums of money, they could better support themselves and their families. [6]As a result, he started a bank to serve the needs of the poorest people, and it has reduced poverty significantly. [7]Second, Muhammad Yunus is a practical problem-solver. [8]For example, Yunus had to figure out how to secure the loans made to poor people. [9]Banks usually lend only to people who own property, but poor people have no property that a bank can use to secure a loan. [10]Yunus's solution was to require borrowers to join groups because the social pressure of group membership encourages people to pay back their loans. [11]In addition, Yunus has worked to solve other problems in Bangladesh such as communication problems and malnutrition. [12]I admire Muhammad Yunus greatly and hope to cultivate compassion and a practical approach to problems in my own life.

Yunus, Muhammad. *Banker to the Poor: Micro-lending and the Battle against World Poverty*. New York: Public Affairs, 1999.

The Writing Process

Making an outline. An **outline** shows the structure of a three-level paragraph. Writers use outlines to organize their ideas before they write.

Main Idea (Topic Sentence)
  I. Major Supporting Point
      A. Specific Support (examples, explanation, quotations)
      B. Specific Support (examples, explanation, quotations)
  II. Major Supporting Point
      A. Specific Support (examples, explanation, quotations)
      B. Specific Support (examples, explanation, quotations)
  III. Major Supporting Point
      A. Specific Support (examples, explanation, quotations)
      B. Specific Support (examples, explanation, quotations)

EXERCISE 3

Read the paragraphs. Underline the topic sentences, put a double line under the major supporting points, and put brackets [ ] around the specific support. Then complete the outlines. Note that these paragraphs have concluding sentences. You should not include the concluding sentences in the outlines.

1.   **Lionel Messi**

¹The Argentinian soccer player, Lionel Messi, is my role model because of his fighting spirit and ability to shoot goals. ²First of all, Messi, who has played for both Barcelona and Argentina, is a fighter. ³At 1.69 meters (5 feet 7 inches) tall, Messi, who was nicknamed "the flea," plays fearlessly against much bigger athletes, moving around them with speed and agility. ⁴Moreover, Messi has fought back from several serious injuries including several muscle tears and a broken bone, and he has come back stronger each time. ⁵Second, Messi, who is left-footed, is able to make fast, accurate goals, even from difficult positions on the field. ⁶He has a career record of over 125 goals, including three hat tricks (games in which a player scores three goals) and one match in which he scored four goals. ⁷Perhaps his most spectacular goal was in the Spanish Cup of 2007, when he ran sixty meters in ten seconds, passed five rivals, and shot past the goalie. ⁸I admire Messi for his spirit and his skill, and I would like to play like him some day.

The Argentinian soccer player, Lionel Messi, is my role model because of his fighting spirit and ability to shoot goals.

    I. Messi is a fighter.

        A. Messi is short, but he plays fearlessly against much bigger athletes.

        B. After several serious injuries, he has come back stronger each time.

   II. _____

        A. career record of over 125 goals

        B. _____

2.   **The Sage Kings**

¹For thousands of years of Chinese history, legendary kings were the role models for the whole society; these sage, or wise, kings had exemplary qualities and showed both rulers and ordinary citizens how to be frugal, resourceful, and devoted to the common good. ²One characteristic the Chinese of the past valued is frugality, and King Yao, who ruled around 2350 B.C.E., exemplified this virtue. ³Yao ate coarse rice and herb soup although he could afford better food. ⁴He lived simply in a thatched-roof house and never got new clothes until his old clothes wore out. ⁵Another characteristic the Chinese valued is resourcefulness, and King Shun, who ruled around 2250 B.C.E., exemplified this

quality. [6]Shun trained an elephant to help him with farming. [7]He also fished and made his own pottery. [8]A final trait admired by the Chinese is devotion to the common good, and King Yu, whose rule began in 2205 B.C.E., exemplified this virtue. [9]Yu stayed with his wife only a few days after their wedding before going into the field to solve China's flood control problem. [10]He worked for thirteen years, digging channels and dredging the rivers, never going home to visit his family, though he passed his house three times. [11]Yao, Shun, and Yu, as well as other exemplary rulers, were admired and imitated by the Chinese for centuries.

For thousands of years of Chinese history, legendary kings were the role models for the whole society; these sage, or wise, kings had exemplary qualities and showed both rulers and ordinary citizens how to be frugal, resourceful, and devoted to the common good.

    I. frugality, King Yao

        A. _____

           _____

        B. lived simply in a thatched-roof house and never got new clothes until his old clothes wore out

   II. _____

        A. trained an elephant to help him with farming

        B. _____

           _____

  III. devotion to the common good, King Yu

        A. stayed with his wife only a few days after their wedding before going into the field to solve China's flood control problem

        B. _____

           _____

NOTE
The first level of an outline (the topic sentence) must be a complete sentence. The second and third levels do not have to be complete sentences.

Exercise 4

*Read the topic sentence and the major supporting points of each brief outline. Then look at the list of specific details, and decide which part of the outline each detail should go in. Write **I**, **II**, or **III** next to each specific detail.*

TOPIC SENTENCE ⌐ 1. My role model is Nestor, a self-made man, a lawyer who is committed to social justice, and a modest person.

    I. Nestor became a lawyer through his own efforts.

    II. Nestor is committed to helping others.

    III. Nestor is modest.

      II a. Nestor spends much of his free time asking for donations to fund his nonprofit organization.

      _____ b. When asked about the number of people he has helped, Nestor smiles and quietly says, "I do what I can."

      _____ c. As an immigrant to the U.S. from Mexico, Nestor learned English in high school and was the first in his family to go to college.

      _____ d. He assists people who experience injustice but who cannot afford to hire lawyers for themselves.

      _____ e. Nestor's legal work does not pay as much as other types of legal work, but he does it because he believes poor communities need his services.

      _____ f. Nestor studied diligently and graduated with honors.

      _____ g. He works on cases involving employment discrimination and immigrant rights.

2. Yao Ming, a star basketball player with the Houston Rockets, is my role model for two reasons.

I. Yao has a cooperative team spirit.

II. Yao is adaptable and able to cross between cultures.

_____ a. When Yao joined the National Basketball Association in the U.S., he had to get used to a new style of play that was more aggressive. He adjusted to the NBA style over the course of his first year in the U.S.

_____ b. When Yao is sitting on the bench and a teammate makes a good play, he stands up and applauds and gives the player high-fives when he returns to the bench.

_____ c. Yao thinks that a team win is much more important than the number of baskets he makes in a game.

_____ d. When Yao arrived in the U.S., his coaches started talking to him in English without a translator although he didn't understand. Now, Yao can speak English and even "talk trash" like other NBA players.

Prewriting. To write well, you must do a lot of thinking about the topic before you begin to write. We call the thinking we do before writing **prewriting**. Prewriting means gathering ideas (**brainstorming**) and selecting ideas that are related to each other and that you can develop (**focusing**). There are a number of techniques you can use to brainstorm and focus. One of the most common is making **lists** of ideas and then selecting items from the lists. In this section, you will learn how to use lists and outlines to prepare to write a paragraph.

In each chapter in this book, you will see how one student accomplished prewriting, focusing, organizing, and writing the first draft. As you read through this section, you will see how Miguel, a student from Mexico, used a series of steps as he prepared to write a paragraph about his role model.

Complete steps 1–3, do Exercises 5–7 on pages 23–25, and then write your first draft.

Miguel's Steps

STEP 1

Make a **list** of three or four characteristics of a (kind of) role model. Write the characteristics across the top of another piece of paper. Under each characteristic, write details and examples. If you can remember any quotations, include them too. Then review your notes, and cross out any information that is not closely related to one of the characteristics.

Miguel wrote down three characteristics of his high school physical education teacher and made three lists. Then he crossed out ideas that were not related.

Fairness:
- stressed knowing the rules and playing by them
- He showed equal interest in every student; he had no favorites.
- ~~talked to us about the rules of international competitions~~
- "Fairness is one goal we all can share."

Patience:
- never raised his voice in anger

Self-discipline:
- worked out with every P.E. class he taught all day, every day
- was assistant principal, and he used to get to work at 7:00 A.M. to do his office work
- wore nothing but white, and his clothes were always fresh and clean
- ~~made us do push-ups, sit-ups, chin ups, and jumping jacks, and we had to run more laps than the soccer team~~
- ~~made us wear a clean white uniform; no uniform, no practice; dirty uniform, lose points~~
- was never late for class

STEP 2 Evaluate your lists to see how much supporting information you have for each characteristic, and select the characteristics that you can best develop in your paragraph. Draft a topic sentence. You can revise the topic sentence later.

Miguel decided to focus on two characteristics, fairness and self-discipline, because he did not have enough information for a third supporting point. He drafted the following topic sentence.

> *Mr. Jimenez, my high school physical education teacher, was an excellent role model because he set an example of fairness and self-discipline.*

STEP 3 Use the ideas on your lists to make an **outline**. Decide how to organize the major supporting points and the specific details as you work on the outline.

Miguel's outline shows three levels of development: first, the topic sentence (**TS**), then the major supporting points (**SP**), and, finally, development with examples, explanation, and a quotation (**DEV**).

> *Mr. Jimenez, my high school physical education teacher, was an excellent role model because he set an example of fairness and self-discipline. (TS)*
>
>   I. *Mr. Jimenez was fair. (SP)*
>   A. *Even during practice, he stressed knowing the rules and playing by them. (DEV)*
>   B. *used to remind us, "Fairness is one goal we all can share." (DEV)*
>   C. *showed equal interest in every student; he had no favorites (DEV)*
>   II. *He modeled self-discipline. (SP)*
>   A. *was never late for class (DEV)*
>   B. *wore nothing but white, and his clothes were always fresh and clean (DEV)*
>   C. *He was the assistant principal, and he used to get to work at 7:00 A.M. to do his office work before he began teaching. (DEV)*
>   D. *worked out with every P.E. class he taught all day, every day (DEV)*

With his outline complete, Miguel was ready to write.

Miguel's First Draft

Draft #1 ○	Miguel Reyes September 8, 2010 Mr. Jimenez, Always in My Memory
	[1]Mr. Jimenez, my high school physical education teacher, was an excellent role model because he set an example of fairness and self-discipline. [2]First, Mr. Jimenez did everything in a way that was fair. [3]Even during practice, he stressed knowing the rules and playing by them. [4]He used to remind us, "Fairness is one goal we all can share." [5]He showed equal interest in every student; he had no favorites. [6]Second, Mr. Jimenez taught us self-discipline because he modeled it for us. [7]For instance, he was never late for class. [8]He wore nothing but white, and his clothes were always fresh and clean. [9]He worked extremely hard. [10]He was the assistant principal, and he used to get to work at 7:00 A.M. to do his office work, and then he worked out with every P.E. class he taught all day, every day. [11]Mr. Jimenez taught me two very important lessons, fairness and self-discipline, and I will always remember him.

Find the three levels of development in Miguel's first draft paragraph on page 22. Underline the topic sentence, put a double line under the major supporting points, and put brackets [ ] around the specific support (examples, explanations, and quotations).

After Miguel worked through the rest of this chapter, he completed this final draft.

Miguel's Final Draft

Miguel Reyes
September 17, 2010

Mr. Jimenez, Always in My Memory

¹Mr. Jimenez, my high school physical education teacher, was an excellent role model because he set an example of fairness and self-discipline. ²First, Mr. Jimenez did everything in a way that was fair. ³Even during practice, he stressed knowing the rules and playing by them. ⁴For example, those who cheated had to stand on the sidelines and watch. ⁵He used to remind us, "Fairness is one goal we all can share." ⁶He showed equal interest in every student; he had no favorites. ⁷He advised every one of us on ways to do better and praised us when we improved. ⁸Second, Mr. Jimenez taught us self-discipline because he modeled it for us. ⁹He had high standards, and he never failed to meet those standards. ¹⁰For instance, he was never late for class. ¹¹He wore nothing but white—white shirt, white shorts, white socks, white shoes, white visor cap—and his clothes were always fresh and clean. ¹²He worked extremely hard. ¹³He was the assistant principal, and he used to get to work at 7:00 A.M. to do his office work, and then he worked out with every P.E. class he taught all day, every day. ¹⁴Mr. Jimenez taught me two very important lessons, fairness and self-discipline, and I will always remember him.

EXERCISE 6

Review Miguel's final draft.

1. Can you find any information that Miguel added as he wrote his final draft? If so, put brackets around that information.

2. What kind of information did Miguel add? In the margin next to each sentence you have bracketed, write **example** or **explanation** to identify the kind of information Miguel added.

After studying the following section about paragraph form, follow the sequence of steps Miguel used and write your first draft.

Paragraph form. Miguel's first draft is handwritten, and his final draft is typed. Whenever you write a paragraph to hand in to your teacher—whether you write it by hand or type it—follow these guidelines.

- Put the title in the middle of the top line of your paper. Always use a capital letter for the first word in the title. Use capital letters for all other words except for articles, prepositions, and conjunctions, such as *and* or *but*.

An Important Role Model in My Life

- Indent the first line of the paragraph five spaces.
- Use a capital letter for the first letter of the first word in each sentence.
- Each line should end at about the same place on the right.
- If you are handwriting, use lined paper with a margin line on the left. Except for the first line of the paragraph (which is indented), your writing should start next to the margin line.
- If you are typing, double space and use a 12-point type.

 For more on capital letters, see page 289 in Appendix IB.

Review Miguel's first and final drafts for correct paragraph form. Answer these questions by putting checks (✔) after each rule Miguel followed.

	Miguel's First Draft	Miguel's Final Draft
1. The title is in the center at the top of the page. If the paper is handwritten, it is on the top line.	✔	
2. The first word in the title has a capital letter, and all other words except for articles, prepositions, and conjunctions also have capital letters.		
3. The first line of the paragraph is indented five spaces.		
4. In the handwritten draft, Miguel wrote inside the margin line on the left. He also left a margin on the right.		
5. In the typed draft, there is a margin on both the left and the right.		
6. Miguel wrote his name and the draft number on the top of the page.		

■ REVISING

All writers revise, or rewrite, to improve their writing. Even experienced writers cannot produce good writing in just one attempt; sometimes it takes many drafts. Students usually need to write about three drafts in order to produce a piece of writing that is complete, clear, and correct.

Tips for Revising

- After you've written your draft, set it aside for a few hours or days. When you pick it up again, you will be better able to see it as others see it. This helps you determine what information to include and what connections to strengthen.

- Look at your draft often. Don't be afraid to cross words out or add new ideas. The more often you read and revise your work, the better it will be.
- Keep the paper you are working on in a special folder. Taking special care of your work can help you become a more successful writer because it makes you feel proud of your work. Always have this folder with you in class; you will revise your composition as you learn more about writing.

The lessons and exercises in the Composition Focus and Language Focus sections will help you revise. You will be using the information in the lessons and the **Revision Checkpoints** to develop your sentences and your composition as a whole, so keep your draft nearby.

Composition Focus

The controlling idea of the topic sentence and the major supporting points. A topic sentence usually has two parts: the *topic* and the *controlling idea*. The topic tells you what the general subject of the paragraph is. The controlling idea limits the topic. Notice that you can express the controlling idea in different ways.

TOPIC	CONTROLLING IDEA

Nora is my role model for two reasons.

TOPIC	CONTROLLING IDEA

Nora is my role model because she has two great qualities.

TOPIC	CONTROLLING IDEA

Nora is my role model because she is focused and level-headed.

The controlling idea also tells you what parts of the topic the writer wants to focus on; that is, it points to the major supporting points in the paragraph.

TOPIC SENTENCE
My Uncle Max is my role model because of his *cooperative* spirit and *practicality*.

MAJOR SUPPORTING POINTS
First, Uncle Max *works with others cooperatively*.

Second, Uncle Max is a very *practical* man.

Notice that the controlling idea of the topic sentence and the major supporting points say the same thing in slightly different words. When you write the topic sentence and the major supporting points, you can use word forms to avoid repeating exactly the same vocabulary.

A. *Circle the parts of the controlling idea in each topic sentence and the corresponding parts of the major supporting points. On the line, write the word forms (n. = noun, adj. = adjective) that the writer used to avoid repetition.*

1. My role model is Clara because she exemplifies (focus), (determination), and (diligence).
   I. First, Clara is always (focused) on her goals.
   II. In addition, Clara was (determined) to get an education and lead a responsible life.
   III. Finally, Clara was a (diligent) student and now is a diligent journalist.

Word forms: *focus (n.), focused (adj.); determination (n.), determined (adj.); diligence (n.), diligent (adj.)*

2. Bing has had a great influence on me, and I consider him my role model because he is level-headed, trustworthy, and persistent.
   I. One reason I admire Bing is his level-headedness.
   II. Another reason I look up to Bing is his trustworthiness.
   III. A final reason Bing inspires me is his persistence.

Word forms: _____

3. Aunt Monica is my role model. She has left an imprint on my life because of her ambition, ingenuity, and commitment to excellence in her career as a Web page designer.
   I. First, Aunt Monica is ambitious.
   II. Second, Aunt Monica is an ingenious person.
   III. Finally, Aunt Monica is an inspiration to me because she is committed to excellence in her career as a Web page designer.

Word forms: _____

_____

4. Juan stands tall in my memory because he was modest, resourceful, and devoted to our family.
   I. First, Juan had the quality of modesty.
   II. Second, Juan possessed the characteristic of resourcefulness.
   III. Finally, Juan was important in my life because of his devotion to our family.

Word forms: _____

_____

B. *Compare your answers with a partner's.*

These two paragraphs need topic sentences. To write a topic sentence for each paragraph, first find the major supporting points in the paragraph and underline them. Notice the nouns or adjectives used in the supporting points, and find word forms for them. You may need to use a dictionary. Then write a topic sentence for the paragraph, using the word forms you have found.

1. ### My Role Model, Emi

_____

_____

²One of Emi's fine qualities that I admire is her sincerity. ³Emi never wears makeup, and she never exaggerates when she speaks. ⁴She tells you exactly what she likes, what she doesn't like, and why she feels that way. ⁵She admits her shortcomings readily. ⁶One time I asked Emi if she had ever tried to diet. ⁷She laughed and said, "Too many times to count. ⁸But I can't say no to ice cream." ⁹Another reason I admire Emi is her level-headedness. ¹⁰One rainy morning Emi and I were driving to the airport to catch a flight when Emi suddenly realized that she had forgotten her plane ticket. ¹¹Emi debated whether to go back home for a few minutes, and then decided that doing so might cause us to miss the flight. ¹²She drove calmly to the airport, got a replacement ticket at the counter, and managed to catch the flight. ¹³Finally, I admire Emi's warmth. ¹⁴When Emi's at a party, she circles the room, her kind smile and hearty laugh touching everyone. ¹⁵Emi is a remarkable woman, and I respect her greatly and aspire to be like her.

2. ### Ricky Martin

_____

_____

²First, Ricky Martin has always been self-assured, that is, certain about who he is and what he wants. ³From an early age, he knew that he wanted to be a performing artist. ⁴At age seven, Martin told his parents that he wanted to go into show business. ⁵He made commercials and then joined the popular boys' band Menudo. ⁶Since his years with Menudo, Martin himself has actively managed his career, guiding it toward success in Latin America, Europe, Asia, and the U.S. ⁷Second, Ricky Martin is an accomplished performer. ⁸His music ranges in style from pop rock and salsa to flamenco and hip-hop.

[9]He has collaborated with performers such as Madonna and Christina Aguilera. [10]Martin has made more than twenty albums and performed all over the world—in Berlin, Beirut, Egypt, and Japan. [11]Finally, Ricky Martin is generous. [12]As a performer, he holds nothing back, giving everything he has to the audience. [13]When he is not on stage, he works with various charities, including the Ricky Martin Foundation, which sponsors camps for children. [14]Ricky Martin has set an example for me because of his amazing qualities.

REVISION CHECKPOINT 1

The Controlling Idea of the Topic Sentence and the Major Supporting Points
Check your paper. Make sure that it has a topic sentence with a controlling idea and clearly written major supporting points. Circle the parts of the controlling idea in your topic sentence, and underline the corresponding parts in the major supporting points. Check your vocabulary to see if you have used word forms to avoid repetition. If you need to make changes, make them now.

Background information. Sometimes you need to supply some information near the beginning of your paragraph to help readers understand your paragraph. For example, in the paragraph "Muhammad Yunus" (page 15), we learned that Yunus is "an economist who started a banking system for the poor," and in "Lionel Messi" (page 16), we learned that Messi is an "Argentinian soccer player." To readers, background information is very helpful, and sometimes it is essential to understanding a paragraph. You can include background information in several ways.

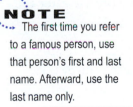

NOTE
The first time you refer to a famous person, use that person's first and last name. Afterward, use the last name only.

- You can put background information in a sentence *before* or *after* the topic sentence.

BACKGROUND	TOPIC SENTENCE

Bahaa Taher is an Egyptian writer. Taher is my role model for several reasons.

TOPIC SENTENCE	BACKGROUND

Bahaa Taher is my role model for several reasons. Taher is an Egyptian writer.

- Sometimes you can put background information *inside* the topic sentence before the person's name.

TOPIC SENTENCE
BACKGROUND

The Egyptian writer Bahaa Taher is my role model for several reasons.

EXERCISE 10

Add the background information in parentheses to these topic sentences by placing it inside the sentences. On another piece of paper, rewrite each sentence with the background information. Underline the background information.

1. My role model is Zaha Hadid because of her dynamic forms and innovative ideas. (the Iraqi architect)

   My role model is <u>the Iraqi architect</u> Zaha Hadid because of her

   dynamic forms and innovative ideas.

2. My role model is Itzhak Perlman because his music is very moving and he works to help the disabled. (the classical violinist)

3. My role model is Daniel Ansari because his research is contributing to our understanding of children's difficulties with math and of ways to help children learn more effectively. (the psychologist)

4. My role model is Paloma Herrera because of her technical skill and her ability to express emotions in her dancing. (the accomplished ballerina)

5. My role model is David Suzuki because he has made wonderful television programs about nature and has informed people about global climate change. (the well-known environmentalist)

- When the background information is too long to place before a person's name, you can put it in an adjective clause or adjective phrase after the name.

ADJECTIVE CLAUSE

My role model is America Ferrera, who is the star of the television comedy *Ugly Betty*, because of her dynamism and acting skills.

ADJECTIVE CLAUSE

My role model is America Ferrera, the star of the television comedy *Ugly Betty*, because of her dynamism and acting skills.

NOTE
Put commas around an adjective clause or phrase after a person's name.

For more on adjective clauses, see Appendix IA, page 229, and for more on adjective phrases, see Appendix IA, page 234.

Exercise 11

Add the background information in parentheses to the topic sentence by placing it in an adjective clause. On another piece of paper, write each sentence and underline the adjective clause that you added (remember to use commas). Then put parentheses around the words you can delete to make the clause a phrase.

1. My role model is Bill Watterson because his drawings are expressive and his comic characters and stories are very interesting to children and adults. (the creator of the comic strip *Calvin and Hobbes*)

   My role model is Bill Watterson, (who is) the creator of the comic strip Calvin and Hobbes, because his drawings are expressive and his comic characters and stories are very interesting to children and adults.

2. Ali Mazrui is my role model because of his vast knowledge and wisdom. (the author of over thirty books about Africa)

3. Eva Habil is my role model for several reasons. (Egypt's first female mayor)

4. For three reasons, my role model is the softball player Lisa Fernandez. (the winner of three Olympic gold medals)

5. Dr. Govindappa Venkataswamy is my role model because he has provided free eye care to the poor and saved millions of people from going blind. (the founder of the Aravind Eye Hospital)

REVISION CHECKPOINT 2

Background Information

Review your paragraph to see if you need to add background information. If you wish, you can show your paragraph to a classmate and ask him or her if you need to add background information. If your paragraph needs background information, decide how to include that information, and add it now. If you have questions about background information, write a note to your teacher in the margin of your paper.

The third level: Specificity. You have learned that you can develop the third level of your paragraph with examples, explanation, and quotations. The more clear and specific you make the third level of your paragraph, the more effective your writing will be. Look at these examples.

TOPIC SENTENCE	Jorge is my role model because of his unselfishness and compassion.
MAJOR SUPPORTING POINT	Jorge is a compassionate person.
EXPLANATION THAT IS TOO GENERAL	Jorge cares about his friends.
EXPLANATION THAT IS SPECIFIC ENOUGH	Jorge listens to his friends when they have problems, and he brings food to them when they are sick.

TOPIC SENTENCE	Laura is my role model because of her discipline and frugality.
MAJOR SUPPORTING POINT	Laura is a frugal person.
EXPLANATION THAT IS TOO GENERAL	For example, Laura never wastes money.
EXPLANATION THAT IS SPECIFIC ENOUGH	For example, Laura shops at stores that are going out of business and at garage sales whenever she needs to buy clothing or furniture.

EXERCISE 12

A. These two paragraphs each have three major supporting points. In each paragraph, two of the major supporting points are developed well, and the other is not specific enough. Put brackets [ ] around the point that is not developed well in each paragraph. On the lines, write one or two questions to help the writer develop that supporting point.

1.
My Grandmother, My Role Model

¹My grandmother brought my brothers and me up, and she is my role model to this day because she was practical, ingenious, and supportive. ²First, my grandmother was very practical. ³She encouraged me to pursue business rather than art because she believed that with a business degree, I would have no difficulty finding work. ⁴My grandmother was also ingenious. ⁵She could find a clever solution to any problem. ⁶Finally, my grandmother supported me in a number of ways. ⁷She treated me exactly like my brothers and believed I could achieve no less than they did. ⁸Whenever I was studying for exams, my grandmother studied along with me. ⁹We used to quiz each other on historical facts, scientific terms, and math concepts. ¹⁰Grandmother always said, "If you want to learn something, child, you can. ¹¹All it takes is a little effort." ¹²My grandmother was a very special woman, and I admire her a great deal. ¹³I think she was exceptional in her practicality, ingenuity, and supportiveness, and I try to be like her.

_____

_____

2.   **Horatio Alger's Exemplary Characters**

[1]In the late nineteenth and early twentieth century, some of the popular role models for boys in the United States were the leading characters in stories by Horatio Alger. [2]Alger wrote dozens of stories, and all of them were similar in that the central character was a young boy. [3]Young readers saw these characters as role models because they were always successful in life and because they had admirable qualities that contributed to their success. [4]One quality of these heroic figures is that they started out in life poor and rose to the middle class through diligence and hard work. [5]For example, Ragged Dick was a poor boy who made his living shining shoes in New York. [6]Dick worked hard, saved his money, studied to improve himself, and eventually moved up to the middle class. [7]Another quality of Horatio Alger's heroes is that they were courageous. [8]For example, the character Robert Rushton risked his own life in order to stop a train that was coming toward a tree that had fallen across the tracks. [9]He stood on the tracks and waved a red flag until the conductor put on the brakes. [10]This brave act saved the lives of the people on board the train. [11]Another characteristic of these figures is trustworthiness. [12]For instance, Luke Larkin kept a secret. [13]Alger's stories were popular, so his heroes had a great deal of influence on young boys one hundred years ago.

_____

_____

B. Compare your work with a partner's work. Discuss 1) how you could improve the parts of the paragraph that you have identified as not specific enough, and 2) which development strategies (example, explanation, quotation) the writers of these paragraphs used in the other parts of the third level.

The third level: Quotations. Quotations bring life into writing because they give readers a sense of the speaker's personality. Reread "Se Ri Pak" on page 14 without the quotation. Does it seem less true-to-life without the quotation?

Tips for Including Quotations

- Make sure that the quote relates clearly to the major supporting point it follows.
- Make sure to punctuate quotations correctly.

For more on punctuating quotations, see pages 190–198 in Part II and page 294 in Appendix IB.

EXERCISE 13

Read the paragraph, and find a place in it for the quotation. On another piece of paper, you will write three sentences. First, copy the sentence from the text that should go before the quotation. Then you need to write a sentence beginning with **Murthy said** *and include the quotation. Finally, copy the sentence from the text that should follow the quotation.*

Quotation: "The real power of money is the power to give it away."

N. R. Narayana Murthy

¹My role model is N. R. Narayana Murthy, the founder and former CEO of Infosys, a global consulting and IT services company based in Bangalore, India. ²I admire Murthy for his foresight and his generosity. ³First, Murthy has foresight, or the ability to see the future. ⁴In the 1970s, Murthy observed that many technically skilled Indians were emigrating to find work, and he thought that they would stay in India if they could find good jobs. ⁵Therefore, in 1981, Murthy founded the software company Infosys, which attracted highly skilled employees with high wages and amenities such as recreational facilities. ⁶Infosys grew rapidly and kept its loyal workers, showing other Indian entrepreneurs what could be done and contributing to the growth of the software industry in India. ⁷Second, Murthy's generosity is exemplary. ⁸ Murthy believes that business must benefit society, so with his wife, Murthy started the Infosys Foundation, which provides vocational training, libraries, and hospital wards in poor rural areas. ⁹Murthy has set an outstanding example for people in business not only in India, but worldwide.

REVISION CHECKPOINT 3

The Third Level: Specificity and Quotations
Check the third level of your paragraph. Make sure that your explanations and examples are specific enough. If you have not used any quotations, ask yourself if you have a quote that you could add. If you want to make changes to the third level, make them now.

Transitions. A paragraph that contains two or three major supporting points and some examples usually needs some signals, known as **transitions**, that help readers follow its organization. There are various kinds of transitions.

- One type identifies items in a list or sequence: *first, second, one, another,* etc. *First* and *second* come at the beginning of a sentence and are followed by a comma.

  First, Jacques is independent.

  Second, Jacques is resourceful.

- *One* and *another* are adjectives, so they come before nouns.

  One quality I admire in Jacques is his independence.

  Another quality I admire in Jacques is his resourcefulness.

TRANSITIONS TO SIGNAL A LIST	
Transitions That Introduce Sentences	**Transitions That Come Before Nouns**
first	one
second also in addition	another
third finally	another/the other final

 For more on **one, another,** *and* **the other,** *see Appendix IA, page 268.*

see Appendix IA, page 268.

EXERCISE 14

Turn back to the paragraphs in Exercise 12 on pages 32 and 33. Find the transitions listed in the chart above and circle them.

Another type of transition signals that an example is coming. These transitions are *for example, for instance, such as,* and *like.*

TRANSITIONS TO INTRODUCE EXAMPLES	
Transitions to Introduce Sentence-long Examples	**Transitions to Introduce Words or Phrases Used as Examples Within Sentences**
For example, For instance,	such as like

- *For example* and *for instance* come at the beginning of a sentence and are followed by a comma; they are the same in meaning and use.

  Maria is very diligent. *For example/For instance*, she comes to the office early, does more than her share of the work, and finally leaves after everyone else has gone home.

- *Such as* and *like* are used in the middle of sentences. *Such as* and *like* are prepositions and are followed by nouns or noun phrases; they are the same in meaning and use.

  Maria is very generous. She gives her nieces and nephews gifts *such as/like* computer programs and magazine subscriptions.

 To learn about phrases, clauses, and logical connectors, see Appendix IA, pages 271 and 272.

see Appendix IA, pages 271 and 272.

EXERCISE 15

Read the two paragraphs, and fill in the blanks with transitions from the chart on page 35. Then compare your answers with your classmates' answers.

1.   **Santosh Yadav, Indian Mountain Climber**

My role model is Santosh Yadav, the only woman to climb Mount Everest twice. Yadav, who is from the small village of Jonia, took the initiative to change her own life, took risks, and worked hard for her goals. (a) _____*First,*_____, Yadav wanted something more for herself than the traditional lifestyle of a village woman, so she persuaded her father to let her attend college in Jaipur, where she majored in economics. She seized an opportunity again when she saw a group of mountaineers in Jaipur preparing to go climbing, and she asked them if she could join them. They agreed, and she climbed the "White Needle" in Kashmir on that trip; as a result, she became a mountain climber. (b) _____, as a mountaineer, Yadav has taken many risks. (c)_____, in 1999, she successfully attempted the most dangerous route on Mount Everest, the Kangshung Face. (d) _____, Yadav believes that the only way to reach one's goals is through hard work. While she was training to climb the highest mountains in the world, she was also studying for the difficult Indian civil service exam. She was successful in both attempts because she applied herself. I admire Yadav as a role model and would like to be like her, so I plan to take initiative, take risks, and work hard.

2.   **Kira Burenina**

My role model is Kira Burenina, who is editor-in-chief of the popular Russian women's magazine *Liza* and a novelist. I admire Burenina for two reasons. (a) _____ reason I admire Burenina is her ambition. Burenina earned four college degrees—in linguistics, psychology, economics, and public relations management. As editor-in-chief at *Liza*, Burenina works long hours and meets the deadlines of a weekly publication, but she enjoys the challenge of working with creative people (b) _____ designers, illustrators, and photographers. (c) _____ reason I admire Burenina is that her magazine and her novels are helpful to women. *Liza* features columns written by psychologists that advise women on issues (d) _____ careers, marriage, and family life. Her novels are about successful women in professions (e) _____ show business and journalism. They inspire women to aim high and, like Burenina, to achieve their full potential.

Concluding sentences. A concluding sentence is a signal to the reader that the paragraph is finished. Most one-paragraph compositions seem more complete with the addition of a concluding sentence. Reread "Santosh Yadav, Indian Mountain Climber" on page 36 without the conclusion. Does it seem less complete without the concluding sentence?

Tips for Writing Concluding Sentences

- You can repeat the vocabulary of the controlling idea (the major supporting points) or use word forms or synonyms. Or you can just refer to the topic sentence in a general way.
- You can add a final thought, but do not introduce new information that readers would want you to explain or a new opinion that readers would want you to support.

EXERCISE 16

With a partner, review the concluding sentences in three of the model paragraphs in this chapter, and check (✔) the appropriate boxes in the chart.

	Uncle Wei (page 13)	N. R. Narayana Murthy (page 34)	Santosh Yadav, Indian Mountain Climber (page 36)
Refers to the topic in a general way; does not repeat the controlling idea/ major supporting points			
Refers back to the controlling idea/ major supporting points with some word forms or synonyms			
Repeats the vocabulary of the controlling idea/ major supporting points			

EXERCISE 17

A. *Read the paragraph, and write a concluding sentence for it on the lines that follow.*

An Admirable Entrepreneur

¹My father's friend Gunnar is my role model because he is an innovative, confident, persistent entrepreneur who started a company that makes shoes out of recycled materials. ²First, Gunnar is an innovator: He designed the shoes he makes and invented the production process he uses to make them. ³Working in his parents' basement, he used his knowledge of physics, chemistry, and materials science and experimented with various recycled materials including plastic, rubber, cloth, and metal. ⁴He made shoes of different styles for himself and wore them to test their durability. ⁵Second, although at first Gunnar had no money, he had the confidence that he would be able to begin manufacturing shoes in a few years. ⁶With this self-assurance, he met investors and showed them his sample shoes and explained his business model. ⁷He sold his car to have the money to start manufacturing, feeling sure that his company would make it. ⁸Above all, Gunnar has enormous persistence. ⁹He worked on his start-up business in his free time every day for six years—while working as a teller in a bank—before his business made a profit. ¹⁰He didn't sell many shoes the first two years, but he kept going to trade shows and fairs to show people his products and let them try them out.

_____

_____

B. *Compare your concluding sentence with a partner's. Did you repeat the vocabulary of the controlling idea (the major supporting points), use word forms or synonyms, or refer to the topic sentence in a general way?*

REVISION CHECKPOINT 4

Transitions and Concluding Sentence
Check your paragraph. If your supporting points or examples need transitions, add them now. Also, review the end of your paragraph, and consider adding a concluding sentence. If you have already written a concluding sentence, review it to see if you have used synonyms and related words whenever possible.

Language Focus

Sentence combining. You can make your writing more effective if you combine sentences. By combining sentences, you can show logical relationships and include more information in your sentences. Two kinds of conjunctions, *coordinating conjunctions* and *subordinating conjunctions,* let you do this.

Each conjunction adds a different meaning. Here are the most common coordinating conjunctions and their meanings.

Coordinating Conjunctions	Examples	Meanings
and	Al has confidence, *and* he is proud of his accomplishments.	signals addition of a similar idea
so	Al has confidence, *so* people respect him.	introduces a result
but	Al has confidence, *but* he is modest, too.	introduces a contrasting idea

NOTE
When a coordinating conjunction joins two clauses, put a comma between the clauses.

For more on coordinating conjunctions, see Appendix IA, page 252.

EXERCISE 18

Use coordinating conjunctions to combine the underlined sentences in this paragraph. Write the new sentences on another piece of paper. Be sure to use commas where you need them.

Steven Spielberg

My role model is the movie director and producer Steven Spielberg because he has two qualities I admire. The first reason I admire Spielberg is his imagination. a) <u>Spielberg has said, "I dream for a living." He has translated his dreams to movie scenes that are unforgettable.</u> Who was not terrified when watching two men on a leaky old boat trying to kill a 25-foot man-eating shark in *Jaws*? Who didn't cry when watching three children say a sad good-bye to their friend, the alien visitor E.T.? Who can forget the hungry dinosaurs chasing people around an island in *Jurassic Park*? b) <u>Spielberg has been telling stories in film since age eleven. He has not run out of imaginative ideas.</u> The second reason I admire Steven Spielberg is his passion. Spielberg does not spare any effort to make a movie excellent. c) <u>First, he does thorough research. He knows as much as possible about the story and the characters before he starts to film.</u> Then he spends as much time filming as he needs. For example, before making *Saving Private Ryan*, Spielberg interviewed veterans of World War II. Then he spent almost a month shooting the first twenty-five minutes of the movie in order to get the realistic effects in the battle scene that he wanted. d) <u>No, I will never achieve what Steven Spielberg has done in movies. I hope to have the same kind of imagination and passion in my own career.</u>

Here are some of the most common subordinating conjunctions and their meanings. Notice that there are two ways to order the clauses in sentences with subordinating conjunctions.

Subordinating Conjunctions	Examples	Meanings
when	People listen *when* Simone speaks. *When* Simone speaks, people listen.	signals either two actions happening at the same time or a sequence, with the action following *when* happening first
because	People listen to Simone *because* she speaks with confidence. *Because* Simone speaks with confidence, people listen to her.	introduces a reason
although	People listen to Simone, *although* they may not agree with her. *Although* people may not agree with Simone, they listen to her.	introduces a contrasting idea

For more on subordinating conjunctions and other logical connectors, see Appendix IA, page 272.

NOTE
When the subordinating conjunction is in the middle of the sentence, do not use a comma, except before *although*. When the subordinating conjunction is at the beginning of the sentence, always put a comma at the end of the subordinate clause.

Exercise 19

Use the subordinating conjunctions when, because, *and* although *to combine the pairs of underlined sentences in this paragraph. Write the new sentences on another piece of paper. Be sure to use commas where you need them.*

Mohammad Bah Abba

My role model is the Nigerian inventor Mohammad Bah Abba, who developed a refrigeration device called "pot-in-pot" that does not need electricity. A "pot-in-pot" is very simple: It consists of two clay pots, one inside the other, with wet sand in between. a) "Pot-in-pot" works. The evaporation of water lowers temperatures. b) I admire Abba. He is a resourceful problem-solver and a caring person. c) First, Abba went to college. He studied science. d) Then he understood chemistry and physics. He was able to invent this device. Second, Abba is caring. e) <u>He invented "pot-in-pot." He was concerned about the struggle of farmers in his country</u>. In Nigeria's hot, dry climate, farmers cannot keep vegetables fresh easily. f) <u>Farmers pick the vegetables. They have to sell them immediately</u>. With "pot-in-pot," farmers can keep their produce longer so they can sell more of it and increase their income. g) <u>Abba could have charged money for his device. He gave it to farmers for free</u>.

Exercise 20

Use coordinating and subordinating conjunctions to combine the pairs of underlined sentences in this paragraph. Write the new sentences on another piece of paper. Be sure to use commas where you need them.

Wangari Maathai, Planter of Trees

My role model is Wangari Maathai, a Kenyan woman who started a tree-planting movement. I admire Maathai for her devotion to people and to the environment and her resolve in the face of opposition. First, Maathai recognized serious environmental and human problems in Kenya: a) <u>Trees had been cut down to plant coffee and tea. The land was becoming a desert</u>. b) <u>There was no firewood. People could not cook.</u> Children were malnourished. c) <u>Maathai had studied biology. She realized that planting trees would help solve these problems</u>. d) <u>She started the Greenbelt Movement in 1977. So far it has planted 40 million trees in Kenya</u>. e) <u>The Greenbelt Movement has provided jobs. The trees it has planted provide fruit and firewood</u>. f) <u>The tree roots protect Kenya's water supply and soil. It rains</u>. g) <u>The Greenbelt Movement has benefited Kenya. Maathai has faced opposition from the Kenyan government</u>. h) <u>Maathai was arrested. She protested the destruction of a park</u>. i) <u>Maathai was forced into hiding. She never lost her resolve</u>. j) <u>Maathai has run for Parliament three times and for the presidency once. She finally won a parliamentary seat in 2002</u>. Maathai said, ". . . others told me that I shouldn't . . . raise my voice, [but I saw] that if I had a contribution I wanted to make, I must do it . . . it was all right to be strong."

Sears, Priscilla. "Wangari Maathai: 'You Strike the Woman.'" <u>In Context: A Quarterly of Humane Sustainable Culture</u> 28 Spring 1991. 5 Aug. 2009. <http://www.context.org/ICLIB/IC28/Sears.htm>.

REVISION CHECKPOINT 5

Combining Sentences

Review your draft to see if you used any coordinating or subordinating conjunctions. If you did, put a check () in the margin next to those sentences. If you think you can combine any more sentences with coordinating or subordinating conjunctions, make those changes now. Finally, make sure that you used commas correctly.

■ FINAL DRAFT

1. Before you write your final draft, look over your paragraph one last time to decide if you want to make any further changes.

2. Prepare a final draft of your composition. Make sure that you have used capital letters at the beginning of your sentences and periods at the end, and check your spelling.

3. Exchange papers with one or two classmates. Read each other's papers carefully. Turn to page 296 in Appendix II, and fill out the Peer Review Form.

4. Check your paper again and make any necessary corrections. Turn it in to your teacher.

■ CHAPTER REVIEW

Look back at what you have accomplished in Chapter 1. Check off (✔) what you have learned and what you have used as you have written and revised your composition.

Chapter 1 Topics	Learned	Used
organizing ideas from general to specific, and making an outline for a three-level paragraph (pages 12–19)		
presenting major supporting points in sentences that link the topic sentence and the examples (pages 12–13)		
using specific examples, explanation, and quotations to develop the major supporting points (pages 13–15)		
writing a topic sentence with a controlling idea (page 26)		
using transitions to mark the major supporting points and to signal examples (pages 34–35)		
writing a paragraph conclusion (pages 37–38)		
using coordinating and subordinating conjunctions to combine sentences (pages 38–41)		

CHAPTER TWO

Culture, Identity, and Homeland

Writing a Division Paragraph and Essay

Who are you? Very likely your answer to this question has several parts. Your response will probably include your name, where you were born, and what cultural or ethnic group you belong to. It may also include your ancestry; the history of your homeland; and your language, customs, and beliefs. In this chapter, you will reflect on and then write about a topic related to your cultural or ethnic identity.

This chapter will help you

- analyze a topic by logical division.
- expand a paragraph to an essay by developing supporting points as body paragraphs.
- use parallel structure in thesis statements.
- increase cohesion by using repeated words, synonyms, and transitions to create links between a thesis and the topic sentences of body paragraphs.
- use background information to write an essay introduction.
- expand noun phrases and use adjective clauses to include additional information.

Before You Read

With a partner or a small group, read this statement and the questions that follow it. Make some notes to answer the questions, and then share your ideas.

> *Culture* is a broad term. It includes all the customs, values, and beliefs of a group of people. *Ethnic identity* is an even broader term. It is the sense of connection a person feels to a particular group and can be based on shared customs, race, language, religion, or homeland.

1. Are children usually aware of their culture or ethnic identity?
2. How do children learn about their culture or ethnic identity?
3. What gives children either positive or negative feelings about their culture or ethnic identity?

Reading

TO BE AN AMERICAN, BLACK, CATHOLIC, AND CREOLE
by Alfred J. Guillaume, Jr.

segregated: *divided according to race*

Native Americans: *the original inhabitants of the Americas, Indians*

exoticism: *foreignness*

shatter: *destroy*

derogatory: *insulting*

1   I am an American. I am black, Roman Catholic, and Creole. This is how I describe myself 62 years in the making. As a young boy growing up in the South, I was made to believe that I was different. Images of America did not mirror me. The **segregated** South wanted me to believe that I was inferior. The Catholic Church taught me that all of God's people were equal. My French Creole heritage gave me a special bond to **Native Americans**, to Europeans, and to Africans. This is the composite portrait of who I am. I like who I am and can imagine being no other.

2   I'm an American. I was born in New Orleans, Louisiana, whose elegance and **exoticism** make it America's most European city and also its most Caribbean. Natives call it the Big Easy. From its founding, New Orleans has been a place that represents good times—the enjoyment of music, food, and celebration. In 2005, Hurricane Katrina devastated this beautiful American city, **shattering** the lives of people whose cultural heritage spanned generations of European, African, and Native American ancestry. Today the vibrancy of New Orleans is visible in the revitalization of neighborhoods, in the resurgence of age-old traditions like Mardi Gras, All Saints Day, and jazz funerals.

3   I'm an African American. Just within my lifetime, people of African ancestry have been called colored, Negro, black, and various **derogatory** terms that I completely reject. I am proud to have been born black. My

people paid a heavy price through toil and suffering to make America. Their **unparalleled** creative contributions shaped American culture.

4   I am Catholic. I thought everyone was Catholic until I went to school and learned that there were **Protestants**. The **nuns** taught my schoolmates and me to pray for them and for all other non-Catholics. My values were formed in large part by my religious faith. As a child I dreamed of becoming a priest. I left my parents at age twelve to study for the priesthood in New York. I made my first long journey on a train with five other **seminarians** from my parish.

5   I am Creole. I trace my ancestry to Africa, to Europe, and to Native America. The word *Creole* is used to define Europeans who came to the Americas, but *Creole* also refers to blacks in the Americas, mixed-blood people whose ancestry can be traced to Africa as well as to Europe. This is my heritage: a blend of Africa, Europe, and Native America. The first languages of my maternal grandparents were French and Creole, a kind of **pidgin** French. I regret that my siblings and I never learned to speak the language. We lived in the city and the language was spoken primarily in the rural areas. My mother understood the language but never spoke it to us. Speaking English correctly was important, particularly without the **melodic** Creole accent so characteristic of natives of southern Louisiana. Yet even without the language, I speak with a regional accent. On my paternal side were the Houma Indians. Pictures of my great-great grandmother are prized family possessions.

6   I grew up in the segregated South. My parents shielded us from racism. Our upbringing, our religion, and our schooling protected us. We lived in a middle-class neighborhood, attended a Catholic elementary school run by a black order of nuns called the Holy Family Sisters, and went to Mass at a black Catholic church. We lived in a **cocoon** in our black, Catholic, Creole world. Because of all the support Creole society provided, it seemed that segregation did not affect us. It was not until the sixties, during my teenage years, that I became fully aware of the **dehumanizing** effects of segregation.

7   Creole society could not totally isolate us from racial prejudice. I remember sitting with my maternal grandmother in the colored section of the bus, behind the "Colored Only" sign, when a white patron removed the sign and put it behind us, forcing us to stand and relinquish our seat to him. I remember the separate water fountains, the separate entrances to restaurants, the separate playgrounds, the separate schools and churches. In department stores and other businesses, blacks did menial work; the salespeople and bosses were white. I remember the day my dad took me with him to the post office, where he worked. At the desks and the service counters were only whites; I asked my dad to show me his office. I had no notion then that only whites had offices.

8   My first recollection that black meant being inferior occurred one morning as I walked to school. In the segregated South, only white children were bused to school. A young white boy, about my own age—eight or so— yelled out the

(continued)

window of the yellow school bus, "Hey, chocolate boy!" When I related this story to my maternal great aunt her response to me was, "Cher (My dear), you a pretty chocolate boy." Since then I have always taken a particular delight in being "chocolate."

9   Though the message of segregation was hatred and **subjugation**, my parents taught my four siblings and me never to feel inferior to whites. We never heard a **disparaging** word in our home about white people. Rather than thinking that whites were superior, we grew up thinking that we were special. We were Americans. And not only were we colored, we were Creole and Catholic. My father took particular delight in repeatedly saying that each of us was a jewel; we were five dazzling jewels, and each was different. My parents taught us to believe in ourselves above all else, and that we were never to forget where we came from.

10   What I've accomplished professionally I owe to discipline, a good education, and opportunity. Education was stressed in my family. My siblings and I knew from an early age that we would go to college. My parents taught us that everything was within our reach, because success depended on our hard work and persistence. My dad taught us never to give up, that the word "can't" is not in the dictionary. We were Guillaumes, he would say, and a Guillaume never gives up. He told us never to accept **mediocrity**. He encouraged us in our schoolwork always to aim for an *A*. "It is far better to aim high and miss the mark," he would say, "than aim low and make it." We understood that to mean that if we studied for an *A* and failed, then our reward would be a *B* or no less than a *C*. But if we studied for a *D* and succeeded, the results would be disastrous. I consider myself blessed to have had parents who valued education and who understood the limitless potential education affords.

11   I was divorced and am now remarried. I have two sons, ages thirty-two and twenty-three, and two adult step-children, ages thirty-eight and thirty-four. My sons are black; my stepchildren are white. As for my sons, I know that each is trying to find his place in a society that is increasingly multicultural but whose power base remains white. As young black men they struggle with the **stereotypical** images of what being black means in America. This is particularly true for my older son, who learned bitterly what it meant to be black when, as a young boy of eleven, he was stopped by campus police at a Midwest university and escorted off campus because he did not belong there. He was afraid to tell them that his father was the vice president. My younger son, to my knowledge, has not yet experienced racism at its ugliest. He remains open and accepting of others. He hates talk of black people and white people and proudly proclaims that all people are the same. For him, the important quality in a person is whether he or she is nice.

12   I raised my sons as my parents raised me. I taught them that it is less important that the world sees you as black, and it is more important that the

subjugation: *forcing people into an inferior position*

disparaging: *critical or disrespectful*

mediocrity: *the condition of being no better than average*

stereotypical: *having to do with a possibly wrong or unfair idea of what a particular type of person is like*

integrity: the quality of being honest and of having high moral principles

world recognizes you as a person of strength and **integrity**. As my father taught me, I teach them to be strong and independent, to be individuals. Even though they are finding their place in this world, I continue to tell them that they are jewels, that there are no others like them, that they have unique gifts of self, and that they should be willing to share their gifts of self with others. Color is not important; character is. They are special and they honor their father and their heritage.

ABOUT the **AUTHOR**   Alfred J. Guillaume, Jr., Ph.D., is the vice chancellor for academic affairs at Indiana University, South Bend. He has also held the position of provost and vice president for academic affairs at Humboldt State University and St. Louis University. "To Be an American, Black, Catholic, and Creole" is adapted from a longer essay by the same name.

Understanding the Reading

With a partner or a small group, discuss the following questions.

1. In the first paragraph of the essay, Guillaume tells us that he is going to give us a *composite portrait* of himself. What is a composite portrait, and why must Guillaume's be composite?

2. Guillaume develops the parts of his composite portrait with details and examples. Which ones do you remember (without looking back at the essay)? Why are they memorable?

3. Which parts of his composite identity (nationality, race, religion, and culture) does Guillaume emphasize most in this essay? Why do you think he does this?

4. What does the term *Creole* refer to? How does Guillaume seem to feel about being Creole? Which words in Guillaume's discussion of his Creole heritage reveal his attitude?

5. What examples does Guillaume use to illustrate the fact that he experienced racial discrimination at an early age? How did he manage to retain his pride, or his positive self-image, in the face of discrimination?

6. Guillaume also discusses the values that he learned from his parents. What are those values, and why are they important in this essay?

7. In paragraph 11, Guillaume discusses his sons' sense of their own identity and he explains that there is a difference between the two boys. What does this explanation tell us about how children form their identity?

8. Do you, like Guillaume, see yourself as belonging to several groups, or do you see yourself as belonging to just one? Explain.

Vocabulary Expansion

Vocabulary for analyzing cultures. To explain your culture to someone, you could, like Guillaume, begin by identifying its parts.

EXERCISE 1

Complete the following activities.

1. The circular diagram represents a culture. In each of the six wedge-shaped sections of the circle, write an aspect of culture, such as *architecture*.

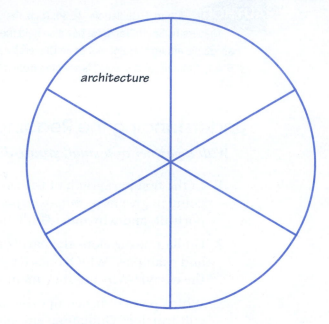

architecture

2. In the word-family chart below, write the six nouns you used in the culture circle. Check the dictionary to see if there is an adjective in the word family of each noun. If you find one, add it to the chart. (You may not find adjectives for all your nouns.)

Nouns	Adjectives
architecture	architectural

■ WRITING

Assignment

You will analyze one of the following topics by logical division. That means you will divide the topic into parts and discuss each part. First you will write a paragraph, and later you will expand it to an essay. Select a topic from the list below that you will be able to divide into parts and whose parts you will be able to develop well.

1. Tell what your culture or ethnic identity is. Identify and describe three or four aspects of your culture or ethnic identity.

2. Write about your home country in terms of its geographic parts or your native city in terms of its neighborhoods.

3. Analyze a holiday that is observed in your culture. Divide that celebration into parts according to time, place, or people's roles.

4. Write about the life of a person in your country in terms of its parts. For example, Mahatma Gandhi's life can be analyzed by *time* (periods of his life: youth, mid-life, old age), *places* he lived (England, South Africa, India), or *roles* he played in his life (student, lawyer, social reformer, religious and political leader). The person you choose does not need to be famous. If you write about an ordinary person, you can analyze either the person's entire life or a day in his or her life.

What Logical Division Is and Why It Is Important

Logical division. **Logical division** helps us understand things that are big, complicated, unfamiliar, or abstract by dividing them into parts. For example, to understand a country such as China, we can divide it into geographic regions (northern, eastern, southern, western) and study each region. Or we can divide it according to the languages people speak in different parts or the way people make their living in different areas. We can also use logical division to study China over time, looking at the many stages in its history.

Finding a basis of division. A **basis of division** is a way to divide a topic. The two most common bases of division are *time* and *place*. These two concepts will help you divide many different topics into logical parts.

EXERCISE 2

*Read each topic idea and decide whether you would analyze it according to time or place. Write **T** (time) or **P** (place). Some topic ideas may be analyzed both ways.*

___P___ 1. the marketplace in San Salvador

_____ 2. New Year's celebration in Japan

_____ 3. a traditional meal in Morocco

_____ 4. economic zones in Portugal

_____ 5. ethnic groups in the former Yugoslavia

_____ 6. language groups in India

_____ 7. the Great Wall of China

_____ 8. the life of Albert Einstein

Compare your answers with your classmates'. Discuss any differences in your responses.

Place and *time* are not the only bases of division you can use in a logical division paper. When you analyze the life of a person like Albert Einstein, you can use *roles* (scientist, teacher, father) as well as *time* and *place*. When you write about a culture, you can select *aspects* such as music or architecture to discuss.

Your **purpose** (why you have chosen to write about a topic and the message you want to express about the topic) will determine the parts or aspects of your topic that you discuss. For example, if you wanted to show that Einstein was a better scientist and teacher than father, you would use *role* as an organizing principle. If you wanted to show that Einstein's life in Switzerland was more productive than his life in Germany or the United States, you would use *place* or *time*.

The Writing Process

Select a topic. Analyze the topics on page 49, or consider how you could divide each one into parts. Ask yourself what purpose you would have in writing about each topic. Notice how Dion, a student from Fiji, analyzed each topic before he selected one to write about. Dion chose topic 3, the celebration of Fiji Day, because it has three parts that he thought he could develop well.

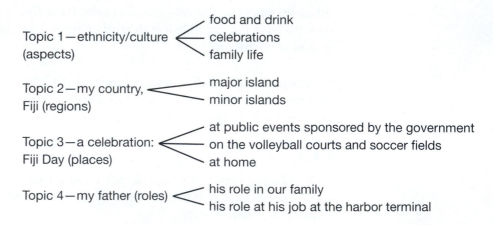

Topic 1—ethnicity/culture (aspects)
- food and drink
- celebrations
- family life

Topic 2—my country, Fiji (regions)
- major island
- minor islands

Topic 3—a celebration: Fiji Day (places)
- at public events sponsored by the government
- on the volleyball courts and soccer fields
- at home

Topic 4—my father (roles)
- his role in our family
- his role at his job at the harbor terminal

> **TIP**
> Choose a topic that has two or more parts you can develop well. The ideal number of parts is three, but two or four will work as well.

Follow the series of writing steps listed below. As you read through the steps, you will see how Dion prepared to write a paragraph about Fiji Day.

T I P

Remember that you can always revise a draft topic sentence as you work on your composition.

Topic sentence. After you have chosen a topic, you will be ready to draft a topic sentence. As you learned in Chapter 1, the purpose of a topic sentence is to help the reader focus on the main idea of the paragraph. Because your paragraph will analyze your topic and divide it in parts, the topic sentence should refer to those parts. Look at these examples.

> Fijian culture has three interesting aspects.

> The island country of Fiji has two regions.

Follow the series of writing steps. As you read through the steps, you will see how Dion prepared to write a paragraph about Fiji Day.

Dion's Steps

STEP 1 Draft a **topic sentence**.

Dion drafted this topic sentence.

> *Fijans celebrate Fiji Day in three places.*

STEP 2 Develop each part of your topic by making a **list** for it. If you have two parts, make two lists; if you have three parts, make three lists, and so on.

Dion decided to divide Fiji Day celebrations according to place. Because he had three locations to discuss, he made three lists.

At public events:

government officials' speeches

singing competition between church choirs

On the volleyball courts and soccer fields:

Young people gather and form casual teams.

After they play, they sit on the grass and chat.

Winners tease the losers, but there is no serious competition.

At home:

Relatives help prepare the meal, which includes palusami, a mixture of chicken or beef, onion, and tomato wrapped in a taro leaf and cooked in coconut milk.

The head of the household makes yaqona, our traditional drink, and offers it to the guests in coconut shell cups.

STEP 3 *Outlining.* Make an **outline**. Your outline must have three levels: **topic sentence, major supporting points**, and **development**.

Dion marked his topic sentence (*TS*), his supporting points (*SP*), and finally his development (*DEV*).

Fijians celebrate Fiji Day in three places. (TS)

I. The public events give a feeling of national pride and provide some fine traditional Fijian entertainment. (SP)

   A. Public speeches are delivered by elected officials. (DEV)

   B. Awards are presented for the young people's essay contest. (DEV)

   C. There is a singing competition between church choirs. (DEV)

II. Soccer and volleyball games give us a chance to meet and play together with friends. (SP)

   A. Winners tease the losers, but there is no serious competition. (DEV)

   B. Players stay to chat after the game. (DEV)

III. At home, a big celebration is underway. (SP)

   A. Friends and relatives arrive early to help make palusami, a mixture of chicken or beef, onion, and tomato wrapped in a taro leaf and cooked in coconut milk. (DEV)

   B. The head of the household makes yaqona, our traditional drink, in a large bowl and offers it to the guests in coconut shell cups. (DEV)

   C. After the drinking, everyone eats palusami, rice, and salad. (DEV)

When your outline is complete, you will be ready to write your first draft. Dion wrote the following paragraph.

Dion's First Draft

○ *Fiji Day*

○ [1] *Fijians celebrate Fiji Day in three places.* [2] *At the public celebrations, government officials' speeches and fine traditional Fijian entertainment stir feelings of national pride.* [3] *Awards are presented to young people for the annual essay competition, and there is a singing contest between church choirs.* [4] *On the beaches and in the parks, informal games of volleyball and soccer give young people a chance to play together and socialize.* [5] *Sometimes winners playfully tease the losers, but there is no serious competition.* [6] *After the games, players stay to chat with their friends.* [7] *Finally, at home a big celebration is underway.* [8] *Friends and relatives arrive early to help make palusami—a mixture of chicken, onion, and tomato, wrapped in a taro leaf and cooked in coconut milk.* [9] *The head of the household makes the traditional drink, yaqona, in a large bowl and offers it to the guests in coconut shells.* [10] *After the yaqona drinking, everyone eats palusami, rice, and salad.* [11] *Fiji Day is our most popular celebration because it incorporates all the things Fijians love most: our national heritage, sports, food and drink, and socializing with family and friends.*

With a partner or a small group, review Dion's paragraph.

1. Find the three levels of development in Dion's paragraph. Underline the first level (topic sentence), put a double line under the second level (supporting points), and put brackets [ ] around the third level (development).

2. How would you divide this paragraph if you were to expand it into a five-paragraph essay? Put slashes (*I*) to show where the introduction and each of the three body paragraphs would end. Discuss what kind of information you might add to the text in order to expand it into an essay.

After selecting a topic from the list on page 49 that you think you can explain well in terms of its parts, follow the sequence of steps Dion used and write your paragraph.

■ REVISING

Composition Focus

Before you expand your paragraph to an essay, check it to make sure that it communicates effectively. Follow the directions in the following **Revision Checkpoint**.

REVISION CHECKPOINT 1

First-Draft Paragraph

Review your paragraph. Ask yourself if it has the three levels a paragraph should have: a clear topic sentence that presents the main idea, supporting points, and development. Review the topic sentence to see whether it informs the reader that you are going to divide the topic into parts. If the topic sentence or the paragraph needs improvement, revise it now.

Expanding a paragraph to an essay. We read paragraphs as units of information. We can read a paragraph of ten or twelve sentences and keep all the ideas in mind. However, when paragraphs become longer than that, we find it difficult to focus on the whole paragraph at once.

   Therefore, when you have too much supporting information in a paragraph, you need to break it down into smaller paragraphs. In order to expand your one-paragraph composition to an essay, you will change your composition in the following ways:

1. **Topic Sentence** ⟶ **Thesis Statement**

   The topic sentence of your paragraph will become the thesis statement of your essay.

2. Supporting Points ⟶ Body Paragraphs

The supporting points will become the topic sentences of your body paragraphs.

3. Development ⟶ More Development

You will add more development to complete the body paragraphs of the essay. This is the most important part of changing a paragraph to an essay.

4. Concluding Sentence ⟶ Conclusion

The concluding sentence of your paragraph will become the conclusion of your essay.

In this chapter, you will learn how to develop the supporting points into body paragraphs and how to write an introduction for your essay. In Chapter 3, you will learn more about essay introductions and you will learn how to write an essay conclusion.

Outlining and expansion. When you expand a paragraph into an essay, you keep the same main idea statement and supporting points. Therefore, it is usually not necessary to make a new outline. The only thing you might add to your original outline is more development of your supporting points.

EXERCISE 4

A. *Read the paragraph and the essay about the culture of Kenya. You will see that the essay is an expansion of the paragraph. Then do the activities that follow.*

PARAGRAPH

The Cultures of Kenya: Enduring Aspects of a Diverse People

[1]Although Kenya has many different ethnic groups and these groups have been affected to various degrees by European colonization, the cultures of people across the nation share some common characteristics. [2]One enduring aspect of the cultures of Kenya is the importance of the family. [3]Traditionally, Kenyan people received all their education from their parents and grandparents. [4]Today there are schools to educate children, but the family is still very important as a social unit. [5]Another enduring aspect of Kenyan cultures is respect for the old. [6]Traditional society was organized around not only family life but also relationships with a group of people of the same age. [7]These same-age groups went through all the stages of life together until they became the much-respected elders who made decisions for the community. [8]Today old people are still respected, but they don't have the responsibility of leadership that they once had. [9]Another enduring aspect of Kenyan cultures is dance. [10]Traditionally, dances marked all the important events in life. [11]Kenyans in both the countryside and the cities still dance,

but most dancing is done simply for pleasure these days. [12]The traditional music of Kenya has been influenced by music from the United States and Europe, and new styles of music and dance have evolved. [13]To sum up, the cultures of Kenya's ethnic groups have undergone many changes, but family, respect for elders, and dance still have an important place in the lives of the people of Kenya.

The Cultures of Kenya: Enduring Aspects of a Diverse People

ESSAY INTRODUCTION

[1]Although Kenya contains many different ethnic groups and these groups have been affected to various degrees by European colonization, the cultures of people across the nation still share common characteristics: Families are important to them, they respect their elders, and they enjoy dance.

BODY PARAGRAPH

[2]One enduring aspect of the cultures of Kenya is the importance of the family. [3]Traditionally, people received all their education from their parents and grandparents in the form of stories, songs, and proverbs. [4]Although this is no longer the case today because schools educate the children, the family is still a vital social unit. [5]Most people in Kenya live on scattered farms with their families or extended families, and their nearest neighbors are relatives. [6]Usually everyone in their region is related to them in some way. [7]Clans or large extended families cooperate in community projects such as the building of schools. [8]To some extent, the growth in recent decades of large-scale farms and cities has put a strain on rural family life. [9]Fathers often go away to work for extended periods of time, leaving mothers and aging parents to manage the family farms. [10]This is a hardship for families, but the money that fathers send home helps with expenses such as school tuition.

BODY PARAGRAPH

[11]Another enduring aspect of Kenyan cultures is respect for the old. [12]Traditional society was organized around not only family life but also relationships with a group of people of the same age. [13]These same-age groups went through all the stages of life together until they became the much-respected elders who made decisions for the community. [14]Formerly, councils of elders were the only government the people had. [15]They made decisions, judged wrong-doing, and initiated social activities. [16]Today Kenya's central government and its regional branches have taken over these functions. [17]Although Kenyans still show respect for elders with gestures and greetings, old people do not have the leadership role they once had.

BODY PARAGRAPH

[18]Another enduring aspect of Kenyan cultures is dance. [19]Traditionally, dances marked all important events in life—coming-of-age ceremonies and weddings, wars

or hunts, planting and harvesting. [20]Traditional dances did not allow much self-expression; they were learned and performed in the same way that generations before had learned them. [21]The dances told stories and thus formed part of the education of the young people in the community. [22]For the most part, these traditional dances are only performed by professional dancers now, but all Kenyans still enjoy dancing. [23]The traditional music of Kenya has been influenced by jazz, rock, and hip-hop music from the United States and Europe, and, as a result, new styles of music have evolved, such as *benga,* which combines traditional rhythms and modern instrumentation. [24]Kenyans enjoy dancing to *benga* and many other styles of music that are a fusion of old and new.

CONCLUSION

[25]Traditional cultures in Kenya have undergone many changes, but family, respect for elders, and dance still have an important place in the lives of the people of Kenya.

B. **Compare the paragraph and the essay.**

1. *Main Idea Statement.* Find the main idea statement in the paragraph (topic sentence) and in the essay (thesis statement), and underline them. What is the difference between the two main idea statements?

2. *Supporting Points.* Find the supporting points in the paragraph and in the essay, and put double lines under them. Where are the supporting points in the essay? What transition words are used to mark the supporting points?

3. *Development.* Find the development for the supporting points in the paragraph and the essay and put brackets [ ] around it. How many sentences did the writer add to each supporting point in order to expand his ideas into an essay?

C. **With a partner, compare how you each marked the text. Discuss your observations with your teacher and classmates.**

D. **With your teacher and classmates, make an outline showing the structure of the paragraph and the essay.**

REVISION CHECKPOINT 2

Preparing to Expand Your Paragraph
Review your first-draft paragraph and the outline you prepared before writing. Put slashes (/) in your paragraph to show where you will divide it when you expand it to an essay. You may find it helpful to cut the paragraph up with scissors and then tape each piece to a separate piece of paper for expanding and revising. Or, if you are working on a computer, simply insert spaces between the various parts of your paragraph.

From topic sentence to thesis statement: Adding supporting points. In Chapter 1, you learned that a topic sentence has two parts, the topic and the controlling idea. The same is true of thesis statements. Because an essay contains a lot of information, it is helpful to the reader if the controlling idea names the supporting points. In a logical division essay, naming the supporting points means naming the parts. Compare the topic sentence and thesis statement below.

TOPIC SENTENCE:

Chinese New Year celebrations have three parts.

THESIS STATEMENT:

Chinese New Year celebrations have three **parts**: the preparations, New Year's Eve and New Year's Day, and the two weeks following New Year's Day.

The controlling idea of the thesis statement names the parts of the celebration (*the preparations, New Year's Eve and New Year's Day,* and *the two weeks following New Year's Day*). This helps the reader anticipate what will appear in the body paragraphs of the essay.

Vocabulary for logical division. In addition to the word *part*, other nouns can be used in the controlling idea of a logical division essay.

Time	Space	Parts or Qualities
period	district	aspect
stage	region	characteristic
	zone	element
		feature
		quality

EXERCISE 5

Complete each thesis statement with an appropriate word from the chart above. Mark each thesis statement C *(complete) if the thesis names the parts of the controlling idea or* I *(incomplete) if it does not name the parts of the controlling idea.*

_____I_____ 1. The island of Cyprus has two distinct ethnic
_____regions_____.

_____ 2. The culture of Haiti has three _____: the people's African heritage, the French language, and cultural influence from Latin America.

_____ 3. Each of Uruguay's four agricultural _____ has a certain type of product: fresh fruit and vegetables, milk and dairy products, grain, and meat.

_____ 4. Over time, the celebration of Christmas that we see in the United States today has developed in a series of _____.

_____ 5. The Brazilian dance called the *samba* has three important _____: rhythm, lyrics, and dance steps.

_____ 6. Dag Hammarskjöld, who was secretary-general of the United Nations from 1953 to 1961, is remembered for these _____: tactfulness, self-discipline, and a strong sense of duty.

_____ 7. The three dominant buildings of Thailand's Royal Palace symbolize three significant _____ in the country's history.

_____ 8. The cellist Yo-Yo Ma is greatly admired for two _____: his personal warmth and the sensitivity of his playing.

_____ 9. The celebration of Holy Week in Guatemala has two important _____: the religious objects that are carried in processions through the streets and the colors worn by the people in the processions.

_____ 10. The city of Salzburg, Austria, has three unique _____: The oldest is the medieval part with narrow, winding streets; the second oldest is the baroque part with wide boulevards and large public buildings; and the newest is the modern, industrial part with factories and high-rise apartment buildings.

REVISION CHECKPOINT 3

Supporting Points in Thesis Statements
Look at your composition. The topic sentence of your first-draft paragraph will become the thesis statement of your essay. Check the controlling idea of your thesis statement to see whether it lists the supporting points of your essay. If not, expand it so that it includes your supporting points.

Parallel structure in thesis statements. When your thesis statement lists your supporting points, the supporting points must be **parallel**. That is, they must be the same part of speech.

Underline parallel elements in the following examples.

1. In our region, most men work in offices, stores, and factories.
2. Our culture is unique because of its architectural, musical, and artistic traditions.

What elements are parallel in sentence 1? What part of speech are they? What elements are parallel in sentence 2? What part of speech are they?

In sentence 1, the words *offices, stores,* and *factories* are parallel. They are all nouns. It would be wrong to write the sentence this way:

INCORRECT: In our region, most men work in offices, stores, and industrial.

Offices and *stores* are nouns. *Industrial* is an adjective. That is why the sentence above is not parallel and is therefore incorrect.

 For more on parallel structure, see Appendix IA, page 254.

EXERCISE 6

Each statement contains a list that is not parallel. Find the word in each list that is not parallel and change its form so that the words are parallel. Then underline the parallel items.

1. The economy is based on ~~agricultural~~ agriculture, mining, and industry.
2. The inhabitants of the two regions share a common history, language, and architectural.
3. The names of cities and towns come from religion, history, or natural.
4. The language, art, and educational of this community have barely changed over the last 100 years.
5. The land can be divided into three parts: forest, grasslands, and dry.
6. The community has well-organized educational, political, and law organizations.
7. The city has three kinds of buildings: public, commercial, and houses.

REVISION CHECKPOINT 4

Parallel Structure in Thesis Statements
Look at your thesis statement again. If you have used a list in the controlling idea of your thesis, make sure that it has correct parallel structure.

Linking the thesis statement to the body paragraphs: Cohesion. When we read, we look for connections. If the parts of a paragraph or essay have clear connections, we say that the paragraph or essay has **cohesion**.

In essays, the most important connections are between the thesis statement and the topic sentences of the body paragraphs. These connections will be very clear in your essay if you:

1. name the supporting points in your thesis statement.

2. put the supporting points in the body paragraphs in the same order as they appear in your thesis statement.

3. repeat the words you have used in your thesis statement in the topic sentences of your body paragraphs or use *word forms* (members of the same word family) or *synonyms* (words that have the same or similar meaning).

4. use transitions such as *another, second,* and *finally* in the topic sentences of your body paragraphs.

EXERCISE 7

Work with a partner. One of you should read the essay "Fiji Day" below, and the other should reread "The Cultures of Kenya: Enduring Aspects of a Diverse People" on page 56. Find signals of cohesion in your assigned essay, and complete the chart that follows.

Fiji Day

[1]Fiji is an island nation in the South Pacific. [2]An important holiday in Fiji is October 10, Fiji Day, when the country celebrates its independence from British rule in 1970. [3]On Fiji Day we have a wonderful time celebrating at the public events, on the volleyball courts and on the soccer fields, and at home.

[4]At the public celebrations, government officials' speeches and fine traditional Fijian entertainment stir feelings of national pride. [5]Politicians remind us of the value of our independence and the importance of harmony in our multiethnic society. [6]Men wearing grass skirts and women wearing tapa cloth perform *meke*, a performance of dance and singing which tells a story. [7]Awards are presented to young people for the annual essay competition, and there is a singing contest between church choirs.

[8]On the beaches and in the parks, informal games of volleyball and soccer give young people a chance to get together and socialize. [9]Fiji Day comes in early October, when the weather is not too hot or humid, so the games can last for hours. [10]Sometimes the winners playfully tease the losers, but there is no serious competition. [11]After the games, players sit on the grass and chat, catching up with old friends and making new acquaintances.

[12]Finally, at home, friends and relatives arrive carrying baskets of breadfruit as the women prepare a celebratory feast. [13]They gossip in the kitchen as they make

palusami—a mixture of chicken, onion, and tomato, wrapped in a taro leaf and cooked in coconut milk. [14]Someone plays the guitar while the head of the household makes the traditional drink, *yaqona*, in a large bowl and offers it to the guests in coconut shells. [15]People sit on handwoven mats in a circle, celebrating as their ancestors have done: Upon receiving the cup they clap once, drink, say "Bula," and clap three times in appreciation. [16]After the *yaqona* drinking, everyone eats *palusami*, rice, yams, salad, and fish roasted in banana leaves. [17]The celebration can last long into the night.

[18]Fiji Day is our most popular celebration because it incorporates all the things Fijians love most: our national heritage, sports, food and drink, and socializing with family and friends.

Signals of Cohesion in _____
                                                    (Name of Essay)

1. Words or **phrases** from the thesis statement that are **repeated** in the topic sentences of the body paragraph:

_____

_____

2. Word forms used in the topic sentences of the body paragraphs that refer to words or phrases in the thesis statement:

_____

_____

3. Synonyms used in the topic sentences of the body paragraphs that refer to words or phrases in the thesis statement:

_____

_____

4. Transitions that link the topic sentences to the thesis statement and the body paragraphs to one another:

_____

_____

Discuss the signals of cohesion that you found with your partner. Why are signals of cohesion important? Do these two essays illustrate good cohesion?

REVISION CHECKPOINT 5

Cohesion

Check your thesis statement and the topic sentences of your body paragraphs for cohesion. If you have not used repeated words, word forms, synonyms, and transitions to link the thesis and the body paragraphs, add them now.

Using background information to write an essay introduction. Your readers may not be familiar with your topic, so providing some background information at the beginning of your essay is a good idea. Background information can answer the questions *Who, What, Where, When, Why,* and *How*. Read the introduction to "Fiji Day," and notice how it introduces the topic by answering readers' questions and, at the same time, leads readers to the thesis statement. The thesis statement is usually the last sentence in an introductory paragraph.

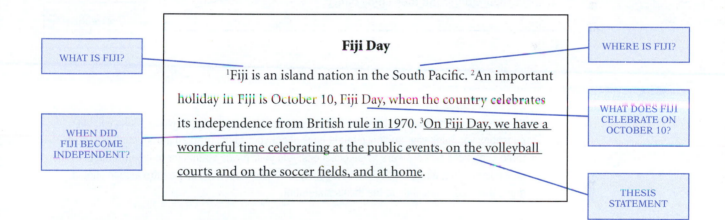

WHAT IS FIJI?

WHERE IS FIJI?

WHEN DID FIJI BECOME INDEPENDENT?

WHAT DOES FIJI CELEBRATE ON OCTOBER 10?

THESIS STATEMENT

Fiji Day

[1]Fiji is an island nation in the South Pacific. [2]An important holiday in Fiji is October 10, Fiji Day, when the country celebrates its independence from British rule in 1970. [3]On Fiji Day, we have a wonderful time celebrating at the public events, on the volleyball courts and on the soccer fields, and at home.

EXERCISE 8

Read this introduction to "The Cultures of Kenya: Enduring Aspects of a Diverse People," and write some questions that the introduction answers.

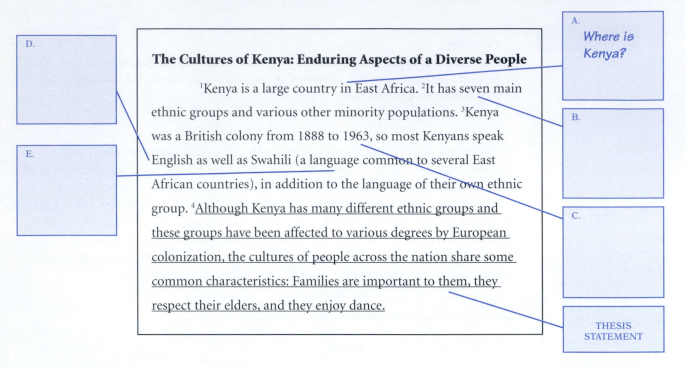

A. *Where is Kenya?*

B.

C.

D.

E.

THESIS STATEMENT

The Cultures of Kenya: Enduring Aspects of a Diverse People

¹Kenya is a large country in East Africa. ²It has seven main ethnic groups and various other minority populations. ³Kenya was a British colony from 1888 to 1963, so most Kenyans speak English as well as Swahili (a language common to several East African countries), in addition to the language of their own ethnic group. ⁴Although Kenya has many different ethnic groups and these groups have been affected to various degrees by European colonization, the cultures of people across the nation share some common characteristics: Families are important to them, they respect their elders, and they enjoy dance.

REVISION CHECKPOINT 6

Essay Introduction
Consider your audience and how much it knows about the topic of your essay. Make a list of questions you think your audience might have about your topic. Draft an introduction of two or three sentences that answers these questions. Add your thesis statement to the introduction, and check to see that all the sentences fit together well. The sentences in the introduction should guide the reader smoothly to the thesis statement.

Development of body paragraphs. The most important part of expanding a composition from a paragraph to an essay is developing its body paragraphs. The two main types of development are **examples** and **explanation**.

1. **Examples** are references to specific things or events that help readers understand general or abstract ideas. In Chapter 1 you learned to introduce examples with *for example, for instance, such as,* and *like*.

   In the celebration of Nawruz, or Persian New Year, symbolic things are displayed on a table. *For example*, there are silver coins, which represent prosperity, and eggs, which represent fertility. There are also herbs *such as* sumac and rue.

2. **Explanation** means providing information of various types to readers. Explanation can include:

   a. giving the meaning of words or symbols

> In the Nawruz celebration, the table is covered with a *sofreh*. This is a special tablecloth for the occasion.

   b. presenting a reason that something occurs

> Nawruz has its roots in the Zoroastrian religion. It is celebrated on March 21 because that is the birthday of the Zoroastrian prophet Zarathustra.

   c. telling the process by which something occurs

> Preparation for Nawruz begins weeks in advance. First, the whole house must be cleaned from top to bottom. Then new clothes are purchased, or old clothes are washed so that they can be worn on the holiday. Finally, special foods must be purchased and prepared according to tradition.

   d. describing how something looks or sounds

> Nawruz is a time of light-hearted fun. In the evening, people gather around bonfires, talking and laughing as they try to jump over the flames, following an ancient custom.

EXERCISE 9

Read the following essay. Two of the body paragraphs are well developed, but one needs additional examples and explanations. Write a message to the writer, telling him or her which paragraph needs development and suggesting ways to develop that paragraph.

Shanghai: Long-time Residents and Newcomers

[1]The population of Shanghai has grown very fast in recent years with a great influx of migrants from all over China, so there are now two groups of people in Shanghai: long-time Shanghai residents and newcomers. [2]The members of each group identify themselves by their language, clothing, and food.

[3]Language separates long-time Shanghai residents from newcomers. [4]Although Mandarin has replaced the local dialect as the official language of the city, long-term residents prefer to speak the local dialect in some situations. [5]New residents in Shanghai come from all parts of China, so they speak many different dialects.

[6]Clothing also distinguishes long-time Shanghai residents from newcomers. [7]Long-term residents are very fashion conscious. [8]Young people wear blue jeans, while older adults prefer suits. [9]Men and women alike respect brand names, which they sometimes display on handbags, footwear, or even business suits. [10]Women wear muted color combinations. [11]Newcomers often dress in traditional Chinese jackets and

work clothes. [12]The newcomer women tend to wear brighter colors than the long-term residents.

[13]Not only language and clothing, but also food serves to identify long-time Shanghai residents and newcomers. [14]The long-time residents eat rice porridge, flat bread, and fried dough sticks for breakfast, while the newcomers from the provinces prefer steamed bread or soup. [15]Also, because Shanghai is an international city, the original Shanghainese are more likely to sample Western foods. [16]For example, for lunch a long-time Shanghai resident might order a sandwich and a soda, while a newcomer would select a traditional meal of rice, vegetables, and bean curd.

[17]As Shanghai's population has grown, it has become apparent that there are two social groups in the city. [18]The residents of Shanghai identify themselves as either long-term residents or as newcomers by the way they speak, dress, and eat.

To the writer: _____

_____

_____

_____

REVISION CHECKPOINT 7	***Development of Body Paragraphs*** If your body paragraphs lack examples or explanation, add some now. Try to use various types of development (examples as well as explanations, which include the meaning of words, reasons, processes, or description) in your essay.

Language Focus

Expanding the noun phrase. One way to develop your body paragraphs is to expand the noun phrases in your sentences. There are several kinds of changes you can make.

- Use more specific nouns.

  a structure → a *hospital*

  a worker → a *technician*

- Add descriptive adjectives.

  a region → a *mountainous* region

  a group → a *musical* group

- Add noun modifiers.

    a building → an *apartment* building

    a market → a *fruit* market

- Add prepositional phrases.

    an area *of small family farms*

    a political leader *in the 1990s*

 For more on the order of adjectives and noun modifiers, see Appendix IA, page 236. For more on noun modifiers, see Appendix IA, page 236. For more on prepositions, see Appendix IA, page 264.

EXERCISE 10

*With a partner, read the phrases. Then label the adjectives (**adj.**), the noun modifiers (**n.m.**), the nouns (**n.**), and the prepositional phrases (**prep. ph.**) Use a dictionary if necessary, but note that the dictionary will identify a noun modifier as a noun.*

       (n.m.)   (n.) ┌─── (prep. ph.) ───┐

1. the business district with its skyscrapers
2. the final evening of the festival
3. an important German film director in the twentieth century
4. the largest ancient palace complex with 980 buildings
5. beautiful love poems in Farsi

EXERCISE 11

With a partner, replace each general noun with a more specific noun. Then add an adjective or a noun modifier and a prepositional phrase to each specific noun.

1. celebration   _____wedding_____   a large wedding in June
2. artist   _____painter_____   a well-known landscape painter from China
3. meal   _____   _____
4. text   _____   _____
5. event   _____   _____
6. leader   _____   _____
7. area   _____   _____

Specific Noun Phrases
Review your body paragraphs, and underline the noun phrases. Consider making some of your noun phrases more specific. Check to see if you can improve your writing by using more specific nouns or by adding adjectives, noun modifiers, and prepositional phrases to your noun phrases.

Adjective clauses. An adjective clause is a dependent clause that modifies a noun. Adjective clauses begin with the relative pronouns *who, whom, which, that, whose, where,* and *when.* Adjective clauses provide a way to combine short sentences and show relationships between ideas. Look at the following examples.

1a. King Sejong ruled Korea during a time of peace and prosperity. He invented the Korean alphabet.

RELATIVE
PRONOUN

1b. (King Sejong), **who** *invented the Korean alphabet*, ruled Korea during a time of peace and prosperity.

2a. The Korean alphabet is relatively easy to learn. It has fourteen consonants and ten vowels.

RELATIVE
PRONOUN

2b. The (Korean alphabet), **which** *has fourteen consonants and ten vowels*, is relatively easy to learn.

In the examples above, notice that the relative pronouns **who** and **which** follow the nouns that they modify. In example 1b, **who** refers to *King Sejong*, and in example 2b, **which** refers to *Korean alphabet*.

 For more on adjective clauses, see Appendix IA, page 229.

EXERCISE 12

A. *This essay contains <u>seven</u> adjective clauses. Underline the adjective clauses and circle the nouns they modify.*

¹The (Nile,) <u>which is the longest river in the world</u>, flows through northeastern Africa from Lake Victoria to the Mediterranean Sea. ²The history of the relationship between the Nile and the people of Egypt has two parts: the period before the Aswan Dam was built and the period since.

³Over 4,000 years ago, the Nile made ancient Egypt a birthplace of civilization. ⁴The river brought water to this extremely dry land, where agriculture would not have been possible without its annual flooding. ⁵The floodwaters also distributed a fine dark soil called silt, which is rich in nutrients. ⁶The ancient Egyptians learned to trap the waters of the Nile for irrigation and to raise enough food to support their thriving

civilization. [7]The Nile also provided food in the form of fish and waterfowl, and the plant called *papyrus* grew along its banks, from which the ancient Egyptians made paper. [8]While Egyptians still depend on the Nile today, their relationship to the river, and the river itself, have changed.

[9]The Nile was altered in 1971, when the Aswan High Dam was completed. [10]The river does not flood its banks anymore, so the Egyptian people, most of whom live along its banks, no longer have to worry about annual floodwaters destroying their homes. [11]Egyptian farmers today are able to raise food year round because there is a constant supply of water, whereas in centuries past, they could produce only one crop a year. [12]When the dam went into operation, new lands were opened to farming in the Upper Nile, but at the same time, agricultural lands were lost in the delta region, where saltwater from the Mediterranean flooded the fields and made them unusable.

[13]The two-part history of the Nile has an important lesson: People have benefited from this great river, which has allowed civilization to flourish for over 4,000 years, and so people must take responsibility for the Nile's future.

B. *Now read the essay without the adjective clauses. Notice how much information the clauses contribute.*

EXERCISE 13

*Read each paragraph and the list of sentences following it. Find a place in the paragraph for each sentence, change the sentence to an adjective clause, and insert it in the paragraph. To help you, the part of the sentence which must be changed to a relative pronoun (*who, which, where,* or *when) is underlined. Rewrite the sentences to which you have added adjective clauses on another piece of paper. Punctuate all the adjective clauses in this exercise with commas.*

Example

Another region in Brazil is known as the Pantanal, which means *swampland* in Portuguese. . . .

1. This paragraph is from an essay that describes geographic regions in Brazil.

[1]Another region in Brazil is known as the Pantanal. [2]This vast lowland area in western Brazil is completely flooded in the rainy season from November to April. [3]The Pantanal is not suitable for farmland because of its poor soil, but it has been used for cattle grazing since the eighteenth century. [4]The Pantanal has remarkably varied wildlife

including jaguars, wild pigs, giant river otters, large crocodilians called caimans, and capybaras. [5]There are at least 700 species of birds, including twenty-six kinds of parrots. [6]There are 260 species of fish. [7]In the dry season, when the lakes and ponds shrink to small pools, flocks of birds and caimans gather to feast upon the numerous fish trapped in them. [8]Brazilians say, "O Pantanal é vida," and the Pantanal is truly a very important part of the web of life on the South American continent.

    a. <u>Pantanal</u> means *swampland* in Portuguese.

    b. <u>In the eighteenth century</u> cowboys first staked out tracts of land as large as 12,000 square kilometers.

    c. <u>Capybaras</u> are the biggest rodents in the world.

    d. Many of <u>the species of fish</u> survive on fruits and nuts during the annual floods.

    e. <u>"O Pantanal é vida"</u> means "The Pantanal is life."

2. This paragraph is from an essay about aspects of Arab culture.

    [1]Another important aspect of Arab culture is hospitality. [2]In Arab countries from Morocco to Iraq, visitors are very warmly welcomed. [3]Relatives, friends, and even strangers are always offered coffee or tea and perhaps some bread or sweets, and if they happen to arrive at mealtime, they are urged to stay and eat. [4]Guests cannot refuse these offers without offending their host. [5]This tradition of hospitality dates back thousands of years. [6]To survive in the desert, nomadic tribesmen had to depend on one another, so it became a matter of honor to give and receive hospitality. [7]The Quran and the books known as the *hadith* have helped preserve this tradition of hospitality by urging people to practice kindness. [8]But the holy books do not say that kindness and hospitality must be given without limit. [9]Guests must know when to leave, and hospitality must be returned. [10]Hospitality can strengthen the bonds between the members of society only when its rules are followed well.

    a. <u>Their host</u> feels that how well he treats his guests is a measure of the kind of person he is.

    b. Water and food are scarce <u>in the desert</u>.

    c. <u>The Quran</u> is the chief holy book of Islam.

    d. <u>The *hadith*</u> relate the life story and teachings of the prophet Mohammed.

    e. <u>Hospitality</u> is actually part of a system of mutual obligations.

3. This paragraph is from an essay about economic zones in Mexico.

[1]The *maquiladora* zone is in the north, especially in the cities of Tijuana, Ciudad Juarez, and Matamoros. [2]*Maquiladoras* produce plastics, clothing, furniture, appliances, and electronic and automobile components. [3]*Maquiladora* owners take advantage of the relatively low cost of labor in Mexico. [4]The *maquiladora* workers have migrated to this border region from central and southern Mexico. [5]Most *maquiladoras* are owned by U.S., Japanese, and European companies such as IBM, Sony, and BMW. [6]As long as trading conditions remain favorable, international companies are likely to continue opening new *maquiladoras*.

a. <u>Tijuana, Ciudad Juarez, and Matamoros</u> are located near the U.S. border.

b. <u>Plastics, clothing, furniture, appliances, and electronic and automobile components</u> are shipped to the United States and other countries around the world.

c. Workers <u>in Mexico</u> earn a fraction of what U.S. industrial workers earn.

d. <u>The *maquiladora* workers</u> cannot find employment in their villages and towns.

e. <u>U.S., Japanese, and European companies such as IBM, Sony, and BMW</u> can import machinery and materials to Mexico duty-free.

 ***For the use of commas with adjective clauses, see Appendix IA, page 231.***

For the use of commas with adjective clauses, see Appendix IA, page 231.

REVISION CHECKPOINT 9

Adjective Clauses
Make sure your body paragraphs are well developed. Check to see if your composition has some adjective clauses. If you think your body paragraphs need more development, look for ways to use adjective clauses to include more information in your body paragraphs.

■ FINAL DRAFT

1. Before you write your final draft, look over your essay one last time to decide if you want to make any further changes.

2. Prepare a final draft of your composition. Make sure that you have used capital letters at the beginning of your sentences and periods at the end, and check your spelling.

3. Exchange papers with one or two classmates. Read each other's papers carefully. Turn to page 297 in Appendix II, and fill out the Peer Review Form.

4. Check your paper again and make any necessary corrections. Turn in your paper to your teacher.

■ CHAPTER REVIEW

Look back at what you have accomplished in Chapter 2. Check (✔) what you have learned and what you have used as you have written and revised your composition.

Chapter 2 Topics	Learned	Used
using logical division by time, place, or another organizing principle to analyze a topic (pages 49–54)		
expanding a paragraph to an essay by developing the supporting points in body paragraphs (pages 54–57)		
expanding main idea statements and using parallel structure to list supporting points in thesis statements (pages 58–60)		
using repeated words, word forms, synonyms, and transitions to link the thesis statement to the topic sentences of the body paragraphs to increase cohesion in the essay (pages 61–63)		
using background information to write an essay introduction (pages 63–66)		
expanding noun phrases to make your writing more specific (pages 66–67)		
using adjective clauses to include more information in sentences and develop body paragraphs (pages 68–71)		

Full Pockets, Empty Pockets

Writing a Cause-and-Effect Essay

Around the world people find themselves in very different living conditions—some rich and comfortable, some harsh and miserable—and they often live their whole lives without realizing that their situation is not typical of the other 6.8 billion Earth-dwellers. A look at the contrast that exists today invites serious questions.

This chapter will help you

- write a complete essay with an introduction and a conclusion.
- practice two methods of organization: time order and order of importance.
- use transitions to make the essay's organization clear.
- write well-developed body paragraphs that have unity.
- use the language of cause and effect.

■ READING FOR WRITING

Before You Read

A. *Discuss this question with a partner or a small group.*

This map shows the relative wealth of the world's countries as measured by the value of all goods and services produced by each country within a year. Which countries are the wealthiest? Which regions of the world have some of the poorest countries?

Gross Domestic Product ($US)

15 trillion

5 trillion

1 trillion

100 billiion

5 billion

Source: CIA World Factbook 2008 figures

B. *Complete the following tasks.*

International Monetary Fund (IMF): *an international organization that works with the World Bank to coordinate economic policies among nations*

Periphery countries: *countries on the outside and so not as involved or important as others*

1. Economists have different ways of classifying countries. Sometimes they call the richest countries *developed countries* because these countries have the most industry and the highest *GDP* (GDP, or *gross domestic product*, means the value of all goods and services produced in the country). The richest countries are also known as *Core countries* because they play a central role in global relationships: They have the most international trade, the largest number of Internet users, and the most influence in global organizations such as the United Nations and the **International Monetary Fund (IMF)**. The poorest countries are sometimes called *underdeveloped countries* because they have the least industry and the lowest GDP. These countries are also known as **Periphery countries** because they are outside of most global trade and global decision making. Finally, countries in the middle—those with a moderate amount of industry and mid-range GDP—-are called *developing countries* or *New Core* countries.

Using the information in the map, write the names of two Core countries, two New Core countries, and two Periphery countries on this diagram. Then compare your answers with your classmates'.

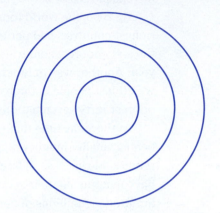

2. Core (developed) and Periphery (underdeveloped) countries have very different characteristics. Write **C** next to a characteristic if you think it refers to Core countries and **P** if you think it refers to Periphery countries.

_C_   a. The country has a high *per capita income*. (Per capita income means the average personal income in a country.)

_____   b. The citizens of the country consume a large percentage of the world's resources (oil, minerals, water, forests, fish, etc.).

_____   c. The country has borrowed a lot of money from the *World Bank*. (The World Bank is an international organization that loans money to governments and private companies for economic development.)

disparity: *inequality*

Reading

GLOBAL ECONOMIC DISPARITY
by Bruce Clark and John Wallace

1   Globalization is a trend toward greater economic, political, and cultural connection between the world's nations. Most observers agree that economic globalization has created more wealth in the world. Unfortunately, the economic growth has not been shared equally among all nations and among the people within each country. While the wealthier nations have seen their economies grow, poorer countries have not. At the same time, some people— whether in rich countries or poor—are much better off financially than others.

Disparity among Nations

2   For the world's poor, the situation has been described as "a race to the bottom." The United Nations has reported that per capita incomes in 100 countries, with a combined population of 1.6 billion, have dropped from

(continued)

the highest levels ever reached. This decline has not been just a recent **phenomenon**. Sadly, almost twenty countries reached their maximum per capita income in 1960 or before, and fifty more reached theirs in the 1960s and 1970s.

3   By 2006, the world found itself in the sad situation in which its twenty richest countries had per capita incomes of more than US$30,000, while the sixty poorest countries had per capita incomes of less than $3,000 per year. Another way of looking at the problem is that the assets of the three wealthiest people in the world total about the same as the total GDP of the poorest forty-seven nations.

4   At the same time that many countries have become poorer, there have been a smaller number of economic winners, some of whom have enjoyed remarkable success. While the traditional "fat cat" countries of the **Old Core** have maintained their economic growth, they have been joined by many hundreds of millions of people who live in New Core countries. The most notable of these New Core countries are China and India, whose economies have been growing at enormously fast rates. In each of these countries, hundreds of millions of people have benefited from rising standards of living, although even more people remain dreadfully poor.

5   Supporters of globalization have used a **metaphor** to explain how it should work: They say that "a rising tide lifts all boats." **Critics** of globalization would change the metaphor to "a rising tide drowns those who do not own boats." Some observers say that what seems to have happened is not that poorer countries are being harmed by globalization, but rather, they are being ignored.

Extreme Poverty in the World

6   Hundreds of millions of people live on a few dollars or less per day. The United Nations calls this situation extreme poverty. Compare this amount to how much you spend to go to a movie or buy a new pair of jeans. More than 900 million people have to survive for a day on less than what you might spend for popcorn at a movie theater.

Causes of Economic Disparity

7   The causes of the world's economic disparity are complex. As you look at the reasons that follow, remember that economic disparity between countries is often a product of poor or unfair political and economic decisions in the past, rather than a result of fundamental differences in the richness of the **resource base** of different countries. The obvious solution for the future would be to make better decisions.

Impact of Colonialism

8   Most developing countries were, at one time or another, colonies. Colonization produced **distortions** in the economic structures of these countries that still have a huge impact, even though they may have been independent for a half century or more.

Population Growth

9   In general, developing countries have experienced (and are still experiencing) **substantially** higher rates of population growth than the developed world. This means that economic growth in developing countries has provided at best a miserable level of existence for more and more people, rather than a higher standard of living for a more **stable** population.

Foreign Debt

10   In 1977, the sixty poorest countries owed US$650 billion for various loans that they had received. In the next thirty years, they made US$540 billion in loan payments and still owed US$523 billion to foreign governments and private lenders. Another way of looking at this sad reality is that developing countries paid US$13 in debt repayment (almost totally for interest) for every dollar they received in aid. The result is that they had little money left to invest in vital economic development, education, and health care.

War

11   The poorest countries, especially those in Africa, have often had to deal with the devastation of wars and **civil unrest** arising from tribal conflicts and the ambitions of warlords. Some civil conflicts, like those in Colombia, Mozambique, and the Democratic Republic of the Congo, have been going on for decades.

Leadership Issues

12   Many of the poorest countries in the world have had to deal with leaders who had little interest or skill in improving the economic **lot** of the citizens of their countries. Far too often they have used their positions to steal millions— and in some cases, billions—of dollars for their own use.

Trade Inequities

13   The Core nations have traditionally used **tariff** and **non-tariff barriers** to restrict imports from developing countries. For example, the tariffs placed by these countries on cloth and clothing produced in Africa and the Middle East are four times as high as the tariffs on similar products from Core countries. At the same time, the Core nations, and in particular the E.U., the U.S., and Japan, subsidize their agricultural products so that they are often as cheap or cheaper than **commodities** from developing countries. Trade policies in the Core that are fair to all would help poorer countries to reach their economic **potential** without relying on direct aid from richer countries.

Local Control

14   Citizens of developing countries complain that they lack the power to control their own affairs. They point out that far too many **critical** decisions are made outside their countries by international groups like the United

(continued)

substantially: *a lot*

✱stable: *unchanging*

✱civil unrest: *conflict between groups in a nation's population*

lot: *condition*

inequity: *unfairness*

tariff: *a tax on imported goods*

non-tariff barrier: *subsidy or government action to stop the movement of goods into a country*

✱commodity: *a product that is bought and sold*

✱potential: *ability to grow in the future*

critical: *important*

Nations, the World Bank, and the International Monetary Fund (IMF), by transnational corporations and the powerful governments of Core nations.

interact: *affect each other*

15   The solution to the problem of global inequity is complex. It requires an understanding of each of the factors listed above and of how they **interact** in each country. Those who work to solve the problems of poor countries must also remember that the problems and solutions for each country are different.

ABOUT the AUTHOR

Bruce Clark and John Wallace are high school instructors in Canada who have written several textbooks together. They both hold multiple degrees in geography and education, and together they have over sixty years teaching experience.

Understanding the Reading

With a partner or a small group, discuss the questions.

1. The poorest people in the world lack a great many things that you may have. For example, they may not have three meals a day. Make a list of the things you believe the poorest people lack. After making your list, rank the items in order of importance from 1 (least important) to 5 (most important).

2. Do the authors have an optimistic or a pessimistic view of the global economy today? What words or phrases in the title and first four paragraphs provide clues to their point of view? What do you think was their purpose in writing this passage?

3. In paragraph 5, Clark and Wallace present two opposing opinions of the impact of economic globalization on the disparity among nations. What does the metaphor "a rising tide lifts all boats" mean? What does "a rising tide drowns those who do not own boats" mean? In your opinion, which view is correct? Why?

4. a. In paragraphs 7–14, Clark and Wallace list seven reasons that developing countries are not catching up with the developed countries. Looking back at the text, check (✔) three problems that you think can be addressed, or fixed, in some way. (It is helpful to have an example in mind, so try to focus on the economic problems of *one* country when you do this.)

   b. Look at the three causes of global inequality that you have identified in item 4a and describe a way to reduce or eliminate the problem. For each cause, tell *who* should do *what* to reduce inequality. For example, referring to paragraph 14, you could say, "To reduce the problem of lack of local control in poor countries, the wealthy countries and international organizations such as the World Bank and the IMF should agree not to interfere with local leaders' rights to set their own economic policies."

Vocabulary Expansion

Adjectives used as nouns. In English, some adjectives are used with *the* to refer to classes of people. Some examples are *the poor, the wealthy, the old,* and *the young.* The following three sentences all have the same meaning. Which sentence is the most concise?

> This magazine is read by **people who are young**.

> This magazine is read by **young people**.

> This magazine is read by **the young**.

EXERCISE 1

A. *Change the sentences, replacing the phrase* **people who are . . .** *with an adjective used as a noun.*

1. In societies and between countries, there is often envy of people who are rich.

   In societies and between countries, there is often envy of the rich.

2. People who are uneducated have a hard time catching up.

   _____

3. It is usually hard for people who are undernourished to be productive.

   _____

4. Governments should not overlook people who are unfortunate.

   _____

5. People who are powerful decide which projects to invest in and which to ignore.

   _____

6. Many people feel that people who are prosperous should share their wealth.

   _____

B. *Each of the adjectives used as a noun in Exercise 1A has an* **antonym** *(a word with the opposite meaning). For example, the antonym of* **the rich** *is* **the poor.** *List the antonyms of the adjectives used as nouns in the exercise above.*

1. __the poor__   4. _____

2. _____   5. _____

3. _____   6. _____

Verbs used as adjectives. In English it is common to find adjectives that are made from **participles**, the *-ed* and *-ing* parts of verbs. Verbs have two participles, a **present participle** and a **past participle**.

VERB: develop

PRESENT PARTICIPLE: developing

PAST PARTICIPLE: developed

Both present participles and past participles can be used as **participial adjectives**.

Developing countries want to have more technology.

Developed countries have a lot of technology.

What is the difference between these two participial adjectives? Which participial adjective indicates that a process is ongoing? Which indicates that a process is complete?

The *-ing* participial adjective indicates that a process is going on. The *-ed* participial adjective indicates that a process is complete.

Participial adjectives provide a way to make sentences more concise. It is sometimes possible to change an adjective clause to a participial adjective. Compare these two sentences:

The *inequality which is rising* is a concern to everyone.

The *rising inequality* is a concern to everyone.

EXERCISE 2

Replace the adjective clause with a participial adjective in each sentence. First, underline the noun and adjective clause. Then, to select the appropriate participial adjective, decide whether the verb in the adjective clause indicates a process that is ongoing or a process that is complete.

1. <u>Countries that have industrialized</u> usually have a large middle class.

   Industrialized countries usually have a large middle class.

2. Countries that are industrializing need tariffs to protect their new industries.

   _____

3. Economies that are growing need infrastructure such as roads and telephone lines.

   _____

4. Rivers and beaches that have been polluted can be restored.

_____

5. Factories that are polluting should be required to clean up their operations.

_____

6. There will be demand that is increasing for technology to reduce pollution.

_____

 For more on participial adjectives, see Appendix IA, page 237.

EXERCISE 3

In order to learn the words that are new to you in Exercises 1 and 2, write statements about your country and its economy on another piece of paper. Underline these new words in your example sentences.

■WRITING

Assignment

Choose one of the following topics and write an essay.

1. Write about the effects of globalization on your country, region, or city.

2. Write about the reasons that your country has a strong or weak economy.

3. Write about the economic effects of an event in your country, region, or city. Some examples of events that can bring about positive or negative economic effects are the following: a new government policy (formal plan of action), a treaty (an agreement between nations), the introduction of new technology, a war, or an environmental disaster.

4. *Migration* (the movement of people from one place to another) is part of globalization. Write about the reasons that people migrate in today's world.

What Cause and Effect Is and Why It Is Important

When we experience change, we want to know *why* things happen and what their *effects* will be. Whether it is a war, an accident, or just the experience of catching a cold, we ask the same questions: What are the reasons that this happened? What will the results be? Understanding cause and effect helps us analyze events, and knowing how to write about cause and effect is essential to being a competent writer.

In this chapter, you will learn to write a cause-and-effect essay. Brainstorming your topic before you write will help you discover several causes (reasons) or effects and organize them.

Organizing a cause-and-effect essay: Time order and order of importance. Generally, cause-and-effect essays are organized by either **time order** or **order of importance**. When organizing a list of causes or effects, look for time order first. If you don't see any time relationships, use order of importance.

Look at the sample question and the two different sets of answers. What is the difference between the first and second set of answers?

> Why did the family become wealthy?
>
> 1. • They saved money from growing wheat.
>
>   • They bought more land and grew more wheat.
>
>   • They bought equipment to save labor.
>
>   • They bought a mill to process the wheat so that they could sell directly to retailers.
>
> 2. • They had five healthy sons.
>
>   • They were quite well educated.
>
>   • They worked very hard together.

The first set of answers gives the process, step-by-step, that the family used to gain wealth. This is time order. The second set of answers lists the reasons they became wealthy in order of importance from less to more important, with the most important last. (People do not always agree on what is most important, so individuals might organize a list by order of importance differently.)

EXERCISE 4

A. *Look at the thesis statements on page 83 and lists of supporting points. Number the supporting points to show how you would organize them. Organize the points by time order or by order of importance. (Look for time order first.) You may want to work with a partner or a small group.*

1. THESIS: Government investment in higher education has several effects.

   __2__ Over time, the skills of the workforce increase.

   __1__ College enrollment increases.

   __3__ The country's economy shows greater productivity.

2. THESIS: Inflation, or an increase in consumer prices, has several effects.

   _____ When prices rise, people buy less.

   _____ When factories slow down, workers are laid off.

   _____ When people buy less, factories must slow their rate of production.

3. THESIS: There are several reasons that a product costs more when it is imported.

   _____ Sellers can ask the highest price that they think customers will pay.

   _____ There are transportation costs involved in moving the product from the country where it was made to the country of sale.

   _____ Exchange rates and tariffs affect the price of imported products.

4. THESIS: When a country opens its markets to imports, there are several effects.

   _____ The new items compete with domestic goods.

   _____ Domestic industries have to adjust by lowering production costs and reducing prices.

   _____ People rush to buy the new items.

5. THESIS: Poor people need bank credit for several reasons.

   _____ When people suffer hardships such as natural disasters or illness, small loans can make the difference between life and death.

   _____ People can sometimes escape poverty if they can borrow small amounts to start small businesses.

   _____ There is a lot of unemployment in poor communities. If there are loans, there will be more business, so unemployment will decrease.

Note that when one point is clearly much more important than the others, the normal order of importance (least to most important) is sometimes reversed. Writers often put a point that is obviously important first because readers anticipate it. For example, the first choice under item 5 above says, "small loans can make the difference between life and death." A matter of life and death is of obvious importance, so many writers would put this idea first.

B. Discuss your answers with your classmates.

The Writing Process

Before you write, do the following prewriting activities. As you read through the steps, you will see how Chong Ho, a student from South Korea, prepared to write about the effects of economic growth on his city, Seoul, the capital of South Korea.

Chong Ho's Steps

STEP 1 Make a **list**, and, if possible, discuss it with friends or classmates. Then use your list to draft a **thesis statement**.

Chong Ho made a list of all the effects of economic growth he had seen in Seoul.

- many more cars, some fancy cars
- air pollution
- more roads, bridges, and buildings
- more factories; People now manufacture electronics and automobiles, whereas they used to make shoes and clothing.
- The city's boundary is constantly expanding.
- loss of farmland
- New suburbs are continually being built; entire satellite cities arise from farmland over the course of two or three years.
- Although people have little leisure time, golf is popular, and some people belong to private clubs to play.
- People who were farmers now dwell in high-rise apartments.
- People used to cook at home only; now they can afford to eat out.

After discussing his list, Chong Ho was able to focus on the two most important effects, which he used to draft his thesis.

Draft Thesis Statement

Over the past forty or fifty years, my city, Seoul, has experienced great economic growth. This growth has had two major effects: The city has grown, and the people have a better standard of living.

STEP 2 **Number** the items on your list according to how they relate to the controlling idea of your draft thesis statement. **Cross out** the items that do not relate to the supporting points that you plan to address in your body paragraphs.

Chong Ho went back to his list and numbered items relating to urban growth (1) and items relating to the standard of living (2). He crossed out the items that did not relate to either point.

(2) • many more cars, some fancy cars

~~• air pollution~~

(1) • more roads, bridges, and buildings

(2) • more factories; People now manufacture electronics and automobiles whereas they used to make shoes and clothing.

(1) • The city's boundary is constantly expanding.

~~loss of farmland~~

(1) • New suburbs are continually being built; entire satellite cities arise from farmland over the course of two or three years.

(2) • Although people have little leisure time, golf is popular, and some people belong to private clubs to play.

(2) • People who were farmers now dwell in high-rise apartments.

(2) • People used to cook at home only; now they can afford to eat out.

STEP 3 Make a **cluster** for each supporting point to make sure that you have enough information for each body paragraph. (A cluster is a diagram of connected circles that shows cause-and-effect development.) Clustering will help you see the relationships between your supporting ideas.

Chong Ho made one cluster about each of these two major effects: urban growth and improved standard of living.

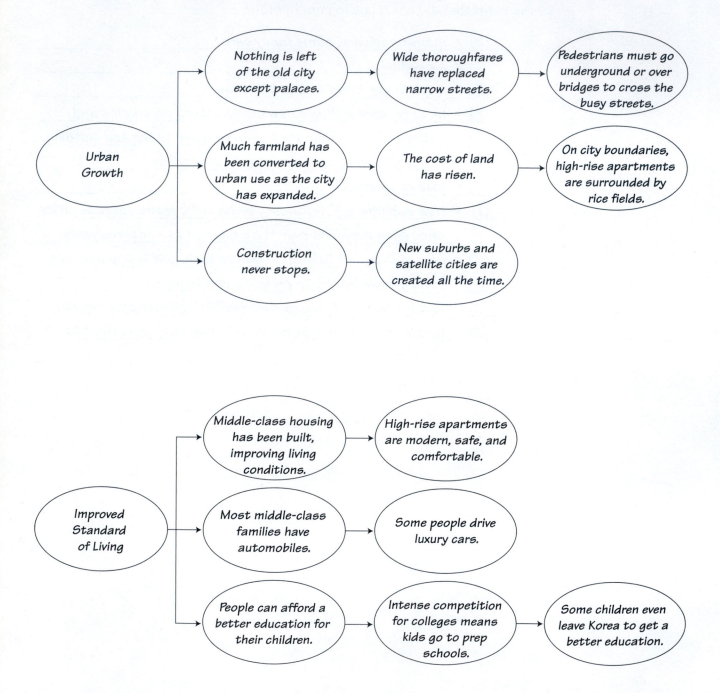

STEP 4 Make an **outline** that shows three levels of development. You may organize the supporting ideas on your outline according to **time** or **importance**.

Chong Ho labeled the three levels of development: thesis statement (**TS**), supporting points/topic sentences for body paragraphs (**SP**), and development of the supporting points (**DEV**).

Over the past forty or fifty years, my city, Seoul, has experienced great economic growth. This growth has had two major effects: urban expansion and an improved standard of living. (TS)

I. *Economic growth produced urban expansion. (SP)*
   A. *The city center has been transformed. (DEV)*
   B. *Much farmland has been converted to urban use. (DEV)*
   C. *There is ongoing construction of suburbs and satellite cities. (DEV)*

II. *Economic growth has improved people's standard of living; there is now a large middle class. (SP)*
   A. *New housing means improved living conditions. (DEV)*
   B. *Most middle-class families have automobiles. (DEV)*
   C. *People can afford to invest more in their children's education. (DEV)*

When your outline is complete, you will be ready to write your first draft, which will be an essay consisting of a thesis statement and body paragraphs. You will develop your introduction and conclusion later—in the process of revising.

After several drafts, Chong Ho wrote his finished essay.

Chong Ho's Final Draft

The Effects of Economic Growth on Seoul

1   [1]My family is from Seoul, the capital of South Korea, a city that has been completely transformed since our country began a great push for economic growth in the 1960s. [2]This phenomenal growth has had two major effects: urban expansion and an improvement in the standard of living.

2   [3]One effect of economic growth is urbanization. [4]Seoul is now many times larger than it used to be. [5]The city center has been transformed. [6]Where there used to be narrow winding streets lined by one-story houses, today there are glass skyscrapers and such wide, busy thoroughfares that pedestrians can only cross via underground tunnels. [7]The only remnants of the past in central Seoul are three magnificent palaces with their stately grounds and five gates that marked the boundaries of the old walled city. [8]Much of the land under present-day Seoul was farmland fifty years ago. [9]As the economy expanded, land values rose. [10]Farmers became rich by selling their fields for the construction of factories and high-rise apartment buildings. [11]This process has not stopped; new suburbs and satellite cities are being created all the time. [12]A strange sight is seen on the boundaries of Seoul: Gray high-rise apartment buildings rise up from brilliant green rice fields. [13]Farmland is now nearly as scarce as places for people to live.

3   [14]Another effect of economic growth is the rise of the middle class. [15]Before the industrial age in Korea, there was almost no middle class. [16]Now there is a large middle class that can afford to dine out in traditional Korean restaurants or enjoy American-style fast-food snacks. [17]They can afford automobiles, cell phones, and computers, and they may even find a little time for golf. [18]The government has used the profits from a growing economy to invest in education. [19]This means that all Koreans attend good public

schools, so even children from lower-class families have a chance to go to universities. [20]Competition for the best universities is intense, however, so parents who can afford it send their children to prep schools that coach the youngsters to pass the entrance exams. [21]Those who are able may even send their children overseas to improve their chances of getting ahead.

4   [22]Forty or fifty years of dramatic economic growth have transformed Seoul. [23]As a result, its residents, who now number over 10 million, have had to adapt to a very urban environment that is continually changing. [24]Fortunately, this rapid growth has resulted in more equality in Korean society, which has made it easier to accept the changes.

EXERCISE 5

With a partner or a small group, review Chong Ho's essay and discuss the following questions.

1. Can you find three levels of development in Chong Ho's essay? Tell a partner what they are.

2. Does Chong Ho's essay have good cohesion? Check the order of the supporting points in the thesis statement and in the topic sentences of the body paragraphs. Look for repeated words or phrases, word forms, and synonyms, and underline them. Circle the transitions.

After selecting a topic from the list on page 81, follow the sequence of prewriting steps Chong Ho used, and then write your first draft.

■ REVISING

This part of the chapter will show you how to expand and improve the first draft of your cause-and-effect essay. As you work through the lessons presented here, pay close attention to the **Revision Checkpoints**, which will give you suggestions for revising your essay.

Composition Focus

Essay introductions. Just as a topic sentence introduces the topic and controlling idea of a paragraph, a formal **introduction** serves the following purposes in an essay:

- It identifies the topic.
- It gets the reader's attention.
- It leads the reader to the thesis.
- It states the thesis.

Reread the introduction to Chong Ho's essay.

> My family is from Seoul, the capital of South Korea, a city that has been completely transformed since our country began a great push for economic growth in the 1960s. This phenomenal growth has had two major effects: urban expansion and an improvement in the standard of living.

Now discuss the following questions with a partner.

1. Where does Chong Ho first introduce the topic? Draw a circle around the words that first introduce the topic.

2. Does Chong Ho engage your interest? If so, put brackets around the phrases that you find engaging.

3. Where does Chong Ho present the main point of the essay? Underline the thesis statement.

You should have noted that Chong Ho introduces the topic with the words *Seoul, South Korea* and *economic growth* in the first sentence. In the same sentence he offers background information about himself, *My family is from Seoul*, and background information about Korea, *our country began a great push . . . in the 1960s*. At the end of the paragraph, he presents the thesis statement containing the controlling idea, *This phenomenal growth has had two major effects: urban expansion and an improvement in the standard of living.*

Strategies for writing an introduction to a formal essay. Essay introductions not only identify the topic, lead the reader to the thesis, and state the thesis; they also must engage readers' interest. Here are some popular strategies that writers use to catch readers' attention.

1. *Background.* You learned about this strategy in Chapters 1 and 2. Background information is what you think readers need in order

to understand your topic well. Writers often provide background information in the introduction to an essay about a historical event or a current problem or situation. For example, Chong Ho might have begun his essay this way:

> After the Korean War, South Korea needed to rebuild, and its leaders chose a path of economic development. In the 1960s, the South Korean government instituted land reform, which improved agricultural production, and it also invested heavily in education. In the 1970s, it invested in industries such as shipbuilding, chemicals, and electronics.

2. *General Statement*. A common technique is to begin with a general statement and follow with statements that become increasingly specific as they move toward the thesis statement of the essay.

> The last fifty years have seen a great deal of economic development around the world. Growth has been especially rapid in the countries known as the "Asian tigers." Among them, South Korea is known as a growth leader.

3. *Anecdote*. An essay can begin with a brief anecdote or story.

> My uncle left Seoul twenty years ago and moved to the United States. When he came back to visit last autumn, he could not believe the transformation in his hometown. The neighborhood where he had grown up had disappeared, and now there were tall skyscrapers and busy thoroughfares where he used to play tag with his friends in the alleyway. The fields on the edge of town where he had picked strawberries after school had long ago disappeared, replaced with factories, warehouses, and high-rise apartments.

4. *Definition*. An introduction may begin with a definition of a key term or concept that helps the reader understand the topic of the essay.

> *Urbanization* refers to the growth of cities. In recent years, cities in developing countries have attracted people who are seeking employment because economic globalization has made cities the center of manufacturing and the distribution of goods. This transformation is evident in Seoul, South Korea.

Exercise 6

With a partner or in a small group, discuss the following questions.

1. Of the four introduction strategies, which do you think is most appropriate for Chong Ho's essay about urban growth and an improvement in the standard of living in Seoul?

2. Chong Ho chose to include some personal information in his introduction. When is personal information appropriate in an introduction?

EXERCISE 7

Read the following introductions, and identify their types (as described on pages 90–91) on the lines below them. Underline the thesis statement in each introduction.

1.   **The Industrial Revolution in Europe**

   [1]By around 1750, Europeans had discovered that coal and iron could be made into steel, and inventors were using this new material to create steam engines and machinery for manufacturing. [2]At the same time, changes in the laws concerning agricultural land had displaced agricultural workers and made agriculture more productive. [3]With new technology and surplus labor and food, conditions were right for what is called the Industrial Revolution. [4]It is called a revolution because <u>it had enormous effects on life in Europe: People moved to the cities and a new social class of urban workers formed, trade increased, and with the new wealth, the standard of living improved</u>.

   <u>background</u>

2.   **India's Economic Miracle**

   [1]*Capital* refers to money or resources that are used to produce more wealth. [2]*Human capital* refers to a country's workers. [3]A country with a large, young, or educated population has a lot of human capital; on the other hand, a country with a small, aging, or less-educated population has less human capital. [4]There are two reasons for India's economic growth: its human capital and the government's economic policies.

   _____

3.   **Foreign Aid**

   [1]Humans are social creatures and often turn to others for help in time of need. [2]Just as individuals ask their relatives and neighbors for assistance when they cannot pay their bills, countries ask their allies for help when they face an economic downturn. [3]In the global community, foreign aid, meaning gifts or special low-interest loans given by rich countries to poor countries, is essential for two reasons: Foreign aid reduces the suffering of people who have been displaced by war and natural disasters, and it helps struggling economies catch up over time.

   _____

4. **Globalization**

[1]The other day I was riding a bus and I witnessed the effects of globalization with my own eyes and ears. [2]Two women—one wearing a T-shirt bearing the name of an Italian company and the other with a French name on her jeans—were speaking about what Indian movies they had seen, what African music they enjoyed, and what South American newspapers they had been reading on the Internet. [3]One of the women got a call on her cell phone and started to speak in Farsi. [4]I was intrigued. [5]I couldn't have imagined this transfer and mixing of information, goods, and cultures ten or fifteen years ago. [6]This phenomenon would not have been possible without investments in communication, improvements in transportation technology, and the creation of multinational corporations.

_____

EXERCISE 8

This cause-and-effect essay has a thesis statement, body paragraphs, and concluding paragraphs, but it does not have an introductory paragraph. On another piece of paper, write an introductory paragraph for it, using one or more of the suggestions for writing introductions listed on pages 90–91. (You can combine methods if you like.) Include the thesis statement that is given, placing it at the end of your introduction.

Why I Left the Farm

THESIS: The reasons I did not want to stay on my family farm were the difficulty of farm work and my desire to learn to program computers.

[1]First of all, I left the farm because life there was extremely hard and frustrating due to lack of water and poor soil. [2]There was no irrigation to water the crops that we planted, so we prayed for rain every year. [3]Periodically, there was a drought. [4]As a result of the drought, there was not even enough water for the cattle to drink, and we had to let the crops die. [5]In addition, the soil was poor in nutrients, and we did not have the money to buy fertilizers to improve it. [6]There were, however, some years when we had a good crop of fruit and corn, but then we had another obstacle to face. [7]Since we didn't have a truck to transport our produce, we had to sell it to people in our village who could transport it to the market town. [8]They would pay us very little because they knew we had no choice but to sell our goods to them.

[9]Second, I left the farm because I knew that I would not have any possibility of getting an advanced education if I remained there. [10]The farm was far from any major city. [11]I attended high school in the nearest town, but there was no college in the area. [12]When I was in my freshman year in high school, a counselor came to our class

and asked what we wanted to do after we graduated. [13]Even though I had never seen a computer, I raised my hand and said that I wanted to learn how to be a programmer. [14]I had little idea about what programmers actually do, but I thought programming would be a very exciting and important job. [15]But at the time, studying computer science seemed to be little more than a dream because I knew my father could not provide me with more education. [16]But three years later I graduated from high school at the top of my class. [17]This led to my receiving a scholarship that paid my way through two years of technical training, and eventually I got a good job.

[18]From the time I was about ten, I realized that I did not want to spend my life toiling on a hot, dusty farm. [19]I felt sad to leave my parents to do the work on the farm alone, but now I am able to send them some money to help them out.

After you finish, break into small groups and take turns reading aloud the introductions you wrote. Guess which strategies your classmates used.

REVISION CHECKPOINT 1

Essay Introductions

Look at the introduction to your essay. Make sure that it contains a thesis statement that names the topic and the controlling idea of your essay. Ask yourself if the introduction catches the reader's attention. If you can improve your introduction, revise it now.

Organization of body paragraphs and transition signals. If you make your essay cohesive, readers will be able to follow your ideas easily. (To review cohesion, see page 61.) If you arrange the supporting points in your essay according to time order or order of importance, readers will be able to understand your thinking. Use the transition signals in this chart to tell readers which plan of organization you have used:

Transitions to Indicate		
Time Order	**Sequence**	**Order of Importance**
First/First of all . . . Then . . . After that . . . Finally . . .	One reason/result . . . Another reason/ result . . .	The most important reason/effect . . .

EXERCISE 9

The topic sentences of the body paragraphs in the following essay lack transitions. Read the essay, decide which pattern of organization it has (time order or order of importance), and add appropriate transitions from the chart.

Singapore's Economic Success

1 [1]When Britain withdrew from Singapore in 1971, the tiny island nation at the tip of the Malay Peninsula had no way to support itself. [2]Its only resource was people. [3]From the start, the Singapore government determined that the country's survival would depend on foreign investment and expertise. [4]Furthermore, the government itself would need to play an active role in guiding economic development. [5]As a result of these strategies, Singapore developed one of the most productive economies in the world.

2 [6]The Singapore government found Asian investors who were willing to open light industries such as textile and toy manufacturing. [7]It converted the land that had been occupied by the British to industrial parks, and it developed its infrastructure—highways, port, and airport. [8]To make it easy for foreign companies to set up business, the government established the Economic Development Board, which helped investors secure land, power, and water. [9]Singapore also gave early investors tax-free status for five years.

3 [10]Singapore successfully attracted high-tech investors from the United States who were willing to open semiconductor factories and, later on, computer-assembly plants. [11]To help Singaporean workers develop the skills they needed to work with this advanced technology, the government provided free training institutes. [12]To make sure that the labor force was disciplined, the government enacted extensive labor laws, and to make sure that it was cooperative, the government formed the National Wages Council. [13]In the council, representatives from labor unions, management, and the government set guidelines for annual wage increases which both allowed for growth and prevented strikes. [14]Although in the 1950s labor strikes were common, there has been no strike in Singapore since 1986.

4 [15]Singapore has been readying itself for the future by promoting its biotechnology, chemical, information, and service industries. [16]The government sees investing in people as a top priority. [17]It has sent its brightest students to the best universities overseas and has expanded its college and university campuses at home. [18]To encourage innovation and provide high-level jobs, it has built a science park where corporations and institutes conduct research in biotechnology and information science. [19]Nearby is the brand-new biomedical research and development center Biopolis, which opened in 2006 at a cost of 570 million Singapore dollars. [20]Singapore has recruited talented researchers from the U.S. and other countries to work in this facility with offers of salaries that are well above those paid elsewhere.

5 [21]As a result of its economic strategies, Singapore has attracted investments from more than 3,000 multinational corporations and achieved almost 100 percent employment over the past few decades, and it can claim one of the highest per capita gross domestic products in the world today.

Pattern of organization: _____

> *Compare your choice of transitions with a partner's, and discuss how you made that choice.*

Organization of Body Paragraphs and Transition Signals
Make sure that you have arranged your supporting points according to a logical plan of organization and that your thesis statement and the topic sentences of your body paragraphs are cohesive. Check your draft to see whether it has enough transition signals. If you need transition signals, add them.

Development of body paragraphs. In the body of an essay, readers expect to find details that support the writer's main point. For example, in the first body paragraph of his essay, Chong Ho wrote that Seoul has "such wide, busy thoroughfares that pedestrians can only cross via underground tunnels." Specific details like these keep readers interested, help them understand the writer's main point, and help them remember what they read. Here are three ways you can develop the body paragraphs of your essay. The examples are from the essay in Exercise 9, "Singapore's Economic Success."

- include **examples**, especially examples containing **sensory** information about things you can see, hear, feel, smell, or taste.

    . . . light industries *such as textile and toy manufacturing* (paragraph 2)

- **explain** what something means, why someone does something, or how something works.

    . . . the government formed the National Wages Council. *In the council, representatives from labor unions, management, and the government set guidelines for annual wage increases which both allowed for growth and prevented strikes.* (paragraph 3)

- include **facts** or **statistics**

    Although in the 1950s labor strikes were common, there has been no strike in Singapore since 1986. (paragraph 3)

A. *This essay has three body paragraphs. One of the body paragraphs is very well developed, one is fairly well developed, and one is poorly developed. Rank the body paragraphs according to their development as* **very good, adequate,** *or* **weak.**

The Effects of Migration

1 [1]People have always moved—*emigrated* out of their home countries and *immigrated* to new countries—either because the place they lived was unsatisfactory in some way or because they wanted to take a chance on finding something better. [2]Migration has a number of effects. [3]It affects the homeland that migrants leave, the host country that they settle in, and the migrants themselves.

2 [4]First of all, the homeland may be affected either positively or negatively by emigration. [5]If the homeland is overcrowded, emigration can bring some relief because the people who are left behind will have more jobs and more resources after the migrants leave. [6]For example, people emigrated from Ireland when a plant disease there wiped out the potato crop in the 1840s and 1850s; as a result, there were fewer people competing for the limited food supply. [7]Furthermore, if the emigrants get good jobs abroad and send money home, the influx of new money will stimulate the home economy. [8]This has happened in recent years as immigrants from Latin America who have been working in the U.S. have sent part of their earnings to family members in their home countries. [9]The homeland may also suffer as a result of emigration. [10]In particular, if professionals leave, the home country may be affected negatively. [11]For instance, in recent years, many Indian doctors have emigrated, and consequently health care in India has suffered.

Rank: _____

3 [12]Second, the host country can be affected either positively or negatively by immigration. [13]The host country may need immigrants to fill low-wage jobs that the settled population does not want. [14]In addition, immigrants will provide stimulation to the local economy as consumers because, while they are living in the host country, they will have to spend part of their earnings on food, clothing, and shelter. [15]However, the host country may be affected negatively by immigration. [16]Because immigrants tend to settle in cities in the host country where jobs are available, parts of those cities may become overcrowded, and, as a result, tensions may build up between the newcomers and the settled population.

Rank: _____

4 [17]Finally, the immigrants themselves may experience either positive or negative effects. [18]Many immigrants achieve a better standard of living by moving to a new country.

¹⁹They may learn new things as well. ²⁰However, at the beginning, they may have to cope with a language barrier, and they may experience discrimination.

Rank: _____

5   ²¹Migration has been a part of human existence throughout history. ²²The English language has an expression that describes the urge to migrate: "The grass is greener on the other side of the fence." ²³As long as people see better opportunities, they will continue to move, with both positive and negative results for themselves and the countries they emigrate from and immigrate into.

B. *Compare your rankings with a partner's. Analyze the paragraph you ranked number 1 to determine what kind of development it has.*

C. *Review the paragraphs with adequate or weak development, and put a star (*) where you think the writer could add development. Next to each star, write in the margin* **example**, **explanation**, *or* **fact or statistic**. *You and your partner may have different answers.*

Unity in body paragraphs. Readers want writers to make a point in a topic sentence and give specific evidence that supports it, and they don't want any extra unnecessary information that is not related to that point. Therefore, you need to be selective about what to include in your body paragraphs, limiting the contents to those details that support the point you are trying to make.

EXERCISE 11

A. *Read this essay about Mali. Each of the body paragraphs has one problem with unity. Locate the sentence that does not belong in each paragraph, and cross it out.*

Mali's Vulnerable Economy

1   ¹Mali, which is in the northwestern part of Africa, is one of the largest countries on the continent but one of the poorest in the world. ²There are two main reasons for Mali's economic problems: its geography and its relations with the rest of the world.

2   ³Mali's geography presents several challenges to its economic well-being. ⁴First, Mali is landlocked. ⁵That is, it has no coastline, so it depends on ports in neighboring countries to export goods such as cotton and livestock to international markets. ⁶Second, some of northern Mali is part of the Sahara Desert, and the rest is dry grassland. ⁷Some of the sand dunes in the Sahara Desert are 180 meters (600 feet) tall. ⁸Only a small part of southern Mali can be farmed, and that limited area is shrinking because the Sahara

Desert is expanding as much as 30 miles (48 km) per year. [9]Mali's forests are declining because of the growing desert and because the Malian people consume more wood than nature produces. [10]A shortage of wood is not Mali's only energy problem: Mali has no oil or natural gas, so it must purchase supplies at unstable prices from other countries.

3 [11]Mali has suffered in several ways as a direct result of its relations with international organizations and other countries. [12]First, after Mali became independent from France, it borrowed money from the World Bank and the International Monetary Fund. [13]When interest rates rose, Mali could not pay back its loans. [14]In fact, in the 1990s, 60 percent of what Mali paid to its creditors was simply interest charges to service the loans. [15]Mali had little money left over for social programs such as education and health care. [16]In 2005, Mali's loans were canceled by the International Monetary Fund, but the arrangement required Mali to accept foreign ownership of its electricity and water, railroads, banks, telecommunications, and textile industry. [17]This means that foreign companies and foreign workers benefit from Mali's resources, but the citizens of Mali benefit little. [18]In recent years, gold has become a more important export than cotton in Mali. [19]In addition, Mali has suffered as a result of political instability in neighboring countries. [20]For example, in 2002 and 2003, Mali could not export its cotton because the road to the port passing through Cote d'Ivoire was closed because of political conflict in that country.

4 [21]Mali's economy is vulnerable because it has no access to the sea, no oil or gas, little farmland, and too little rainfall. [22]It has also suffered because of the decisions and actions of the international community. [23]To better provide for its people, Mali needs to be free of foreign debt and be able to use the limited resources it has to benefit its own people.

B. *Work with a partner. Compare your answers and discuss how you decided which sentences to cross out.*

REVISION CHECKPOINT 3	**Development and Unity in Body Paragraphs**
	Check your body paragraphs for development. If you think you need to add examples, explanation, or facts, add them now. Also check the appropriateness of the supporting details in your body paragraphs. If you find sentences that do not develop or add to understanding of your main points, omit them. Make sure each of your body paragraphs has both good development and unity.

Essay conclusions. Just as the last sentence in a one-paragraph composition signals to the reader that the writer is finished, a concluding paragraph signals the end of an essay. The most important reason for the **conclusion** is to make the reader *feel* that the essay is finished.

A conclusion can answer any questions that have not been addressed in the body of the essay, but it must not raise new questions. Any new information that is added must be sufficient without explanation. For example, see page 94. In the conclusion to "Why I Left the Farm," the writer informs us that he is able to send his parents some money to help them out. This piece of added information does not raise questions that require further explanation.

Strategies for writing a conclusion to a formal essay. Here are several strategies you can use in conclusions. Most conclusions are a combination of these strategies.

1. *Summary*. In a conclusion, you should help readers remember the key points of the essay by summarizing them. Summarizing means repeating the same key words and phrases used in the thesis statement and topic sentences of the body paragraphs or using word forms or synonyms. For example, in the conclusion of the model essay "The Effects of Economic Growth on Seoul," Chong Ho referred to his thesis when he wrote in the final paragraph, *Forty or fifty years of dramatic economic growth have transformed Seoul. . . . Fortunately, this rapid growth has resulted in more equality in Korean society . . .*

2. *Suggestion*. Many essays are about problems, and the most common way to conclude them is by suggesting solutions. For example, an essay that tells how rapid urbanization can produce unhealthy living conditions may conclude by saying, *People should get as much information as they can before moving to a city where they may not find clean drinking water, decent shelter, or adequate health care.*

3. *Prediction*. An essay about a problem may conclude with a prediction or warning about the future. For example, an essay about overpopulated cities and unhealthy living conditions may conclude by warning, *We will see increased cancer in children and people of all ages if we allow cities to grow without adequate regulation of polluting industries.*

4. *Opinion*. You may conclude by offering your own perspective. For example, in an essay that presents the effects of urbanization, you may finish by saying that you think the positive outcomes from urbanization are greater than the negative.

Note that many essays present an opinion in the thesis and support the opinion with arguments in the body paragraphs. But if the main purpose of the paper is to explain, you can withhold your opinion for the conclusion and present it in a brief statement there.

EXERCISE 12

The following two essays have good introductory and body paragraphs, but there are problems with their conclusions. On the lines below each essay, tell what is wrong with the conclusion. Then, on another piece of paper, write better conclusions for them, using some of the strategies listed on page 100.

1.   **Globalization in Naucalapan**

[1]Globalization refers to the exchange of not only goods and services but also cultural information. [2]Globalization has been good for the economy of Mexico, but the impact that it has had on the community that I used to live in, Naucalapan de Juarez, has not been good. [3]The environment, the people's entertainment, and their cultural traditions have been negatively affected by globalization.

[4]One problem caused by globalization is the destruction of the environment. [5]Naucalapan is one of Mexico City's fastest-growing suburbs. [6]It is the home of some of the biggest factories in the city, manufacturers of clothing, athletic shoes, drugs, plastics, machinery, and more. [7]The pollution these factories produce is affecting the environment. [8]The birds are dying, and the residents can't drink the tap water due to the industrial waste discharged in the canals or nearby lakes. [9]There is less and less open space, and today there are rows of city blocks where not a single tree can be seen. [10]New factories move in constantly and new workers, most of whom are from the countryside, arrive to find jobs. [11]These newcomers have no money, so they have to sleep in the parks and streets. [12]The new factories also provide employment for new management-level workers who need housing, too, and this creates a demand for new homes. [13]Developers are constructing houses over what is left of our open space, and the government doesn't seem to care at all because it can collect taxes on the buildings that are built.

[14]Another problem caused by globalization is the corruption of televised entertainment. [15]Because it is no longer pleasant to be outside in Naucalapan, people stay inside and watch television more and more. [16]But television isn't the way it used to be. [17]Mexican television used to censor explicit language, controversial topics, and graphic violence, but since it started buying programs from the United States, television has changed dramatically. [18]It now shows brutal murders and airs frank talk about sex that the community doesn't want its children exposed to.

[19]The most important result of globalization is that the traditional holidays have been changed. [20]The religious meaning and family celebration of Mexican holidays have been replaced with customs from the United States, which always seem to involve spending money. [21]People used to go to church on Easter, but now they hunt for eggs. [22]On October 31, people used to remember and pray for their dead ancestors, but now it's Halloween, a day for dressing up as witches and going to parties. [23]Last but not least is Christmas. [24]This used to be the most sacred holiday, but now it is just an excuse to get as much as possible from Santa Claus.

[25]We have to respect the environment. [26]People should recycle their cans and bottles and not throw them on the street. [27]Not recycling is wasting valuable resources.

Problems with the conclusion: _____

_____

_____

2.   **Globalization in Peru**

[1]Globalization refers to a shift from distinct national economies to a global economy and involves an exchange of cultural information. [2]Lima, Peru, where I come from, is not immune to this phenomenon. [3]I see both positive and negative changes every time I go back for a visit.

[4]The benefits of globalization are in the area of communication. [5]Peruvians are now able to keep in touch with the outside world affordably. [6]My parents are happy that they can call my sister and me in the United States and my brother in Uruguay cheaply, and the transmission is so clear that it seems we are in nearby towns. [7]Many young people access the Internet regularly. [8]They know what books are being published in New York and London, what styles are worn in Paris and Tokyo, and what technological changes are taking place in Silicon Valley and Bangalore. [9]Through the information superhighway, Peruvians are keeping up with the world.

[10]While globalization has been beneficial to Peru in a number of ways, it has increased inequality. [11]Rapid economic growth means modern airports, computers, express highways, and air-conditioned malls with the latest international fashion for a few, but it has not improved conditions for the many. [12]Big corporations have been investing in Peru, and the government has been forced to keep wages down to attract these investments. [13]As a result of globalization, the gap between rich and poor Peruvians has been increasing at an alarming rate.

[14]Peru has a long history that goes back to the Incas. [15]For thousands of years, change was very slow, but change is now much faster. [16]I think it is time for the Peruvian government to address the problems created by globalization.

Problems with the conclusion: _____

_____

_____

REVISION CHECKPOINT 4

Essay Conclusions
Check the conclusion of your essay. Make sure that it does not introduce new ideas that will need development. If your conclusion does not give the reader the feeling that the essay is complete, revise it.

Language Focus

Verb tense in essays. English has twelve verb tenses, and each verb tense has one or more meanings. When you write, you choose a tense because it fits the meaning you want to express. Sometimes you use only one tense throughout an entire piece of writing, but more often you use various tenses, shifting when necessary. Here are the more common verb tenses and their meanings.

1. *The simple present*
   - Use this tense to make a general statement. A general statement is about something that is true now, was true in the past, and will be true in the future.

     Entertainment **is** a profitable business.

   - Also use this tense to refer to a habitual action.

     People **use** television to relax.

2. *The simple past*
   - Use this tense to refer to an event or action that began and ended in the past.

     Television **appeared** in the 1950s.

3. *The past perfect*
   - Use this tense to refer to an event or action that happened before another event or situation in the past.

     Before the Internet became available, people in many countries **had learned** about U.S. culture from television.

4. *The present perfect*
   Use this tense to connect the present to the past.
   - Use it to refer to an event or action that has happened one or more times in the past at an indefinite time/indefinite times.

     Nearly every television viewer **has seen** Mickey Mouse, *I Love Lucy*, and Tony Soprano.

   - Also use it to refer to an event, action, or situation that began at a point in time in the past and has continued or repeated until the present.

     Television **has contributed** to the globalization of culture.

 For more on the twelve English verb tenses, see Appendix IA, page 279.

TIP
Some of the verbs in the essay are passive forms.

A. Read the essay. Then discuss the questions about its verb tenses with a partner. The verbs are in boldface type.

The Economic Effects of the Tsunami on Thailand

[1]On December 26, 2004, southern Thailand **experienced** a natural disaster called a *tsunami*. [2]A tsunami **is** a huge wave disturbance that **results** from an underwater earthquake. [3]The tsunami that **hit** Thailand **sent** four waves of up to 10 meters (32.8 feet) over coastal areas. [4]This event **had** both immediate and long-term economic effects on Thailand.

[5]In the short term, the economy of southern Thailand, which **depends** mainly on tourism, **suffered** greatly. [6]Hundreds of hotels **were closed** due to damage, and tourists **fled**. [7]The fishing industry **was** also severely **affected** as fishermen **had lost** their boats in the tsunami. [8]The Thai government **responded** quickly to assist the injured, recover the dead, bring in needed supplies, and establish refugee camps for the homeless. [9]International donors **offered** a great deal of financial support. [10]However, the cleanup and rebuilding process **took** time, so the economy **did** not **recover** immediately.

[11]In the years since the tsunami, the overall economy of southern Thailand **has recovered** fairly well. [12]First, the Thai government **cleaned** up the resort areas and **put** a tsunami warning system in place. [13]With government loans and tax relief, hotel owners **restored** their properties, and within about a year, most hotels **reopened**. [14]Tourists, who **were** at first hesitant to return with the memory of the disaster still fresh, **have** gradually **come back**. [15]However, the long-term effect of the tsunami **has been** a widening of the income gap in southern Thailand. [16]The poor people whose coastal villages **were destroyed** by the tsunami **moved** into refugee camps and often **stayed** there for a long time. [17]Some **were** former fishermen who **had lost** their boats and **had** no way to buy new ones. [18]Others **were** people who **had lost** their families and **had** no one to turn to for support. [19]These people **were impoverished** by the tsunami.

[20]The tsunami **has taught** Thailand and the world some important lessons. [21]First, a country with a stable economy **can recover** from a natural disaster. [22]Second, people around the world **are** willing to offer assistance to those who **are affected** by a natural disaster. [23]And finally, a natural disaster **can make** the poor poorer if governments and aid organizations **do** not **try** to help them get out of poverty.

B. Discuss your answers with your teacher and classmates.

Questions:

1. What is the main verb tense in the first paragraph, and why?
2. What other tense did the writer use, and why?
3. What is the main verb tense in the second paragraph, and why?
4. What other tenses did the writer use, and why?
5. What are the three verb tenses in the third paragraph? Explain the reason for the use of each tense.
6. What is the first verb tense in the final paragraph, and why?
7. What is the second verb tense in the final paragraph, and why?

REVISION CHECKPOINT 5

Verb Tense in Your Essay
Underline the verbs in your essay. Where you have changed tenses, draw a line [|] between sentences, and make sure you have a reason for the change. If you are unsure about some of the verbs, write a question to your teacher in the margin of your paper.

The vocabulary of cause and effect: Nouns and verbs. English has several nouns and verbs that are used to discuss cause and effect. Look at the chart.

Nouns	Verbs
cause	cause
reason	result in
factor	lead to
result	affect
effect	

1. *Nouns that refer to a cause*
   - We use the noun ***cause*** for events that are beyond our control.

     The *cause of* the landslide was the heavy rain.

   - We use the noun ***reason*** to explain the thinking behind our actions.

     The *reason* I took English composition was so that I could write more confidently.

   - We use the noun ***factor*** when there are two or more reasons or causes.

     There are two *factors* in the company's success. One *factor* is that it faced little competition in the market. The second *factor* is that it had a very popular product.

2. *Nouns that refer to an effect*
   The two nouns we use to talk about what happens as an outcome of an event are ***result*** and ***effect***. These words are generally the same and can be used interchangeably.

   The *result/effect* of the company's expansion was an increase in profit.

3. *Cause-and-effect verbs*
   Cause, ***result in***, and ***lead to*** all describe change and are followed by a result. However, there is a slight difference in meaning: We use *cause* when the effect is direct and immediate. We use *lead to* or *result in* when the result is less direct or is delayed.

   The election of the new president *caused* excitement.

   The election of the new president *led to/resulted in* economic growth.

Cause, lead to, and *result in* can be followed by noun objects, as in the examples on page 105. But they also can be used with other patterns, as in the following examples.

The election *caused* people to celebrate. (*cause* + someone or something + infinitive)

The election *led to/resulted* in Parliament writing new laws. (*lead to/ result in* + someone or something + gerund)

EXERCISE 14

With a partner, fill in the blanks in the following passage with the cause-and-effect nouns and verbs listed below. Write the part of speech of the word, (n.) or (v.), in the parentheses.

Nouns	cause, effect, factor, reason, result
Verbs	cause, lead to, result in

Addressing Inequality

There are two (1) _____reasons_____ that rich nations should help poor
(**n.**)
nations. First, economic assistance would improve the health of people in poor nations

immediately. Disease is a major (2) _____ of human suffering. Two
( )

(3) _____ are responsible for disease in poor nations: lack of sanitation
( )

(sewage systems) and lack of medical treatment. With clean water and medicine, the

suffering caused by disease could be greatly reduced. Treatment of disease would also

(4) _____ economic growth in poor countries, because when people are
( )

healthy, they can work and feed themselves.

Second, in order to have a brighter future, people in poor countries need

education. Providing education would (5) _____ increased productivity, too.
( )

Furthermore, statistics show that educating people has a positive (6) _____
( )

on the next generation in that educated parents have smaller families and raise healthier

children. If people have smaller, healthier families, they will have a higher standard of

living.

One economist suggested a way to raise money to help the poorest nations: Impose a tax on international financial transactions and use those funds to improve conditions in poor countries. Rich countries trade the most. Taxing the rich to help the poor would (7) _____ no hardship for the rich. The poor would see

          (   )

immediate (8) _____ : better health and education.

      (   )

Cause-and-effect vocabulary: Conjunctions and transition words. We can show cause-and-effect relationships between clauses with subordinating conjunctions, coordinating conjunctions, and transition words. Notice the punctuation in these examples.

1. *Subordinating conjunction*

           EFFECT   CAUSE

The people's lifestyle improved **because** the country's economy grew.

           CAUSE   EFFECT

Because the country's economy grew, the people's lifestyle improved.

 For more on commas, see Appendix IB, page 291.

2. *Coordinating conjunction*

           CAUSE   EFFECT

The country's economy grew, **so** the people's lifestyle improved.

3. *Transition word*

           CAUSE   EFFECT

The country's economy grew. **Therefore**, the people's lifestyle improved.

           CAUSE   EFFECT

The country's economy grew; **therefore**, the people's lifestyle improved.

 For more on semicolons, see Appendix IB, page 295. For more on logical connectors that express cause and effect, see Appendix IA, page 272.

On another piece of paper, combine the pairs of sentences using the words in parentheses. You may need to change the order of the clauses. Make sure you use correct punctuation.

1. The countries with the most technology are richest. Technology is vital to development. (so)

   Technology is vital to development, so the countries with the most technology are richest.

2. Technology can help fight disease and improve the use of agricultural land. Poor countries need technology. (because)

3. Technology is often shared when countries trade with each other. Countries that are isolated from international trade are unlikely to acquire technology. (therefore)

4. Landlocked regions such as central Brazil or inland China are isolated from international trade. They cannot easily acquire technology. (so)

5. Today people can work on the Internet from remote areas. The Internet can help isolated regions overcome the disadvantages of distance. (therefore)

6. Innovation, or the development of new technology, requires both universities and the investment of private companies. The poorest countries cannot acquire technology without help. (because)

Compare your sentences with a partner's. Did you use commas, periods, and semicolons in the same way?

Overview of cause-and-effect vocabulary and structures. Some structures are followed by a cause, and some are followed by an effect.

Vocabulary and Structures Followed by a *Cause*		
Coordinating Conjunctions	**Subordinating Conjunctions**	**Prepositions**
for[1]	because[2] since[2] as[2]	due to[3] because of[3] as a result of[3]

1. When *for* is used as a coordinating conjunction, it has the same meaning as *because*. *For* is more formal than *because* and is used less often.

   The amount of money transferred between countries has increased, *for* most countries have removed their restrictions on the flow of money.

   The amount of money transferred between countries has increased *because* most countries have removed their restrictions on the flow of money.

NOTE
Because only introduces reason clauses, but *since* and *as* introduce other kinds of clauses as well.

2. *Because, since,* and *as* are subordinating conjunctions that introduce reason clauses.

   Multinational corporations have prospered *because* they have found new markets for their goods.

   Multinational corporations have prospered *since* they have found new markets for their goods.

   Multinational corporations have prospered *as* they have found new markets for their goods.

3. *Due to, because of,* and *as a result of* are multiword prepositions, and, like all prepositions, they are followed by nouns. (Do not confuse *because of* with *because. Because* is followed by a clause.)

   Communication improved *due to* the Internet.

   Transportation of goods became faster *as a result of* shipping containers.

   The trucking industry has grown *because of* international trade.

   The trucking industry has grown *because* international trade has created a demand for truck transportation.

For more on adverb clauses, see Appendix IA, page 239.

Vocabulary and Structures Followed by an *Effect*		
Verbs	**Transition Words**	**Coordinating Conjunction**
cause result in lead to	therefore consequently as a result	so

Note: The verb *affect* is used to discuss cause and effect, but it is not listed here because it is not followed by a result. Instead, it is followed by the person or thing that experiences the result. Compare these examples:

The crop failure *caused/resulted in/led to* hunger. (Hunger is the result.)

The crop failure *affected* the farmers' children. (The children experienced the result.)

The crop failure *affected* the economy. (The economy experienced the result.)

EXERCISE 16

Practice using the cause-and-effect vocabulary and structures from this chapter. On another piece of paper, rewrite the sentences below, making one sentence by using the words in parentheses. Note that some words may need to be left out and verbs may need to be changed or removed when you combine the sentences.

1. The cost of computers is lower today. Small businesses can afford them. (due to)

   Due to the lower cost of computers today, small businesses can afford them.

2. The Internet benefits consumers. It allows them to compare prices. (as)

3. The Internet allows people to share new discoveries quickly. Innovations in technology are adopted more rapidly. (because)

4. The use of electronic transfers has grown. There is an increased international flow of money. (so)

5. The Internet reduces the cost of buying and selling goods. It helps small companies. (for)

6. The Internet has affected workers who program computers or process data. They now compete with workers in other countries. (as a result of)

Check the punctuation of your sentences.

Cause-and-Effect Vocabulary and Structures

Review your draft. Underline the cause-and-effect vocabulary and structures you have used. Make sure your composition has a variety of vocabulary and structures. If it does not have enough variety, revise it.

■ FINAL DRAFT

1. Before you write your final draft, look over your essay one last time to decide if you want to make any further changes.

2. Prepare a final draft of your composition. Make sure that you have used capital letters at the beginning of your sentences and periods at the end, and check your spelling.

3. Exchange papers with one or two classmates. Read each other's papers carefully. Turn to page 298 in Appendix II, and fill out the Peer Review Form.

4. Check your paper again and make any necessary corrections. Turn in your paper to your teacher.

■ CHAPTER REVIEW

Look back at what you have accomplished in Chapter 3. Check (✔) what you have learned and what you have used as you have written and revised your composition.

Chapter 3 Topics	Learned	Used
organizing causes or effects by time order or order of importance (pages 82–89)		
writing an introduction that gets the reader's attention and identifies the topic and controlling idea of the essay (pages 90–94)		
using transition signals to help the reader follow the organization of the paper (pages 94–96)		
developing body paragraphs with examples, explanation, and facts or statistics (pages 96–98)		
checking for unity in body paragraphs (pages 98–99)		
writing a conclusion that gives the reader the sense that the essay is finished (pages 100–102)		
checking for correct verb tenses in essays (pages 103–104)		
using the language of cause and effect (pages 105–110)		

CHAPTER FOUR

Marriage and Family

Writing a Comparison/ Contrast Essay

In every part of the world, families are important. Therefore, how people meet one another, marry, and arrange family life are serious matters—not only for individuals, but also for whole societies. Historically, cultures around the world have developed very different values and customs regarding courtship, marriage, and family life. In recent times, however, with the growth of industrialization and cities, families everywhere are experiencing similar changes and adapting in similar ways.

This chapter will help you

- use an appropriate pattern of organization for a comparison/contrast essay.
- learn more about introduction strategies.
- balance development in comparison/contrast essays.
- improve cohesion in your essays.
- use the language of comparison/contrast.

Before You Read

Complete the following questionnaire by yourself. Then freewrite on the topic of marriage for ten minutes.

Questionnaire

Our attitudes about marriage are shaped by our cultures. To reflect on your thoughts about this important social institution, circle the answers that best express your opinions.

1. Marriage ____ necessary to a meaningful adult life.

   a. is

   b. is not

2. Choosing a marriage partner is ____ matter.

   a. an individual

   b. a family

3. The purpose of marriage is ____.

   a. finding one's true love

   b. bringing children into the world and providing a safe, secure environment for them

   c. fulfilling one's parents' expectations

   d. strengthening the social position of one's family

   e. *other*: _____

Reading

LIFESTYLE CHANGES IN JAPAN
by Sumiko Iwao

1   Like many other countries, Japan is in the midst of major social change. The area of Japanese life that has changed the most since World War II is the family. The greatest shifts have been seen in women's lives, but men's lives have been altered as well.

Changes in Women's Lives

2   Two of the most significant changes in the lives of Japanese women are the extension of their average lifespan and the decrease in the average number of children they have. In 1935 the average lifespan for women in Japan was just short of fifty years; in 2007 it had **skyrocketed** to almost eighty-six years.

skyrocket: *to increase suddenly and dramatically*

In the early postwar years, the average Japanese woman gave birth to four children, but by 2007, the number of births per woman had dropped to 1.34. The drop in the birthrate is, in part, a result of women's growing participation in the workforce.

career track: *a pathway in which a person moves upward from one job to another*

3   Women have been steadily increasing their rate of employment outside the home, and Japanese companies are coming to rely more on women in all parts of their operations—on the factory floor as well as in the office. It had been the tradition to assign women to a special secretarial **career track** and to deny them access to both shop floor and managerial positions. Recently, however, more and more manufacturers are taking steps to make it possible for women to do blue-collar jobs which were once reserved for men. Women have been given access to the management track as well, and as a result, the number of women pursuing managerial jobs has grown substantially.

4   It used to be that women would quit working as soon as they married, but that is no longer the case. However, many women interrupt their careers for several years to raise a family. When broken down by age, the female workplace participation rate represents an "M" shaped curve. A low percentage of women between the ages of thirty and thirty-four work because they leave the labor market temporarily to take care of young families. This represents the dip in the "M." Comparing the situation in 1998 with 2008, the participation rate of women in the thirty to thirty-four age group rose 9.3 percentage points. Thus, there has been a noticeable change in the "M"-shaped curve, which has become flatter over the decade.

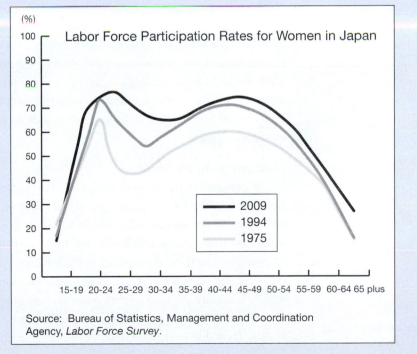

Labor Force Participation Rates for Women in Japan

Source: Bureau of Statistics, Management and Coordination Agency, *Labor Force Survey*.

(continued)

overwhelming: *very large and impressive*

opinion *survey: *questions asked of a large number of people to find out what they think*

autonomy: *independence*

wedlock: *marriage*

toil: *to work hard*

✳colleague: *a fellow worker, especially a fellow professional*

5   The significance of marriage has also changed for women. New employment opportunities for female workers have made it much easier for women to make a life for themselves outside the framework of marriage. Marriage used to be a necessity for women to survive, but today it has clearly become an option, and a woman has the freedom to choose whether to marry or remain single.

6   The **overwhelming** majority of women in Japan do want to marry, however. Recent **opinion surveys** indicate that only a very small number, 6 percent, are determined to remain single all their lives. But since single women can get just about everything they desire without marrying—a challenging job with a good salary, a nice apartment, and even male companionship—they are delaying marriage. In the last forty years, the average age at which people married for the first time rose steadily, from twenty-six to thirty years for men and from twenty-three to twenty-eight for women. The trend among women to wed later is closely related to education. The more education a woman has received, the more likely she is to delay marriage.

7   Young married women, more highly educated and more financially independent than ever before, are also seeking new demands from the relationship with their husbands. They desire to maintain their freedom and **autonomy** even after **wedlock**. This has seen the divorce rate begin to rise in Japan, although it remains considerably lower than in other advanced industrial countries. Japan's numbers are rising, however, and the younger generation has an increasingly tolerant view of divorce.

8   Divorce among older couples is a new phenomenon in Japan. It is in part a product of the tradition in older couples for the husband and wife to form two separate social worlds. For this generation, the man usually leaves management of the home and education of the children in the wife's hands while he **toils** long and hard at the office. His detachment from household affairs has the effect of making his wife psychologically independent. However, divorce is still seen as a last resort, as it brings sacrifice for both women and men.

Changes in Men's Lives

9   In contrast to the dramatic changes that have taken place in women's lives, men's lives have changed to a lesser degree. Furthermore, there is a difference between men of the older generation and younger men. Men in older age groups have wives who are full-time housewives. They did not have women as their classmates in their college days. For them, women and children still form a single group in need of a man's protection.

10   By comparison, younger men are accustomed to women classmates and coworkers. They are quite open to accepting a person based on his or her ability. They find nothing unusual or unsettling about having a female boss or female **colleagues**. When married, these men hope their wives will continue

working even after the children are born. They share as much as possible in the domestic responsibilities (though the amount of their contribution is still limited due to long working hours).

individualistic: *independent, not influenced by other people*

11   In the workplace, the younger generation is much more **individualistic** than their parents were. Their fathers thought it natural to place work before family and personal wishes, but young Japanese are much more interested in placing their individual needs and concerns before their company's. Japan's rapid economic development since World War II, often described as an "economic miracle," was partly due to the Japanese custom of putting the well-being of the group as a whole before individual needs and desires. Such behavior enhanced group harmony, which in turn **reinforced** the importance of a group-centered society.

reinforce: *to support*

pseudo: *false*

12   For many Japanese men, the workplace became a **pseudo** family. These businessmen worked until late at night and then, before returning home, went out drinking with work colleagues. On the weekends, they met again for golf. Their life was focused on their work and prevented them from spending time on personal hobbies or meeting new friends.

13   I expect these men sacrificed their private life to their company because they were working toward building up their country and also they thought they would be rewarded sufficiently and fairly by the company for their service. However, the **so-called restructuring** now underway in the Japanese economy has left many of them **disillusioned**. Their years of hard work have been rewarded by "a seat by the window," a Japanese expression meaning that a worker is pushed aside in the office, although not formally laid off.

so-called: *incorrectly known as*

restructuring: *reorganizing a company, usually to reduce the number of management levels*

disillusioned: *disappointed because of a mistaken belief*

14   The children of these men have watched what happened to their fathers. They have learned quickly that instead of being dependent on the company, they should do what they themselves wish to do as individuals. This generation does not hesitate to take paid holidays if they are entitled to do so. Or if they have a previous engagement, they will refuse to stay late in the office to do overtime work. Some see this change among the younger generation as negative, while others see it as positive.

optimist: *a person with a positive point of view*

pessimist: *a person with a negative point of view*

crossroads: *a point in life when one is forced to make a decision*

15   Whether **optimist** or **pessimist**, all would agree that Japan is at a **crossroads** in her history. In the last 60 years, the Japanese family has experienced major changes. While women's lives have changed the most, men's lives have been altered as well. On every level of society, the Japanese are adapting to these changes.

ABOUT the **AUTHOR**   Sumiko Iwao is a professor emeritus at Keio University. She was a member of the Gender Equality Council in the office of the Japanese prime minister, where she advised the government with respect to gender equality. Dr. Iwao received her Ph.D. in psychology from Yale University, and she has taught at Harvard University. This text is adapted from a speech Dr. Iwao gave in Lima, Peru, in 1996 on the topic of changing lifestyles in Japan.

Understanding the Reading

With a partner or small group, discuss the following questions.

1. Sumiko Iwao makes several comparisons in this text. What are they? Which comparison did you find most interesting, and why?

2. a. In this chapter, you will write an essay that compares two things. To do this, you will select two or three **points of comparison**. To help you prepare for the chapter assignment, compare the lives of women in two countries. First, find the aspects of Japanese women's lives that Iwao discusses, and write them in the column in the chart under *Points of Comparison*. Then, write the names of two countries at the top of the other two columns. (One may be Japan, if you wish.) Complete the chart with information about each point of comparison. (It is not necessary to do research to complete this exercise. Just use your general knowledge.)

Points of Comparison	Women in ＿＿＿＿	Women in ＿＿＿＿
lifespan (paragraph 2)		

   b. Make three or four comparative statements about women in the two countries you chose. For example, *Women in country X are living longer than they used to, while women in country Y are not living as long as they used to.*

3. When a society experiences dramatic change, both positive and negative effects can be seen. In your opinion, what is one positive and one negative effect of the social change in Japan?

4. *Status* refers to a person's position in society relative to other people. How have the changes in Japanese society affected the status of women? Explain.

5. What vocabulary and grammatical structures does Iwao use to present comparisons? Give examples of three different words, phrases, or sentence patterns from the reading that show a comparison.

Vocabulary Expansion

Word families. You have learned that in English there are word families—groups of words with the same root and different suffixes. The suffixes show what parts of speech the members of word families are.

EXERCISE 1

Look at the word-family box above each paragraph. Each box contains the nouns, verbs, and adjectives in a word family. Complete the paragraphs with words from the boxes. Some words will need to be made plural; others will be singular.

| marriage (*n.*)　married (*adj.*)　marital (*adj.*)　marry (*v.*) |

1. Most young people expect to (a) _____marry_____, so magazines often print articles about love and (b) _____. These articles tell single people how to find partners, how to plan a wedding, and, once they are (c) _____, how to solve their (d) _____ problems.

| symbol (*n.*)　symbolic (*adj.*)　symbolism (*n.*)　symbolize (*v.*) |

2. Wedding ceremonies contain a great deal of (e) _____. For example, in traditional Western-style weddings, the white bridal gown is a (f) _____ of the bride's purity, and the rings (g) _____ the bride and groom's commitment to each other. Diamond wedding rings are popular because the diamond is the hardest, most enduring mineral, and therefore it is (h) _____ of the couple's lasting love.

partner (*n.*)   **partnership** (*n.*)

3.   Marriage is a lifelong (i) _____, so the choice of a marriage (j) _____ is a critical decision. When looking for a spouse, one should avoid people who do not like to share responsibility, people who do not always tell the truth, and people who cannot make a decision and live with the consequences.

relate (*v.*)   **relative** (*n.*)   **relation** (*n.*)   **relationship** (*n.*)

4.   Sociologists and anthropologists refer to family members as "kin," but most English speakers call their aunts, uncles, cousins, and grandparents (k) "_____" or (l) "_____."

Some families are close-knit. Aunts, uncles, and cousins talk to each other often, and they can (m) _____ to each other easily. Other families do not have such strong (n) _____. They do not see each other often, and when they do get together, they may have trouble communicating.

cooperate (*v.*)   **cooperation** (*n.*)   **cooperative** (*adj.*)

5.   Marriage is an economic and social union. People need to (o) _____ in order to live well. If there is (p) _____ between not only the husband and wife but the couple and other members of their families, life is better for everyone. That is why, in traditional extended families, it is most important that the person who joins the family through marriage be (q) _____.

commit (*v.*)   **committed** (*adj.*)   **commitment** (*n.*)

6.   Marriage is a serious (r) _____.When two people marry, they (s) _____ themselves to remain together whether they are healthy or sick, rich or poor, happy or unhappy. However, over the years, marital relations can change. Loving, (t) _____ spouses can become discontented or even unfaithful partners. That is why a significant number of marriages end in divorce.

7.   In pre-industrial times, marriage was an agreement between families. To arrange a marriage meant to bring a new person into a family. People identified themselves first as members of families and second as (u) _____.

Economic development has changed this. It has promoted (v) _____, the belief that the rights of the individual are the most important rights in society. The reason that economic development has had this effect is that when a person is employed away from his or her family, he or she acquires a new sense of (w) _____. But opinions about this trend vary, and some people say that a person who insists too much on his or her own way of doing things is too (x) _____.

■ WRITING

Assignment

Choose one of the following topics and write an essay using one of the comparison/contrast patterns of organization shown on page 122.

1. Compare single life and married life.
2. Compare the lives of men and women in your country or culture.
3. Compare young people's expectations for marriage and the reality of married life.
4. Compare courtship and/or marriage in your parents' or grandparents' time and courtship and/or marriage in your time.
5. Compare women's roles in two generations.

What Comparison/Contrast Is and Why It Is Important

Comparing is something you do automatically. You routinely compare things like neighborhoods, schools, and vacation destinations. When you compare two things, you use **points of comparison**. (For example, when you answered item 2 in Understanding the Reading on page 118, you compared the lives of women in two countries in terms of their lifespan, number of children, employment, and so on.) As you consider the composition topics, you will also look for points of comparison. For instance, if you are going to write about topic 1, single life and married life, you will search for points of comparison such as free time, money, and companionship.

When you compare two things, you will find both differences and similarities. (The word *compare* means *find differences and similarities*, while *contrast* means *find differences only*.) Many comparison/contrast essays present only differences, but you may prefer to focus on similarities.

Organizing a comparison/contrast essay. Whether you decide to write about differences or similarities, you will have to choose between two patterns of organization, **point-by-point** or **side-by-side**. The two sample outlines that follow compare single life and married life.

Point-by-Point Organization

Introduction and thesis statement

I. Point of Comparison 1
   Single life
   Married life

II. Point of Comparison 2
   Single life
   Married life

III. Point of Comparison 3
   Single life
   Married life

Conclusion

Side-by-Side Organization

Introduction and thesis statement

I. Single Life
   Point of comparison 1
   Point of comparison 2
   Point of comparison 3

II. Married Life
   Point of comparison 1
   Point of comparison 2
   Point of comparison 3

Conclusion

EXERCISE 2

Look at the following outline, and decide what pattern of organization (side-by-side or point-by-point) it has. On another piece of paper, rewrite the outline, using the other pattern of organization.

THESIS: Marriage in traditional societies differs from marriage in industrialized societies.

I. The purpose of marriage
  A. In traditional societies
    1. A marriage creates an alliance between two families.
    2. Through marriage, children are born who will continue the family line.
  B. In industrialized societies
    1. Marriage serves the needs of individuals.
      a. status and security
      b. an opportunity to have legitimate children

II. The selection of a marriage partner
  A. In traditional societies
    1. A marriage partner is usually selected by the parents of the bride and groom.
  B. In industrialized societies
    1. Individuals choose their own partners.

III. Marriage customs
  A. In traditional societies
    1. Customs symbolize the exchange between two families.
      a. the dowry
  B. In industrialized societies
    1. Customs symbolize the exchange between two individuals.
      a. wedding rings

Pattern of organization: _____

Point-by-point organization is used more often than side-by-side because it helps readers focus on the points of comparison. Point-by-point is particularly useful for papers that contain a lot of information. However, side-by-side is more dramatic and therefore is effective for discussing a change over time or for contrasting an impression of reality with the way things really are. For example, to compare young people's idealistic ideas about marriage with the reality of married life, you might write the first body paragraph about a fantasy of marriage as an extended courtship during which the wife receives frequent gifts of flowers and jewelry. The second body paragraph might be about the unromantic reality of the first few months of marriage when the couple has to decide who will pay the bills, clean the floor, and take out the trash.

When you select a topic, consider both point-by-point and side-by-side (make brief outlines with each to compare them), and then choose the pattern of organization that will be most effective for your essay.

Combining similarities and differences in the comparison/contrast essay.
While many comparison/contrast essays discuss only differences or only
similarities, some discuss both. If you decide to discuss both, put the aspect
you wish to emphasize (either similarities or differences) last. For example,
if you decide to emphasize differences, you can (1) mention similarities
in the introduction before concentrating on differences in the body, or (2)
include a body paragraph about similarities before discussing differences in
one or more additional body paragraphs.

The Writing Process

Once you have selected a topic, following the prewriting steps will help you
gather information and organize it effectively.

Marie, a student from France, decided to write about the differences
in the lives of men and women in her culture because she knew several
married women who had jobs and children, and she had concluded that
their lives were more difficult than their husbands'. She did her prewriting
in the following way.

Marie's Steps

STEP 1   Write down the two things that you plan to compare, and make a **list** for the
first one. Then create a **parallel list** for the second one.

First, Marie wrote a list about men. Then she created a parallel list about
women.

Men	Women
• tend to work away from home more hours than they work at home	• tend to work at home nearly as many or even more hours than they work away from home
• tend to have more leisure time than their wives; tend to spend their leisure time doing outdoor activities or watching sports on television either alone or with friends	• tend to have less leisure time than their husbands; tend to spend their leisure time with their children
• tend to be employed at higher positions and paid more	• even when as well educated as men, tend to be hired at lower positions and paid less
• tend to have higher status in society	• tend to have lower status in society

STEP 2 At this point, you may need to **narrow your topic** and cross out the items on your list that do not fit in your topic focus. Then write a **thesis statement**.

Marie decided to focus on men's and women's work, so she crossed out the point about leisure time. Then she drafted a thesis statement.

Today in France, when married couples both work outside the home, the lives of the husband and wife differ.

STEP 3 Look for **points of comparison** on your lists and check (✔) them. If you can, discuss them with your classmates and teacher. Then write **focused questions** and answers to develop each one.

Marie decided on three points of comparison, which she wrote as focused questions. She then answered each one.

1. *How much time do men and women spend working outside and inside the home?*
   - *Men tend to work away from home more hours than they work at home.*
   - *Women tend to work at home as many or more hours than they work away from home.*

2. *What type of work do men and women do outside and inside the home?*
   - *Men tend to hold managerial positions.*
   - *Women tend to hold lower-level positions such as clerks and food service workers.*
   - *Men tend to choose which household tasks they will perform.*
   - *Women do not choose which household tasks they will perform.*

3. *How are men and women rewarded for the work they do outside and inside the home?*
   - *Men tend to be given more promotions and to be paid more.*
   - *Women, even when as well educated as men, tend to be given fewer promotions and paid less.*

- Men are rewarded for their work at home because it is not expected.
- Women are not rewarded for their work at home because it is expected.

STEP 4 Consider the two **patterns of organization** (point-by-point and side-by-side), and select one. Make an **outline**, using each **focused question** as a **point of comparison**.

Marie decided to use point-by-point organization. She made the following outline.

> Today in France, when married partners both work outside the home, their lives differ <u>in terms of the amount of time they spend on work, the type of work they do, and the rewards they receive both outside and inside the home.</u>

I. Time they spend on work

A. Men

1. spend more hours working away from home

2. spend less time working at home

B. Women

1. some hold part-time jobs near their homes

2. some hold full-time jobs and struggle to do work at home in less time

II. Type of work they do

A. Men

1. managerial positions outside

2. select the household tasks they do

B. Women

1. lower-level positions outside

2. cannot choose the household tasks they do

III. Rewards they receive
    A. Men
        1. higher salaries and more promotions
        2. efforts in the home are acknowledged more
    B. Women
        1. lower salaries and fewer promotions
        2. efforts in the home are not acknowledged

With her outline complete, Marie was ready to write a first draft. Then, as she worked through the chapter, she wrote several drafts before completing her final draft.

Marie's Final Draft

The Lives of Working Husbands and Wives in France Today

[1]Today a significant number of French women work outside the home, some full time and others part time. [2]However, when housewives and mothers enter the labor market, their lives do not become exactly like their husbands'. [3]In fact, the lives of working husbands and wives differ in terms of the time they spend on work, the type of work they do, and the rewards they receive both outside and inside the home.

[4]First, men and women spend different amounts of time working both away from and in the home. [5]Men spend, on average, more time working away from home than women do because most men hold full-time jobs. [6]At home, men average only twenty minutes of work per day while women average about four hours. [7]Many women with young children opt to take part-time jobs so that they can spend more time caring for their children. [8]Women who hold full-time jobs struggle to complete their household tasks and care for their children in less time; for example, they may attempt to do laundry, cook dinner, and help their children with homework all at the same time.

(continued)

⁹Second, the type of work that men and women do differs. ¹⁰In the workforce, more men than women rise to the managerial level, whereas more women occupy low-level jobs such as secretaries, food service workers, and domestic workers. ¹¹At home, men often see housework as voluntary for them and therefore tend to select the tasks they perform. ¹²Thus, the husband may vacuum for twenty minutes and then leave the rest of the housework for his wife. ¹³Unless they can afford to hire other women to clean for them, women have no choice but to do all the housework their husbands cannot or will not do.

¹⁴Third, the rewards men and women receive from work are different. ¹⁵In the workforce, men are paid higher salaries and are promoted more quickly. ¹⁶At home, men receive more praise from their partners for their efforts than women because men are not expected to do housework. ¹⁷Women in the workforce are paid lower salaries and awarded fewer promotions, and at home, because they are expected to do housework, their efforts are not acknowledged as often as their husbands'.

¹⁸The differences we see in the lives of working men and women lead to lower status for women: Women work fewer hours and so cannot advance in their jobs; women hold lower-level positions in the workforce, in part because employers do not view them as able to commit themselves fully to their jobs; and due to their shorter hours and lower-level positions, women earn less. ¹⁹Because they are not bringing home as much money as their husbands, women continue to do more housework, and housework does not bring women status or rewards. ²⁰To break this cycle, men must share equally with women in household responsibilities, and employers must give women opportunities equal to those they offer to men.

EXERCISE 3

With your classmates, discuss the following questions.

NOTE

If you wish to use the side-by-side pattern of organization, you can refer to two examples in this chapter. See "Courtship and Marriage in Japan" on page 132 and "Spanish Women's Lives and Courtship and Dating in My Grandparents' Day and Today" on page 141.

1. Does Marie's essay discuss similarities, differences, or similarities and differences?

2. Which strategy (general statement, background, anecdote) did Marie use in her introduction?

3. Does Marie's thesis statement mention the supporting points of the essay? If so, what are they?

4. Which pattern of organization (point-by-point or side-by-side) did Marie use?

5. Which strategies (summary, suggestion, prediction, opinion) did Marie use in her conclusion?

After selecting a topic from the list on page 121, follow the sequence of steps Marie used, and then write your first draft.

■ REVISING

This part of the chapter will show you how to expand and improve the first draft of your comparison/contrast essay. As you work through the lessons presented here, pay close attention to the **Revision Checkpoints**, which will give you suggestions for revising your essay.

Composition Focus

The introduction of the comparison/contrast essay. In Chapter 3, you learned about four kinds of introductions: background, general statement, anecdote, and definition (see pages 90–91). In a comparison/contrast essay, you can use another kind of introduction: the **turnabout**. For example, you could write about similarities in the introduction, and then turn about and focus on differences in the body.

Furthermore, introductions may contain more than one strategy. For example, you could begin an introductory paragraph with a general statement about marriage, then give some background information about marriage in a particular culture, and finally present a thesis statement about the differences in marriage customs between two generations in that culture.

EXERCISE 4

Read the following introductions, and identify the strategy or strategies used as general statement, background, anecdote, *or* turnabout. *Underline the thesis statement once and put a double line under the controlling idea.*

1. ### Indian Women's Rights before Marriage Laws and Today

[1]India is a land of many cultures and a long history. [2]Traditionally, India had a great variety of marriage customs, some of them very unfair to women. [3]Since India's independence from Britain in 1947, the Indian Parliament has enacted a number of laws which have given more rights to women and greatly improved their lives. [4]<u>As a result of these laws, women's lives have changed</u> <u>in terms of the age at which they get married and the conditions under which they may divorce</u>.

Strategy: _____ background _____

2. ### Civil and Church Weddings in Colombia

[1]Last year I was fortunate to attend two wonderful weddings in my country, Colombia. [2]In May, my cousin Linda married Geraldo in a civil ceremony, and in September, my long-time friend Maria married Ignacio in a Catholic wedding ceremony. [3]Both weddings were joyous occasions, but they were different in a number of ways. [4]In Colombia, civil weddings and church weddings differ in terms of their elaborateness and their social significance.

Strategy: _____

3. ### Men's and Women's Reasons for Marrying

[1]Men and women marry for many of the same reasons. [2]Both men and women marry because marriage is valued by society, and therefore marriage gives both higher social status. [3]Marriage offers both men and women psychological benefits as well in that married people have more support and companionship than single people. [4]However, some of the motivations of men and women differ: Men tend to be more interested in the attractiveness of their spouses, and women tend to be more interested in the wage-earning capacity of their partners.

Strategy: _____

4. **Marriage in Greece and Turkey**

[1]Religious organizations are deeply concerned with preserving family life, so in a country with one dominant faith, marriage customs tend to be shaped by religion. [2]Greece and Turkey are both countries with a single dominant religion: The Greek Orthodox faith is the principal religion of Greece, and Islam is the principal faith of Turkey. [3]Because of this difference in religion, Greek marriages and Turkish marriages differ in that Turkish parents play a larger role in selecting the marriage partner than Greek parents do, and Greek and Turkish ceremonies contain different symbolism.

Strategy: _____

REVISION CHECKPOINT 1

Strategies for Writing Introductions
Look at your essay. If you have already written an introduction, determine what strategy you have used. Ask yourself if another strategy might work better. If you have not written an introduction, choose one of the strategies discussed on pages 90–91 and 129, and write your introduction now.

The controlling idea in thesis statements. In Exercise 4, you identified thesis statements and their controlling ideas. You may have noticed that controlling ideas for comparison/contrast essays can be introduced by *in* or *in terms of*. *In* is followed by a *that*-clause, and *in terms of* is followed by a noun, a noun phrase, or a *wh*-noun clause. Look at the following examples.

 For more about noun clauses, see Appendix IA, page 258.

In + That-Clauses

CLAUSE

Muslim and Christian weddings differ *in* that Muslim ceremonies are held in

CLAUSE

a mosque or a home while Christian weddings are usually held in a church.

In Terms Of + Noun(s), Noun-Phrase(s), or *Wh*-Noun Clause(s)

NOUN

Muslim and Christian weddings differ *in terms of* location.

Muslim and Christian weddings differ in terms of

NOUN PHRASE   NOUN PHRASE

the selection of the marriage partner and the location of the ceremony.

WH-NOUN CLAUSE

Muslim and Christian marriages differ in terms of how they are arranged

WH-NOUN CLAUSE

and where the ceremony is held.

When you introduce two or three points of comparison after *in* or *in terms of,* you must use correct parallel structure (see page 60). Look at the example.

> Nᴏᴛ ᴘᴀʀᴀʟʟᴇʟ: In Japan, Christian weddings differ from traditional Shinto weddings in terms of the location of the ceremony, the presiding official, and the bride and groom wear Western clothing instead of kimonos.

The location of the ceremony and *the presiding official* are noun phrases, but *the bride and groom wear Western clothing instead of kimonos* is a clause. To correct the parallel structure, the clause must be changed to a noun phrase.

> Pᴀʀᴀʟʟᴇʟ: In Japan, Christian weddings differ from traditional Shinto weddings in terms of <u>the location of the ceremony</u>, <u>the presiding official</u>, and <u>the clothing worn by the bride and groom</u>.

 For more on parallel structure, see Appendix IA, page 254.

Eχᴇʀᴄɪsᴇ 5

Work with a partner. Read the following side-by-side essay about the changes in marriage in Japan. Using the information in the two body paragraphs, complete the statements using in *or* in terms of.

Courtship and Marriage in Japan

[1]Over the last six or seven decades, the cultures of countries around the globe have undergone dramatic changes, and Japan is no exception. [2]A comparison of Japanese courtship and marriage customs in the 1950s with those of today reveals significant changes.

[3]In Japan in the 1950s, marriage was a family matter. [4]The father had the authority in the family, so he would arrange the marriages of his children. [5]An eldest son lived all his life in the family home with his parents and carried on the family line, so his marriage was particularly important. [6]For this reason, when an eldest son reached the age of twenty-five, his father would seek the assistance of a go-between, or matchmaker, who would show him photographs and give him family histories of six or seven young women. [7]The father would then choose one young woman whose family was similar to his own and set a date for a meeting between the two families called an *omiai*. [8]During the *omiai*, the parents would do almost all the talking while the young people would sit with eyes cast down. [9]Afterward, if all had gone well, the young man and woman would be asked to give their consent. [10]In those days, there were more available women than men, so young women and their families had to agree to any reasonable match. [11]Once the marriage was agreed upon, the bride and groom would not see each other again until the wedding day.

[12]Since the 1950s, Japan has changed a great deal. [13]Today marriage is largely an individual matter. [14]Fathers do not have as much authority in the family as they once had, and eldest sons do not always remain at home, though, if they move out, they usually settle near their parents. [15]Young people choose their own marriage partners, often after meeting one another at college or work. [16]Today very few seek the help of go-betweens, but those who cannot find a spouse on their own use the services of computer matchmaking companies, which provide applicants with photographs and information about dozens of potential mates. [17]Because many women are delaying marriage and a few are deciding to remain single, the number of available men is now greater than the number of available women, so young men have to agree to any reasonable match. [18]Typically, a young man selecting a potential spouse through computer dating will first send e-mails to a few candidates, then select one to date, and finally, if the dating goes well, ask her to marry him. [19]Young people still want to have their parents' approval in the selection of a partner, but a lack of parental approval will not necessarily stop them from marrying.

[20]From the *omiai* to computer-assisted courtship, the process of finding a spouse in Japan has changed a lot. [21]At the same time, family authority has been weakened as individual choice has come to play the leading role in marriage partner selection.

1. In Japan, the role of fathers has changed *in that they no longer arrange the marriages of their children.*

2. The role of eldest sons has changed as well _____

_____

3. A go-between and a computer dating service are similar _____

_____

4. An *omiai* and a date differ _____

_____

5. Courtship in Japan today differs from courtship fifty years ago _____

_____

Now share your responses with your classmates.

REVISION CHECKPOINT 2

The Controlling Idea in Thesis Statements
Review your thesis statement. If you have not included points of comparison in your thesis statement, try using *in* or *in terms of* to add them. If you use parallel structure in your thesis statement, check it to make sure that it is correct.

Balanced development in the comparison/contrast essay. Whether your essay compares two events, two situations, two customs, or two ideas, it must present these two things in a balanced way. Therefore, when revising a comparison/contrast essay, you must make sure all parts of your paper are equally well developed.

EXERCISE 6

A. *Reread the body paragraphs in "The Lives of Working Husbands and Wives in France Today" on page 127, and circle the words* men *and* women *every time you see them. (Also circle the synonyms* husbands *and* wives.*) Does each paragraph have about the same number of references to men as to women? _____ Did the writer present information about men and women in a balanced way? _____*

B. *Reread the body paragraphs in "Courtship and Marriage in Japan" on page 132. Then, in the margin, mark the lines in each paragraph that discuss 1) the roles of family members, 2) the selection of a spouse, and 3) the consent or decision to marry. Do the two body paragraphs present about the same amount of information on each of these three topics? _____ Do the body paragraphs have balanced development? _____*

REVISION CHECKPOINT 3

Balance in the Comparison/Contrast Essay
Review your own essay for balance. Make sure that the two things you are comparing are equally well developed. If development in your essay is not balanced, revise it now.

More about cohesion. Clear connections are just as important in comparison/contrast essays as in other kinds of essays. Readers look for connections both between the thesis and the body paragraphs and within body paragraphs.

Cohesion between the thesis statement and the topic sentences of the body paragraphs. On page 61, you learned various ways to link the thesis to the topic sentences of the body paragraphs: You can *name the supporting points in your thesis, make sure the supporting points are in the same order in the body as they appear in the thesis,* and *use repeated words, word forms, synonyms,* and *transitions.*

Here are two more ways to link your thesis statement and the topic sentences of your body paragraphs.

1. *Similar sentence beginnings.* Use similar prepositional phrases or subjects and verbs at the beginning of the topic sentences to link the topic sentences to one another.

   THESIS: Family life in two-career television families differs from actual family life in two-career families in terms of the way family members communicate with one another, care for children, and manage household duties.

   TOPIC SENTENCES:

   In situation comedies and similar programs, family members in two-career families have a lot of time to talk to each other, but in real life, working parents and their children are too busy to interact.

   On TV, men are shown caring for children as often as women, but in real life, mothers care for children more often than fathers.

   On the air, dual-career couples seldom argue about or even appear to do housework, but in real life, getting housework done is a big problem for dual-career couples, and they often disagree about who should do the chores.

2. *Correlative conjunctions.* Use the correlative conjunctions *not only . . . but also* to link the topic sentences of the body paragraphs to one another.

> THESIS: Married and single people lead very different lives in terms of their ability to live economically, to find companionship, and to plan for the future.

> TOPIC SENTENCES:

> Married people can share basic expenses and save money, while single people have to manage household expenses on their own.

> Married people have companionship almost any time they want it, whereas single people have to make an effort to find company.

> *Not only* are married people better off economically and socially than single people, *but* married people can *also* face the future with greater certainty.

 For more on correlative conjunctions, see Appendix IA, page 256.

EXERCISE 7

Identify the cohesion strategies used in these examples. The first item has been done for you.

1. THESIS: In my grandmother's time, a woman's life was very different from what it is today: Taiwanese women's lives have changed in terms of their responsibilities, their rights, and their social status.

   TOPIC SENTENCES:

   First, Taiwanese women's lives have changed since my grandmother's generation in terms of what their duties are.

   Second, Taiwanese women's lives have changed since my grandmother's generation in terms of what they are permitted to do.

   Finally, Taiwanese women's lives have changed since my grandmother's generation in terms of how much they are respected by others.

✔ repetition of key words	✔ transitions
____ word forms	✔ similar sentence beginnings
✔ synonyms	____ correlative conjunctions

2. THESIS: Extended families and nuclear families differ in three ways: the education of children, the division of work, and the distribution of property.

TOPIC SENTENCES:

First, the way that babies and young children are educated in extended families and nuclear families is different.

Second, the way that work is divided among family members in extended families and nuclear families is different.

Finally, the way that property is distributed in extended families and nuclear families is different.

_____ repetition of key words	_____ transitions
_____ word forms	_____ similar sentence beginnings
_____ synonyms	_____ correlative conjunctions

3. THESIS: Catholic weddings in the Philippines and Muslim weddings in Indonesia differ in three significant ways: the choosing of the marriage partner, the marriage proposal, and the giving of gifts.

TOPIC SENTENCES:

One important difference between Catholic weddings in the Philippines and Muslim weddings in Indonesia has to do with the way marriage partners are selected.

Another important difference between Catholic weddings in the Philippines and Muslim weddings in Indonesia has to do with the way marriage is proposed.

Not only are the selection of partners and the marriage proposal different, but gift giving at a Catholic wedding in the Philippines is different from gift giving at a Muslim wedding in Indonesia.

_____ repetition of key words	_____ transitions
_____ word forms	_____ similar sentence beginnings
_____ synonyms	_____ correlative conjunctions

Cohesion within body paragraphs. Just as the thesis statement and the topic sentences of body paragraphs need to be connected, the sentences within each body paragraph must also be connected. All of the cohesion strategies you have already learned, including *repetition*, *word forms*, *synonyms*, and *transitions*, create links within body paragraphs. Here are some other strategies you can use.

- **related words**—Words that are used in the same context, like *family*, *father*, and *son*, contribute to paragraph cohesion.
- **pronouns and possessive adjectives**—Pronouns like *he*, *him*, *himself*, *they*, *them*, and *themselves* contribute to cohesion, as do possessive adjectives like *his* and *their*.
- **pointing words and quantity words**—Pointing words like *this* and *these* and quantity words like *one*, *some*, *several*, *many*, and *most* are used both as adjectives and as pronouns to create links to nouns mentioned earlier in the text.
- **conjunctions**—Coordinating, subordinating, and correlative conjunctions connect ideas by showing logical relationships between words and clauses in a paragraph.
- **time expressions**—Adverbs and prepositional phrases like *since 1940* or *during the summer* help readers understand the chronological relationships in a paragraph.

 For more on pronouns and possessive adjectives, see Appendix IA, page 265. For more on coordinating conjunctions, see Appendix IA, page 252, and for more on subordinating conjunctions, see Appendix IA, pages 239 and 272.

EXERCISE 8

Some of the words that provide cohesion in this paragraph from "Courtship and Marriage in Japan" are in boldface type. Identify the strategy used with each boldfaced word, and write its name on the line to the right of the paragraph. (There may be more than one possible answer.)

---

conjunction	repeated word
pointing word (*this*, *these*)	synonym
pronoun or possessive adjective	time expression
quantity word (*one*, *some*)	word form
related word	

---

a) **Since the 1950s**, Japan has changed a great deal.

b) **Today** marriage is largely an individual matter. Fathers do not have as much authority in the family as c) **they** once had, and eldest sons do not always remain at home, though, if they move out, they usually d) **settle** near their parents. Young people choose their own marriage partners, often after meeting one another at college or work. Today very few seek the help of go-betweens, but e) **those** who cannot find a f) **spouse** on their own use the services of computer matchmaking companies, which provide applicants with photographs and information about dozens of potential g) **mates**. h) **Because** many women are delaying marriage and i) **a few** are deciding to remain single, the number of available men is now greater than the number of j) **available** women, so young men have to agree to any reasonable match. Typically, a young man selecting a potential k) **spouse** through computer dating will first send e-mails to a few l) **candidates**, then select m) **one** to date, and n) **finally**, if the dating goes well, ask her to marry him. Young people still want to have their parents' approval in the o) **selection** of a partner, p) **but** a lack of q) **parental** approval will not necessarily stop them from marrying.

a. *time expression*

b. _____

c. _____

d. _____

e. _____

f. _____

g. _____

h. _____

i. _____

j. _____

k. _____

l. _____

m. _____

n. _____

o. _____

p. _____

q. _____

Cohesion
Check 1) your thesis and the topic sentences of your body paragraphs and 2) the sentences within your body paragraphs for cohesion. Make sure that you have used cohesive devices (repeated words, related words, word forms, synonyms, transitions, similar sentence beginnings, pronouns and possessive adjectives, pointing words and quantity words, conjunctions, and time expressions) to create connections. If you can improve the cohesion in your essay, do it now.

Consistent point of view. When you write, you must choose a **point of view**. Point of view refers to the kind of subjects you use in *most* of the sentences in your paragraph or essay. You can use **first person**, **second person**, or **third person** point of view.

First Person: (singular) *I* and (plural) *we*

Second Person: (singular or plural) *you*

Third Person: (singular) *he*, *she*, and *it,* and (plural) *they*

To write a cohesive essay, you must use point of view consistently throughout your paper. That means that you should change point of view only when you need to. In the paragraph in Exercise 8, the following subjects are used:

. . . Japan . . . marriage . . . fathers . . . they . . . sons . . . they . . . they . . . young people . . . few (young people) . . . those (young people) . . . women . . . a few (women) . . . number (of available men) . . . young men . . . young people . . . lack (of parental approval) . . .

Notice that all of the subjects are third person (*Japan, marriage, fathers, sons*). The third person is the most common point of view in academic writing. When you write about people, the third person plural is the easiest point of view to use because you do not have to select between masculine and feminine pronouns and you do not have to use the longer expression *he or she*. Compare these examples.

When a teenager gets married, *he* grows up quickly.

When a teenager gets married, *she* grows up quickly.

When a teenager gets married, *he or she* grows up quickly.

When teenagers get married, *they* grow up quickly.

Note: While some people say that the first person singular pronoun *I* should be avoided in essays, *I* is actually acceptable in most kinds of writing. In fact, the pronoun *I* is frequently used for including personal opinions or examples.

> Where *I* grew up, many teenagers marry as soon as they graduate from high school. *I* think this is too early. For example, *I* got married when I was twenty-two, and *I* believe that the early twenties are a good age to marry.

The point of view that most often causes problems in writing is the second person pronoun, *you,* because writers tend to shift to *you* unintentionally, making their writing less cohesive.

> The media can influence **people** to change their long-held beliefs. For
>
> example, U.S.-made TV programs and movies, which **people** around the world
>
> have access to, often show couples flirting, but in traditional societies, flirting
>
> _people_
> is not allowed. After ~~you~~ have watched a number of U.S. TV shows or movies,
> _they_
> ~~you~~ tend to question traditional beliefs.

Exercise 9

As you read the essay below, find and correct the three inappropriate changes in point of view.

Spanish Women's Lives and Courtship and Dating in My Grandparents' Day and Today

1 [1]My grandparents were teenagers in the 1940s, when Spain was recovering from a civil war. [2]The country was poor in the postwar years, the government tried to control all aspects of political and social life, and Spain remain closed to foreign influences. [3]By comparison, my teen years in the first decade of the twenty-first century in Spain have been a period of prosperity, more political freedom, and greater openness to Europe and the rest of the world. [4]Spanish society today is very different from the way it was seventy years ago; the changes are particularly apparent in women's lives and in courtship and dating customs.

2 [5]In the 1940s, Spanish women's lives were governed by custom and routine. [6]Women's social lives centered around their families. [7]After graduating from high school, women generally did not go to college; if they did not need to work, they stayed at home and

helped their mothers. [8]Spanish families at that time all followed exactly the same daily routine: They ate their midday and evening meals at the same hour every day and before each meal took a stroll through the streets of their city or town, where they met their friends and neighbors.

3 [9]In the 1940s, dating and courtship customs followed rigid rules. [10]If you broke the rules, you faced strong social disapproval. [11]Girls and boys attended separate high schools, so school did not offer a place to meet the opposite sex. [12]Moreover, young men and women could not date until they finished school, and young men who went to college generally could not begin to look for girlfriends until they had passed their professional examinations. [13]Thus, men were usually over twenty and women at least seventeen before they began to date. [14]When a young man or woman reached the age when it was permissible to look for a partner, the daily strolls offered an opportunity to meet members of the opposite sex. [15]In those days, groups of young men and groups of young women strolled through the streets, and when they passed one other, a man and woman could exchange glances. [16]Then if the young man wanted to meet the woman whose eye he had caught, he would need to find a friend or relative to introduce him to her. [17]The next step for the man might be to offer to escort the woman to a party or to the movies, or he might write her a letter. [18]In the forties, a woman could not ask to be introduced to a man, could not write a man a letter unless he wrote to her first, and could not call a man on the telephone. [19]In addition, you would never see couples kiss or hold hands in public.

4 [20]Now, seventy years later, the social customs that influence both women's lives and courtship and dating customs in Spain have changed significantly.

5 [21]Today, most women's lives are governed by the same rules that govern men's lives. [22]That is, women are expected to pursue an education that will lead to employment. [23]Women now make up close to 50 percent of college students in Spain and 40 percent of the workforce. [24]Consequently, the family no longer plays the central role in women's lives that it once did. [25]Women's lives are governed by school and work schedules—just

as men's are—and this is true for many married women with children as well. [26]There is no more midday family meal, and working families do not have time in the evenings for a leisurely stroll before dinner.

6 [27] Today courtship and dating in Spain do not follow the rigid rules of the past. [28]Girls and boys attend the same high schools, and teenagers mix freely with the opposite sex in social clubs where they enjoy activities like hiking or biking. [29]Dating starts as early as age fourteen or fifteen, and the period of dating may continue for many years, as professional couples usually delay marriage until we have saved enough money to buy a home. [30]Today women do not have to wait for men to act first; they can introduce themselves to a man and then call him and ask him out. [31]In addition, society now tolerates couples who freely display their affection for each other in public.

7 [32]Spanish society has seen major changes over the past seventy years, and these changes are especially apparent in the lives of women and in the norms that govern dating and courtship. [33]In my grandparents' time there was a narrow set of rules that applied to everyone. [34]Today the rules are relaxed, and women have much more freedom in all areas of their lives, including their selection of partners. [35]Future generations will probably not see changes in social life as dramatic as the changes that have occurred over the last seven decades in Spain.

REVISION CHECKPOINT 5

Consistent Point of View
Review the subjects of the sentences in your essay. Make sure that you have changed point of view only when necessary. If you find unnecessary shifts in point of view, correct them. If you have questions about the point of view in your essay, write a note to your teacher in the margin of your paper.

The conclusion of the comparison/contrast essay. As you learned on page 100, in conclusions you try to give readers a sense of completion. Use summary, suggestion, prediction, opinion, and other strategies to accomplish this.

Exercise 10

A. *Examine the conclusions of "The Lives of Working Husbands and Wives in France Today" and "Spanish Women's Lives and Courtship and Dating in My Grandparents' Day and Today," and check (✔) the methods that were used in each.*

"The Lives of Working Husbands and Wives in France Today" (pages 127–128)	"Spanish Women's Lives and Courtship and Dating in My Grandparents' Day and Today" (pages 141–143)
_____ summarizing	_____ summarizing
_____ predicting	_____ predicting
_____ recommending	_____ recommending
_____ offering an opinion	_____ offering an opinion
_____ drawing conclusions about why or how things occur	_____ drawing conclusions about why or how things occur

B. *Write a conclusion for the following essay using the methods that you think were successful in the essays you have just reviewed.*

Later Is Better

[1]Because I am now approaching thirty years of age, I have had the opportunity to see most of my friends get married. [2]Some married in their late teens, and, unfortunately, some of those early marriages haven't lasted. [3]Others married in their mid- or late twenties, and these later marriages appear more stable. [4]I have concluded that there is a significant difference between early and late marriage in that mature couples know better what they want in life, are more able to make joint decisions based on their shared goals, and are more willing to make sacrifices.

[5]To succeed in marriage, people must know what they value in life. [6]Young people in their late teens or early twenties are still in the process of getting to know themselves. [7]Trying to discover what they want in life, they may move from one place to another, start school and later drop out, and even alter their idea of an ideal partner. [8]Because people change so much at this age, a person who marries at eighteen may look at her spouse five years later and ask herself, "Is this the same person I married?" [9]On the other hand, those who marry after the age of twenty-five have had time to experience life. [10]They have studied a range of subjects in school or held various jobs; they have dated a number of people and have developed a good sense of what they want in a mate. [11]After the age of twenty-five, people are less likely to undergo major shifts in their interests or values. [12]Therefore, more mature marriage partners are less likely to grow apart.

[13]To succeed in marriage, people must not only know what their own values and goals are, but they must also know how to establish common goals with their spouses and decide together how to reach those goals. [14]Some eighteen-year-olds expect everything to go their way. [15]Others are very impatient and expect problems to be solved quickly. [16]Even the most mature eighteen-year-olds are not practiced in the give-and-take of negotiations with a peer. [17]People of twenty-five or older, in contrast, have learned that they cannot always get what they want. [18]They know that it takes time to work problems out. [19]Through their experience in other relationships, they have learned to cooperate and compromise, so they are more successful at agreeing upon common goals with their spouses.

[20]Finally, to succeed in marriage, people must be ready to sacrifice. [21]Teenage newlyweds are sometimes shocked to discover that they can't watch their favorite TV program when their spouse wants to watch another, that they can't buy a new CD player because they need the money to pay the rent, or that they can't hang out with their old buddies every Friday and Saturday night. [22]They become angry and refuse to give up what they want. [23]More mature newlyweds will also discover that adjusting to married life can be difficult, but they are better able to meet the challenge. [24]Because they have learned that to get along with others requires compromise, they can give up their favorite TV show, wait to buy the CD player, and forgo seeing their old buddies. [25]Such sacrifices create a bond of trust between the couple.

_____

_____

_____

_____

_____

_____

REVISION CHECKPOINT 6

Strategies for Writing Conclusions
Check the conclusion of your essay. Determine which strategies you have used, and ask yourself whether you want to include other strategies. Make sure that your conclusion does not introduce new ideas that require development. If your conclusion can be improved, revise it.

Language Focus

The vocabulary of comparison and contrast. English has many ways to signal similarity and contrast. Look at the chart.

Vocabulary and Structures That Signal Similarity				
Coordinating Conjunctions	**Subordinating Conjunctions**	**Correlative Conjunctions**	**Transitions**	**Other Parts of Speech**
and (can be used with adverbs such as *also*)	as just as	both . . . and neither . . . nor	likewise similarly also in the same way	alike, similar (*adj.*) as well, so, the same, too (*adv.*) similarity (*n.*) like (*prep.*)

EXERCISE 11

Choose a signal of similarity from the chart above to complete each sentence. Write **c.c.** *(coordinating conjunction),* **s.c.** *(subordinating conjunction),* **cor.c.** *(correlative conjunction),* **tr.** *(transition),* **adj.** *(adjective),* **adv.** *(adverb),* **n.** *(noun), or* **prep.** *(preposition) in the parentheses.*

1. _____Like_____ Moroccan brides, Sudanese brides have their hands and feet decorated with designs made of a vegetable dye prior to the wedding. (*prep.*)

2. One _____ between Hindu and Christian weddings is the use of marriage vows. (   )

3. At Catholic weddings in _____ Spain _____ Mexico, the groom gives the bride coins which represent his willingness to support her. (   )

4. Greek and Kazakh weddings are _____ in that the bride and groom drink from a common cup that symbolizes their union. (   )

5. _____ young Italians usually live with their parents until they marry, young Greeks remain at home until married as well. (   )

6. In Chile, a couple transfers the rings from their right to left hands during the marriage ceremony, _____ an Egyptian couple does the same. (   )

7. In Ecuador, the godparents of the bride and groom participate in the wedding ceremony. _____, in Bolivia, the bride and groom's godparents take part in the wedding ceremony. (   )

To avoid repetition in comparative statements, use synonyms and auxiliary verbs.

1. Instead of repeating the same words, phrases, and clauses, use **synonyms** and **synonymous phrases**.

   In Ecuador, the godparents of the bride and groom *participate* in the wedding ceremony. Similarly, in Bolivia, the godparents of the bride and groom *take part* in the wedding ceremony.

2. Instead of repeating long verb phrases, use **auxiliary verbs**.

   In Ecuador, the godparents of the bride and groom participate in the wedding ceremony, just as godparents *do* in Bolivia.

3. With *and,* use **auxiliary verbs** along with **adverbs**.

   In Ecuador, the godparents of the bride and groom participate in the wedding ceremony, and godparents *do the same* in Bolivia.

   In Ecuador, the godparents of the bride and groom participate in the wedding ceremony, and godparents *do* in Bolivia *also/as well/too*.

   In Ecuador, the godparents of the bride and groom participate in the wedding ceremony, and *so do* godparents in Bolivia.

Vocabulary and Structures That Signal Contrast			
Coordinating Conjunctions	**Subordinating Conjunctions**	**Transitions**	**Other Parts of Speech**
but	while	however	differ (*v.*)
	whereas	in contrast	difference (*n.*)
		by comparison	different (*adj.*)
		on the other hand	unlike (*prep.*)

*Choose a signal of contrast from the chart on page 147 to complete each sentence. Write **c.c.** (coordinating conjunction), **s.c.** (subordinating conjunction), **tr.** (transition), **v.** (verb), **n.** (noun), **adj.** (adjective), or **prep.** (preposition) in the parentheses.*

1. In South Africa, weddings are held on Sundays, _____but_____ in the United States, weddings are held on Saturdays. (*c.c.*)

2. _____ a bride in Yemen, who wears a dress of gold fabric, a bride in Pakistan wears a dress of red fabric. (   )

3. Christian weddings and Muslim weddings are _____ in that, in a Christian wedding, the bride and groom make vows, while in a Muslim wedding, they sign a contract. (   )

4. Christian weddings include an exchange of rings to symbolize the bride and groom's union. _____, Hindu weddings include an exchange of necklaces or flower garlands. (   )

5. One _____ between weddings in India and weddings in the United States is the fact that in India the bride's family often pays a dowry to the groom's family. (   )

6. In Singapore, intermarriage, that is, marriage between people of different religions, is common. In India, intermarriage is unusual, _____. (   )

7. Weddings in the Netherlands _____ from weddings in Switzerland in that in the Netherlands, guests throw flowers on the couple after the wedding ceremony, and in Switzerland, they throw rice. (   )

8. Dancing and feasting go on from three to eight days after a Russian Orthodox wedding ceremony, _____ wedding receptions usually last only four or five hours in the United States. (   )

EXERCISE 13

Practice using the comparison/contrast signals. On another piece of paper, rewrite each sentence using the suggested structure. Remember to use synonyms and auxiliary verbs to avoid repetition, and check your punctuation.

1. Twenty-five years ago, Russians lived under a socialist system, but today they live under a capitalist system. (whereas)

   Twenty-five years ago, Russians lived under a socialist system, whereas today they live under a capitalist system.

2. In Russia today, women are as well educated as men, and they were under the socialist system, too. (just as)

3. Unlike twenty-five years ago, when, under the Soviet system, most Russian women between the ages of twenty and sixty were employed, today many Russian women are unemployed. (however)

4. Under the socialist system, women did the same heavy work in agriculture and manufacturing that men did. In contrast, today most of the job opportunities for women are in office work or sales. (while)

5. Today in Russia, some female employees work part time or have flexible schedules, but a generation ago, all female employees worked full time. (by comparison)

6. Twenty-five years ago, Russian women did all the housework, and they continue to do all the work at home today. (just as)

7. For Russian women, one important difference between the socialist and capitalist systems has been that working women had affordable child care under socialism, whereas they have to pay a substantial amount for child care under capitalism. (differ)

8. In contrast to the Soviet period, when by law women made up 34 percent of the lawmakers in the government, today women make up less than 10 percent of the lawmakers. (but)

9. During the Soviet period, women were seen in only two roles, as mothers and as workers. Today in Russia women are seen in a variety of roles, including those of fashion models, television personalities, and journalists. (difference)

Compare your answers with your classmates'. Discuss any questions you have with your teacher.

REVISION CHECKPOINT 7

Signals of Similarity and Contrast
Underline the comparison/contrast signals in your essay. Review your essay to see whether it is easy for a reader to follow. If you think adding more signals would make your paper easier to read, add them now. Make sure you have used commas, periods, and semicolons correctly.

■ FINAL DRAFT

1. Before you write your final draft, look over your essay one last time to decide if you want to make any further changes.

2. Prepare a final draft of your composition. Make sure that you have used capital letters at the beginning of your sentences and periods at the end, and check your spelling.

3. Exchange papers with one or two classmates. Read each other's papers carefully. Turn to page 300 in Appendix II, and fill out the Peer Review Form.

4. Check your paper again and make any necessary corrections. Turn in your paper to your teacher.

■ CHAPTER REVIEW

Look back at what you have accomplished in Chapter 4. Check (✔) what you have learned and what you have used as you have written and revised your composition.

Chapter 4 Topics	Learned	Used
using point-by-point or side-by-side comparison/contrast organization (pages 121–129)		
applying strategies for writing introductions to comparison/contrast essays (pages 129–131)		
using *in* or *in terms of* to state the controlling idea in the thesis statement of a comparison/contrast essay (pages 131–134)		
using balanced development in the body of a comparison/contrast essay (page 134)		
using the strategies of cohesion to link the thesis statement and the topic sentences of the body paragraphs as well as the sentences within body paragraphs (pages 135–139)		
using consistent pronoun point of view (pages 140–143)		
applying strategies for writing conclusions to comparison/contrast essays (pages 143–145)		
using the vocabulary of comparison and contrast (pages 146–149)		

From School to Work

Writing an Argumentative Essay

When young people start to work, they assume the role of adults. Preparation for this important step is critical for both youth and their society. In this chapter, we will look at some of the choices people face as they proceed from school to work and ask what society should do for them to make their transition successful.

This chapter will help you

- define, analyze, and limit your topic.
- write a thesis, introduction, support, and conclusion for an argumentative essay.
- present and respond to opposing points of view.
- use modals, conditionals, and qualifiers to make your argument effective.

■ READING FOR WRITING

Before You Read

A. *You are going to read two argumentative essays about high school education. First, reflect on your own opinions about what high schools should do to prepare youth for the future. Mark each opinion statement* **A** *(agree) or* **D** *(disagree).*

_____ All high school students should have an opportunity to prepare for college if they choose to make that their goal.

_____ High schools should give extra help to students who have been disadvantaged by poverty or racial discrimination so that they can better compete with students who have had more advantages.

_____ High schools should respond to the needs of the economy and train students for the kinds of jobs that will be available to them.

B. *Each of the following two argumentative essays contains 1) a main argument in favor of or against a "college-for-all" policy, and 2) supporting arguments (reasons why readers should accept the main argument). As you read each essay, look for the main and the supporting arguments. After you finish each reading, complete the outlines of the arguments on the lines that follow.*

Reading

SHOULD THE PURPOSE OF A HIGH SCHOOL EDUCATION BE TO SEND ALL STUDENTS TO COLLEGE?

YES

1   Worldwide, people understand college to be the **benchmark** of achievement and the gateway to a better life. Yet sadly many poor and minority students have been denied the opportunity to attend college. Denying anyone the opportunity to go to college is a loss, not only for individuals, but for a society as a whole.

2   In past decades, many U.S. high schools have had two tracks, that is, distinct programs of study

NO

1   Educational **policies**, which are the agreements that determine how schools function, are often the topic of public debate. In recent years, some people have proposed that every student in the United States should plan to attend college. This suggestion is misguided, or based on misunderstandings, because it does not address the real needs of young people, the actual **capabilities** of the high school

benchmark: *a standard against which other things are measured*

policy: *an official way of doing things chosen by those in positions of authority*

✳ capability: *an ability that can be developed*

for groups of students based on their ability. One was for college-bound students and one for work-bound students—and this led to a practice of advising poor and minority students to take the career or vocational track. Classes in the career track were typically not as rigorous, or challenging, as those in the academic track, so once students entered the career track, they quickly dropped behind their peers. Because the curricula (programs of study) and the rate of study of the two tracks were so different, students in the career track found it nearly impossible to transfer into the academic track. To make matters worse, the vocational track did not always prepare students for employment. Too often, students graduated from vocational programs without the skills that they needed to secure well-paying jobs. The **inevitable** result of an inferior, that is, low-quality, education is a lifetime of work in low-skill, low-paying jobs without the opportunity to enjoy a middle-class lifestyle, and this has been the **fate** of too many underserved students.

3   If a society is committed to fairness, it cannot exclude any of its people from its benefits. College is a unique experience for youth in that it offers them an **abundance** of resources. It offers intellectual stimulation of all kinds, opportunities for social **networking**, and, most importantly, the chance to acquire

population, or the demands of today's job market. Instead of advising all high school students to plan on college, we need to make high school education better.

2   All young people need to have realistic goals and must understand how to reach their goals. Whether a teenager's goal is to complete a four-year college degree, get a two-year degree, enter a **trade school**, or find a job immediately after graduation, the teen needs to understand that making steady progress throughout high school will bring him or her to that goal.

3   The problem in secondary schools in the United States today, according to James Rosenbaum of Northwestern University, is that most students are not given realistic information. They are told that they can go to college—even those students whose academic skills are well below their actual grade level—but they are not informed that they need to study and make progress in high school in order to succeed in college (6). While community colleges accept all applicants and offer **remedial courses** to bring students up to college level, research shows that students who are significantly below grade level in high school are unlikely to finish college (4). However, high school counselors do not explain this to students (3), so students do not think their high school grades matter. Moreover, as Rosenbaum reports, few employers care

(continued)

✳ **prospective:** *potential*

post-secondary: *college*

asset: *something useful that can help one succeed*

✳ **eliminate:** *get rid of*

align: *to adjust to fit*

revitalize: *bring new life into*

the skills and knowledge that are the key to satisfying employment and economic security.

4   Yet a **post-secondary** education is much more than a benefit to individuals: An educated population is an **asset** to an entire society. Educated people are the innovators who start new businesses and develop new products. They design the systems that help companies run smoothly, and they guide and inspire others. Furthermore, in today's challenging business environment, educated people are essential to a country's economic competitiveness. Technology is rapidly changing, and, at the same time, transnational corporations are shifting operations across borders with growing frequency. According to Anthony Carnevale (25), director of the Global Institute on Education and the Economy at Georgetown University, "workers with the most education are likely to be the most effective learners in the high-performance work organizations" of today. College prepares young people to welcome challenges and to demand the most from themselves. Moreover, college degree programs have become increasingly **aligned** with occupational demand (Carnevale 25). Therefore, the majority of college graduates have knowledge and skills they can apply in well-paying jobs immediately.

5   A final and sometimes overlooked benefit of higher education is that it assures the

about **prospective** employees' high school grades, in spite of the fact that academic performance is a good predictor of long-term earnings (9). In effect, high school students are not being given the information they need to set realistic goals, and society is telling them that their effort in high school is not necessary.

4   High schools have a responsibility to prepare *all* students for the future. While historically they have prepared the students in the upper or middle achievement range for college quite well, they have not helped students who are struggling with academic subjects get ready for the future as effectively. Vocational programs have been underfunded and disrespected. In addition, these programs have been associated with racial and gender discrimination. Yet vocational programs provide an avenue for students who are not inspired by academic subjects, so these programs cannot be **eliminated** in favor of a college-for-all policy. Instead, vocational education needs to be improved, as UCLA professor Mike Rose argues in his book, *The Mind at Work: Valuing the Intelligence of the American Worker*. Rose encourages high school curriculum designers and policymakers to **revitalize** vocational education, based on an appreciation of the intellectual challenge of all kinds of work and respect for workers. He says that classes that teach subjects

viability: *health or likelihood of success*

✱ integrated: *having separate parts that work together as a whole*

✱ formulate: *think carefully and develop*

✱ promote: *help something develop*

viability of democracies. A democratic form of government requires the participation of citizens. Citizens in a democracy must be able to absorb information, evaluate it, and form opinions independently—skills cultivated nowhere as effectively as in college. College students are required to explore subjects in depth; they learn how to gather and analyze data and how to apply their knowledge to real-world situations. Furthermore, college campuses are places where debate is welcome and students are encouraged to **formulate** their own points of view. When people have the experience of studying and debating issues in college, they tend to remain civically engaged all through their lives—a key to the health of a democratic society.

6   In sum, a college-for-all policy, because it is fair and it offers the greatest number of people access to the benefits of higher education and a pathway to a comfortable life, **promotes** individual happiness. In addition, a college-for-all policy is in the self-interest of any country that wants to be economically competitive and fully democratic.

Carnevale, Anthony. "College for All?" *Change.* Jan./Feb. 2008. 9 Oct. 2009. < http://www.changemag.org/>

such as electronics or automobile repair "could be the core of a rich, **integrated** curriculum: one that includes social and technical history, science and economics, and hands-on assembly and repair" (192).

5   In the past decade, the U.S. and global economies have been rapidly changing, and workers today face more uncertainty than in the past. This fact makes a high school education more, not less, important today to individuals and to the nation. While an increasing number of jobs require two- or four-year college degrees, there will always be many jobs that do not. According to the United States Department of Labor (3), one-quarter of all jobs in the United States are found in fourteen occupations, which include customer service representatives, office clerks, bookkeepers, accountants, and managers. Most of these jobs do not require four-year college degrees, but they do require high school level reading and computational (math) skills. Therefore, it does not make sense to encourage all high school students to go to college. Rather, it makes sense to urge all students to set realistic goals and achieve to the best of their ability throughout high school.

6   Students' high school achievement matters for not only college but employment, and students must be made aware of this. Finally, if high

(continued)

school classes deliver more and better instruction and teachers and counselors expect more of students, everyone will value a high school diploma as a ticket to a good future.

Rose, Mike. *The Mind at Work: Valuing the Intelligence of the American Worker*. New York: Viking, 2004.

Rosenbaum, James E. "Beyond Empty Promises: Policies to Improve Transitions to College and Jobs." Office of Vocational and Adult Education, U.S. Department of Education. April 2002. 18 March 2010. <http://www.earlycolleges.org/ Downloads/ EmptyPromisesRosenbaum.pdf>

United States Dept. of Labor. *Chart Book: Occupational Employment and Wages,* May 2008. 17 March 2010. http://www.bls.gov/ oes/2008/may/figure2.pdf

Outline of Essay in Favor of College for All

Main Argument: <u>All students should have the opportunity to go to college because denying anyone the opportunity to go to college is a loss, not only for individuals, but for a society as a whole.</u>

Supporting Argument 1: _____

_____

_____

Supporting Argument 2: <u>If a society values fairness, it cannot exclude any of its people from its resources, and college is a valuable resource for young people.</u>

Supporting Argument 3: _____

_____

_____

Supporting Argument 4: _____

_____

_____

Outline of Essay Opposing College for All

Main Argument: _A college-for-all policy is misguided and should be rejected_ _because it does not address the real needs of young people, the actual_ _capabilities of the high school population, or the demands of today's job_ _market. Instead, we need to make high school education better._

Supporting Argument 1: _All young people need to have realistic goals and_ _must understand how to reach their goals; therefore, telling all students that_ _they can attend college but not telling them that they must prepare for it does_ _not support them._

Supporting Argument 2: _____

_____

_____

Supporting Argument 3: _____

_____

_____

_____

Understanding the Readings

With a partner or a small group, discuss the following questions.

1. Review the main and supporting arguments of each essay. Discuss which individual supporting arguments you think are strong and which you think are weak. (A strong argument is a **persuasive**, or believable, argument—you do not have to agree with it to see that it is strong.) Discuss which essay has a stronger set of arguments *overall*.

2. Note what kind of development is used for each supporting argument. In the margin next to the sentences that develop each supporting argument, write *explanation, cause-and-effect reasoning, facts, comparison,* or *citing an authority*. (An **authority** is a knowledgeable person whose ideas can be quoted or paraphrased as a means of support.) What kind of development do you think makes an argument strongest?

3. Arguments often contain **implicit** (suggested, but not clearly stated) opinions or beliefs. Which of the following opinions are implicit in the essay in favor of college for all, and which are implicit in the essay opposed to college for all? Mark them *in favor* or *opposed*.

_____ a. Fairness means equal opportunity for people according to their ability.

_____ b. High schools need more public support and more resources.

_____ c. All citizens must be educated in order to participate fully in a democratic society.

_____ d. High school counselors are not doing a good job.

_____ e. Discrimination based on ethnicity or social class is wrong.

_____ f. Some young people are just not cut out for college.

_____ g. Educators must prepare people for the jobs that are available.

_____ h. It's not necessary that people *graduate* from college. It's the experience of attending college—for whatever period of time—that matters.

4. Do you agree fully or in part with either essay? Which main and supporting arguments do you agree with, and why? Which of the implicit arguments do you agree with?

Vocabulary Expansion

TIP
Because a definition can make a sentence harder to read, it is best to make the definition brief or write the sentence so that the definition comes at the end.

Brief definitions. When you use a word that is unfamiliar to your readers, you need to define it. You can put a brief definition in a sentence several ways: You can 1) place the definition in parentheses, 2) put commas around the definition and introduce it with *or* or *that is*, or 3) provide the definition in an adjective clause. Look that these examples.

policy (*n.*)   Our school policy (official rule) requires attendance.

Our school policy, *or* official rule, requires attendance.

Our school policy, *that is*, official rule, requires attendance.

Our school policy, *which is* an official rule, requires attendance.

regulate (*v.*)   School attendance is regulated (controlled by laws and policies).

School attendance is regulated, *or* controlled by laws and policies.

School attendance is regulated, *that is*, controlled by laws and policies.

School attendance is regulated, *which means* controlled by laws and policies.

mandatory (*adj.*)   For children, attendance is mandatory (required by law).

For children, attendance is mandatory, *or* required by law.

For children, attendance is mandatory, *that is*, required by law.

For children, attendance is mandatory, *which means* required by law.

EXERCISE 1

Skim the essays about the "college for all" question, and find and underline the following terms and their definitions: track, rigorous, curriculum *(plural:* curricula*),* inferior, educational policies, misguided, *and* computational. *Notice that the definitions are presented in various ways—with parentheses; with commas and* or *or* that is; *and with an adjective clause.*

EXERCISE 2

The boldface terms in these sentences are related to words that appeared in the essays about the college-for-all question. On another piece of paper, rewrite each sentence, and include a brief definition of the boldface term. The cue at the end of each sentence tells you which definition strategy to use in each sentence. Use a dictionary if necessary, and make sure to punctuate correctly.

1. Professional conferences in the field of computer science give me an opportunity to **network**. (that is)

    Professional conferences in the field of computer science give me an opportunity to network, that is, meet people with whom I share personal or professional interests.

2. Lorna devoted several years of work to the **formulation** of her theory about price inflation. (that is)

3. Regarding our plans for the next quarter, Joe and I are in close **alignment**. (parentheses)

4. According to our business plan, the **integration** of the accounts payable department with the collections department will reduce costs. (or)

5. Lack of communication between teammates or coworkers **inevitably** leads to disagreements. (that is)

6. When we needed someone to resolve a conflict, speak diplomatically, and implement an agreement, Paula proved herself to be very **capable**. (adjective clause)

7. The **revitalized** campus quadrangle has become a social center. (or)

Longer definitions. Sometimes a word requires a one-sentence definition. The most common way to write a one-sentence definition is to name 1) the broader **category** that the thing belongs to and 2) the **distinguishing characteristics** that separate the thing from other members of its category.

TERM   CATEGORY   DISTINGUISHING CHARACTERISTICS

An undergraduate is a student who is working on a college degree.

TERM   CATEGORY   DISTINGUISHING CHARACTERISTICS

A major is a program of study that has specific course requirements and leads to a degree.

TERM   CATEGORY   DISTINGUISHING CHARACTERISTICS

Liberal arts is a program of study that includes literature, languages, and history but not technical or career-related courses.

EXERCISE 3

On another piece of paper, write a one-sentence definition for each of these academic terms using a category and distinguishing characteristics. You may need to ask teachers or classmates to explain some of these terms, or you may have to consult a dictionary.

1. chair
2. dictionary
3. dean

4. elective
5. prerequisite
6. registrar

7. syllabus
8. term paper
9. transcript

Example: _A chair is a person that/who leads an academic department in a_

college or university.

Sometimes you need to extend a definition by adding an additional sentence containing examples, a negative definition (an explanation of what the term you are defining is *not*), or a comparison/contrast statement. Look at these examples.

One-Sentence Definition	**Extended Explanation**
Bullying is behavior that is intended to hurt others.	Some examples of bullying are name calling and making physical threats. (examples)
	Bullying is not an accidental occurrence. It is an intentional action. (negation)
	Both bullying and harassment are offensive and can cause the victim stress and loss of self-esteem. However, bullying usually refers to the aggressive behavior of children, whereas harassment usually refers to discriminatory behavior of adults which is based on racial or gender differences. (comparison/contrast)

EXERCISE 4

A. *Read the writing assignment topics below and on page 162, and underline the words that you think may require definition or explanation. Discuss the meanings of these terms with your classmates and teacher.*

B. *With a partner, select a term to define. Write a one-sentence definition using classification and distinguishing characteristics. Then share your definition with your classmates.*

TIP
Try to avoid using the term you are defining or a member of its word family in your definition. Look at this example.

Discrimination is treatment of people that ~~discriminates~~ *is unequal*.

■ WRITING

Before you select a topic for your argumentative essay, you do not need to have an opinion—you can formulate an opinion as you analyze your topic during prewriting. Once you have formed an opinion, however, you will need to develop at least two persuasive supporting arguments to back it up.

Assignment

1. Should high schools offer vocational education, or should students go to trade schools for practical job training?

2. Should a college or university education be tuition free?

3. Should schools provide moral education for youth, or should instruction in values be left to parents?

4. Should the parents of students who misbehave in school be required to do unpaid work for their children's school?

5. Should public schools be designated as discrimination-free zones?

What Argumentation Is and Why It Is Important

In previous writing assignments, your primary goal has been to give your audience information. However, in writing an argumentative essay you have to *persuade your audience to consider your point of view*, even if they disagree with it. This requires some thought and skill: You need to understand your topic thoroughly, take a clear position, and select solid reasons to support your opinion.

Argumentation is an important skill both in school and at work because in both situations you will be expected to present your opinions clearly and to defend them logically.

The Writing Process

Become familiar with your topic. Before you can begin to brainstorm a topic, you need to understand it. Terms such as *vocational education* may mean different things to different people. For example, one person may define *vocational education* in terms of trade schools that teach specific career skills, while another person might say that vocational education refers to the general instruction about how to find a job that is offered in many high schools. After you gather ideas from others about your topic, you will be able to settle on your own definition.

EXERCISE 5

*Choose a topic from the list on pages 161–162, and make a list of questions. (*What is X? What does X include? How is X different from Y? What are the problems or controversies associated with X?*) Then interview three people outside your classroom (your neighbors, people who work in your school, or your friends), and take notes on their answers to your questions.*

Analyze your topic. Before deciding upon a point of view, analyze the **pros** (reasons *for* a point of view) and **cons** (reasons *against* a point of view). By listing a number of reasons both for and against a point of view, you come to understand the issue thoroughly. Later, when outlining your essay, develop some of the reasons you listed as supporting arguments.

Should high school students work during the school year?

<u>Yes</u>

They can make new friends.

They can save for college.

They can learn responsibility.

They may *discover a career for themselves.*

<u>No</u>

They can get better grades if they don't work.

They can participate in extracurricular activities if they don't work.

EXERCISE 6

A. *With your teacher and classmates, make a list of controversial topics. Choose one topic to analyze. Write a yes/no question about the topic using* **Should**.

B. *With a partner, make pro and con lists for that topic. Then share your ideas with your teacher and classmates.*

Limit your topic. While analyzing your topic and drafting a thesis statement, you may realize that the thesis needs limiting. For example, let's say the topic is *Should high school students work?* You feel that work is generally good for teenagers but realize that work may not be good at *all* times of the year or for *all* teenagers. Moreover, you may decide that the *kind* or *amount* of work is important. Therefore, you will need to add one or more limiting statements such as these to the thesis or introduction.

> Teenagers should work *only during their summer vacations*.
>
> *Only* teenagers *who have passing grades in all their classes* should work.
>
> Teenagers should work *if they can find jobs that teach them useful skills*.
>
> Teenagers should work *no more than ten hours a week during the school year*.

EXERCISE 7

Reread the chapter writing assignment topics on pages 161–162, and underline the words or phrases in each topic that you think might require limiting or explaining. Then discuss the limiting ideas that you might add to each topic.

NOTE

Limiting ideas are often included in a thesis statement and sometimes placed in other parts of an argumentative essay. You will learn more about limiting statements in the section on qualifiers in the Language Focus section of the chapter.

Draft a thesis statement. An argumentative essay must express one clear opinion, and the thesis statement of the essay must contain that opinion.

As you analyze a topic, you will form an opinion. At this point, you should begin to draft your thesis statement. Opinions are usually expressed with the modal verb *should* or evaluative words such as *good* and *bad*.

> Teenagers *should* have part-time jobs.

> Part-time work is *good* for teenagers.

A complete thesis statement also contains reasons, or **supporting arguments**.

OPINION	REASON 1	REASON 2
Employers should hire teenagers	because they are eager to work,	they are flexible,

REASON 3
and they have the knowledge and skills required to do many entry-level jobs.

A thesis statement may also contain an **opposing view**.

OPPOSING VIEW
While some people say that teenagers do not have a good work ethic,

OPINION	REASON 1	REASON 2
employers should hire teenagers	because they are eager to work,	they are flexible,

REASON 3
and they have the knowledge and skills required to do many entry-level jobs.

An opposing view in a thesis statement is usually introduced by the subordinating conjunctions of comparison/contrast *while* or *although*.

NOTE You will learn more about opposing views in the Composition Focus section of this chapter.

Exercise 8

*Each piece of text in this exercise is from the introduction to an argumentative essay. In each item, underline the thesis statement, and list the elements that each statement contains (**opposing view, definition** or **explanation, opinion, limiting statement, supporting reasons**).*

1. Although some people say that tracking (placing students in certain classes according to their ability level) unfairly reduces some students' chances of going to college, <u>tracking makes sense for both teachers and students because it decreases the likelihood of the fastest learners becoming bored. Further, the slowest learners become less frustrated, and grading becomes more fair for all students.</u>

   opposing view, definition, opinion, supporting reasons

2. High schools should require all students to take three years of science so that they will develop an appreciation for nature and understand how the rules of mathematics can be applied to the real world.

   _____

3. In a pass/no pass grading policy, *pass* replaces the letter grades A, B, and C, and *no pass* replaces D and F. The pass/no pass grading policy at Green Hills College should be discontinued because it has led to a higher failure rate and a lowering of standards.

   _____

4. Algebra is a branch of pure mathematics. Introductory algebra teaches students how to use *variables* (symbols such as x or y that can represent any number) and perform operations such as $x + y = 8$. Algebra provides valuable mental training: It teaches students to remember and follow rules, and it helps them become comfortable with abstract ideas. In addition, algebra prepares students for college-level math courses and for the kind of calculations that are used in the working world. Therefore, all high school students should be required to take a year of algebra.

   _____

5. While some people say that they want their tax money to go directly to their neighborhood schools rather than to all public schools, I believe that tax revenues should be divided equally among all schools because all students are equal under the law and all schools are required by law to provide the same basic education.

   _____

As you read through the prewriting steps, you will see how Alina, a student from the Philippines, developed an argument and prepared to write an essay on the question *Should young people be required to do community service?*

Alina's Steps

STEP 1 Explore a potential topic by writing questions, discussing the questions with people you know, and taking notes. The questions should help you 1) **define key terms** and 2) **limit the topic**. (You began this process in Exercise 5 on page 162. Refer back to the notes you made, and determine what further information you need. Write some new questions, and discuss the topic some more.)

Alina wrote the following questions and answers.

> Defining
>
> What does "community service" mean?
>
> — Community service is any work done to help people in one's neighborhood or city who need assistance. Some examples are helping elderly people maintain their homes, teaching children to read, repairing or maintaining historic buildings, guiding visitors in a museum, and picking up garbage on beaches or in city parks.

> Limiting
>
> Isn't community service usually voluntary?
>
> — Community service is usually voluntary, but some countries have compulsory community service. For example, in the Philippines, college students and young men who choose not to do military service are required to do community service.

> Limiting
>
> Isn't community service usually unpaid?
>
> — Community service is usually unpaid, but sometimes compensation is offered. For example, in the United States, the AmeriCorps program compensates participants with vouchers for college tuition.

If community service is to be required, how much work would youths be expected to do?

— I think everyone should have to perform the same number of hours, and the amount should not be excessive—perhaps about fifty hours. Young people could work up to twenty-five hours a week during vacations or as little as an hour a week during the school year, so the term of service would vary.

STEP 2 Identify two opposing opinions, and list as many reasons as you can to support each one.

After reviewing her notes, Alina listed the arguments for and against mandatory community service.

Should young people be required to do community service?

<u>Yes</u>

- Community service provides chances for young people to meet others.
- It teaches youth compassion, responsibility, and how to relate to all kinds of people.
- It benefits society.
- It gives youth work experience they can use when applying for jobs in the future.
- It gives young people a chance to apply what they have learned in school.

<u>No</u>

- Community service takes up time young people could spend on their studies.
- Community service programs would be expensive to administer.
- Some teenagers need paying jobs so they can help their families. They cannot afford the time to do volunteer work.

STEP 3 Decide on the opinion you wish to present in your essay, and select the reasons on your lists that you think are most persuasive. (Persuasive reasons are believable, important, and relevant—that is, clearly connected to the topic.) Write a draft thesis statement and outline. Alina's outline follows on page 168.

Young people should be required to do community service because it benefits both the youth themselves and the society as a whole.

I. *Community service gives young people knowledge of the world.*
    A. *It helps them relate information in textbooks to the real world.*

II. *Community service prepares youth for future employment.*
    A. *It helps them understand how organizations work.*
    B. *It provides opportunities to learn to work with all kinds of people.*

III. *Community service benefits society because without it, many vital services would not be provided.*
    A. *Because of community service, more children get vaccinations.*
    B. *Because of community service, disaster relief is provided when it is needed.*
    C. *Because of community service, more poor people have adequate housing.*
    D. *Because of community service, children who need help in school get tutoring.*

IV. *Community service benefits society in that it affects people's values in a positive way.*
    A. *It helps people become less self-centered.*
    B. *It makes people think about the concept of citizenship, and it gives participants a new understanding of citizenship.*
        1. *citizenship course at the University of the Philippines*

After several drafts, Alina wrote the following final draft. You will notice that in the process of writing and rewriting, she limited her thesis statement even more (by adding *about fifty hours of community service*) and added an additional body paragraph which is not represented in her outline. In addition, you will see that Alina used some outside sources in this essay and that she cited those sources in the text and at the end of the text.

Alina's Final Draft

The Benefits of Community Service

1 [1]Community service means committing one's time and efforts to serving individuals and organizations in one's own local area. [2]The service can take many forms: It can be direct person-to-person assistance such as delivering meals to housebound elderly people or caring for children in after-school programs. [3]Or it can involve working for organizations such as libraries, hospitals, museums, and charities. [4]In my view, all young people between the ages of sixteen and twenty should be required to complete about fifty hours of community service because doing so will benefit both the participants themselves and their societies.

2 [5]First of all, community service benefits young people by broadening their horizons. [6]Many youths know little of the world beyond their homes, schools, and neighborhoods. [7]Community service helps them understand who the people in their society are, what problems these people face, and how their lives can be improved. [8]Young people who have performed community service find that it enriches their learning in school because their service experience helps them relate information in their history, civics, and economics textbooks to the real world.

3 [9]Community service also helps young people prepare for future employment. [10]According to a U.S. Department of Labor report, in order to be ready to enter the labor force, a person must understand how organizations function and be able to work well with all kinds of people (15). [11]Because it is not possible to learn these things at home or in school, a youth who has participated in a well-run community service program is better qualified for employment than a youth who has not had such an experience.

4 [12]Community service not only rewards young participants but benefits society as a whole by providing valuable assistance that would not otherwise be given. [13]Without community service,

(continued)

children might not get vaccinations, the Red Cross/Red Crescent could not provide disaster relief, Habitat for Humanity could not build houses for the homeless, low-income children and adolescents would not get free tutoring in reading and math, and public museums and parks might close for lack of people to staff and maintain them.

5   [14]Finally, community service benefits the society in a less tangible but very important way by shifting public values. [15]In the modern world, the competition for schooling and jobs is encouraging people to be increasingly self-centered in their choice of goals. [16]People have started to think of citizenship as a set of individual rights rather than rights and responsibilities that belong to people collectively. [17]This trend can be reversed when young people are required to perform community service. [18]When people get involved in service, they begin to reflect on the meaning of citizenship. [19]In the Philippines, university students are required to perform community service, and at the University of the Philippines, students must take a citizenship course in conjunction with their service (Co, 191). [20]Through the course and their service activities, students gain a deeper understanding of what citizenship means and how it can be applied through direct community action that improves people's lives.

6   [21]Critics say that community service should be voluntary, not mandatory. [22]They point out that young people in financial need cannot spare time to participate because they have to work to support themselves and their families. [23]It is a fact that in the past volunteer service was something the wealthy did for the poor, and thus it increased the social stigma of being poor. [24]But, as Arthur Gilette, author and former Director of UNESCO's Youth and Sports Activities Division, points out, if participation in community service is required of everyone, tolerance, equality, and cohesiveness will increase in society (61). [25]Furthermore, because a well-run community service program will help all young people acquire

knowledge and skills, it should be seen as part of every youth's education.

7   [26]In conclusion, a well-administered community service program will have multiple benefits. [27]It will expand youths' horizons and help them become ready for the world of work. [28]It will benefit the society as a whole by providing needed services and by reshaping the dominant values in a positive way. [29]Therefore, governments should create community service programs and require young people's participation as an investment in everyone's future.

Co, Edna A. "Developing Citizenship through Service: A Philippines Initiative." *Service Enquiry: Service in the 21st Century*. Ed. Helene Perold, Susan Stroud, and Michael Sherraden. Global Service Institute and Volunteer and Service Enquiry Southern Africa. Sept. 2003. 23 Nov. 2003 <http://www.service-enquiry.org.za/first_edition_download.asp>

Gilette, Arthur. "Taking People out of Boxes and Categories: Voluntary Service and Social Cohesion." *Service Enquiry: Service in the 21st Century*. Ed. Helene Perold, Susan Stroud, and Michael Sherraden. Global Service Institute and Volunteer and Service Enquiry Southern Africa. Sept. 2003. 23 Nov. 2003 <http://www.service-enquiry.org.za/first_edition_download.asp>

United States Dept. of Labor. *Secretary's Commission on Achieving Necessary Skills: Identifying and Describing the Skills Required by Work*. 4 June 2002. 6 Dec. 2003 <http://wdr.doleta.gov/SCANS/idsrw/scansrep.pdf>

EXERCISE 9

With a partner or a small group, discuss the following questions.

1. Look at the introduction and find the defining and limiting phrases, clauses, and sentences. Circle the definition of *community service*. Explain why Alina placed the definition at the very beginning of the essay. Underline the limiting phrases in the thesis statement, and explain why they are important.

2. What is Alina's main argument and what are her supporting arguments? What transition signals did Alina use to link the supporting arguments?

3. Do you think the supporting arguments Alina chose are persuasive? Explain.

4. How did Alina develop each supporting argument? What strategies (*explanation, cause-and-effect reasoning, examples, facts, comparison,* or *outside sources*) did she use in each of her body paragraphs?

5. The last body paragraph did not appear on Alina's outline. What does it discuss?

6. What strategies (*summary, prediction, recommendation*) did Alina use in her conclusion?

After selecting a topic from the list on pages 161–162, follow the prewriting steps that Alina used, and then write your first draft.

■ REVISING

This part of the chapter will show you how to expand and improve the first draft of your argumentative essay. As you work through the lessons presented here, pay close attention to the **Revision Checkpoints**, which will give you suggestions for revising your essay.

Composition Focus

Introduction strategies for argumentative essays. Like other essay introductions, introductions to argumentative essays must stimulate interest and lead readers to the thesis. To do this, you can use any of the strategies you learned in Chapter 3—*background, general statement, anecdote* and *definition* (see pages 90–91). In addition, you can also include a *quotation* or the *turnabout*, a strategy which you learned about in Chapter 4 (page 129). To use the turnabout, present an opposing view at the beginning of the introduction, and then respond to that view in your thesis statement. Finally, you can include a *definition* or an *explanation* if you think it is necessary to explain a term or a concept.

EXERCISE 10

*Read these essay introductions, and underline the thesis statement in each one. Then identify the introduction strategies used (**general statement, background, anecdote, quotation, turnabout,** and **definition or explanation**). Write the name of each strategy in the margin next to the text.*

1. **Standardized Tests**

definition and explanation; background

[1]A standardized test is an examination that is given to a whole student population or to representative samples of a population so that students' learning can be measured by comparing scores. [2]U.S. law requires that students' progress in reading and math be measured with a standardized test at least once a year. [3]Standardized testing is beneficial to educators because it allows them to measure student progress and the effectiveness of teaching methods, and it helps schools and school districts improve their curricula.

2. <h1 style="text-align:center">Home Schooling</h1>

[1] "I don't go to school. [2] My home is my school, and my mommy's the teacher!" seven-year-old Liela proclaimed, grinning. [3] Her mother seemed just as pleased: "Leila reads two years ahead of her age group, and she's advanced in math and social studies, too. [4] She's curious about everything, and she absorbs new information like a sponge. [5] It's fun helping her learn." [6] Leila and her mother are part of a growing trend in the United States—home schooling. [7] While most home-schooled children perform very well on standardized tests and are well adjusted socially, home schooling has some negative outcomes: The nation's public schools would be stronger if home-schooling parents got involved in the system instead of withdrawing from it, and the democracy would be stronger if home-schooled children learned that it is better to participate in society than to opt out.

3. <h1 style="text-align:center">Affirmative Action</h1>

[1] In recent decades, a major controversy developed in the U.S. over the use of affirmative action policies in college admissions. [2] Affirmative action policies give special consideration to racial minorities or disadvantaged applicants in the selection process. [3] The number of applicants to the top universities is many times greater than the number of spaces available, so affirmative action policies make a critical difference; in fact, without affirmative action policies, very few of the available spots in top universities would be given to minority or low-income applicants. [4] Therefore, affirmative action policies play an important role in shaping the society of the future for several reasons.

REVISION CHECKPOINT 1

Introduction
Review your introduction. Make sure that it defines and limits your topic, if necessary. Ask yourself if it stimulates readers' interest and leads them to your thesis statement. Finally, consider whether using a different strategy or adding a strategy would make your introduction more effective. If you can improve your introduction, revise it now.

Support: Organizing and developing body paragraphs. Support is the most essential part of an argumentative essay because it is what persuades readers to consider your point of view. If you select reasons to support your opinion that are believable, relevant, and important, organize them well, and develop them fully in your body paragraphs, your argument will be effective.

The way you organize your supporting reasons, or supporting arguments, can impact the overall effectiveness of your essay. You should consider all possible patterns of organization and then decide which is likely to be most persuasive. You can use order of importance and put the most important or persuasive reason last. Or, if one reason seems more obvious than the others, consider putting it first because readers are likely to think of it first. Finally, if your supporting arguments concern both individuals and society as a whole, consider putting those that deal with society last, as Alina did in "The Benefits of Community Service."

Each supporting reason in your essay should be presented and developed in a body paragraph. The topic sentence of each body paragraph should state the supporting argument and should contain a transition to show how that supporting argument relates to the other supporting arguments. You may use cause-and-effect transitions such as *one reason* and *another reason* (see page 94).

As you saw in Alina's essay, you can develop each supporting argument through explanation, cause-and-effect reasoning, examples, facts or statistics, and comparison. In addition, you may refer to **outside sources**. These sources are usually **authorities**, or experts, who have done research and published articles on the topic you are writing about. You can also use a more informal source such as a friend who has shared information with you that illustrates the point you want to make.

Whichever strategies you use in the supporting sentences of a body paragraph, you must make sure that each sentence is logically related to the topic sentence. In addition, you need to use the signals of cohesion (see page 61) to link the supporting sentences to the topic sentence.

NOTE
Whenever you use information from a published source—whether it is an online or printed document—you must provide citations both in the text and at the end of the text. (For more on citations, see Part II, pages 214–218.) If you use a published source without providing citations, you are committing **plagiarism**, an academic offense which may have serious consequences.

EXERCISE 11

Read this essay, paying attention to the development of the body paragraphs. Then locate each kind of support on the list and write the number of the sentence where you found it.

1. cause-and-effect reasoning

   15, 16, 22

2. example _____

3. fact or statistic _____

4. comparison _____

5. outside source _____

A New Alternative—Distance Education

[1]Distance learning is a growing phenomenon. [2]A majority of traditional colleges and universities now offer some distance courses, and there are also many online-only institutions offering certificate and degree programs. [3]Most distance learning today is done through the Internet, but printed materials, DVDs, television, and telephones are used as well. [4]While critics have questioned its effectiveness, distance learning is a valuable option for many people.

[5]Distance learning gives access to higher education to people who would not have the chance to take college classes otherwise. [6]Distance education is ideal for

people in rural areas who live far from a college campus. [7]In addition, distance learning is helpful to people who cannot enroll in college classes due to their work schedules, family responsibilities, or disabilities. [8]For example, a flight attendant can study business administration without giving up his regular job, a mother of young children can complete her teaching credential when her little ones are asleep, and a blind person can earn a bachelor's degree using technology that makes it possible to listen to printed textbooks and articles. [9]Finally, low-income students find that some distance education programs are less expensive than traditional programs, and, if the cost of transportation or on-campus housing is factored in, distance education becomes a real bargain.

[10]A common criticism of distance learning is that students do not learn as well without regular face-to-face interaction with teachers and fellow classmates. [11]Indeed, students with a keen interest in the social opportunities on a college campus are probably not going to be satisfied with distance programs. [12]However, many students find that distance learning serves their need to feel connected to their instructor and fellow students. [13]My friend Carlo, who is completing an online degree in computer science, says, "What matters most is having a qualified instructor who takes the time to answer my questions—and I've had more one-on-one help from my online instructors than I had when I took traditional college classes." [14]Furthermore, online discussions through e-mail or a chat room can be lively and stimulating, especially when the teacher and students are able to interact in real time. [15]In fact, shy students who do not speak up in classroom discussions are more likely to participate in online discussions because they have the opportunity to reflect before answering and because they realize that if they don't join in, they will "disappear." [16]Cathy, a friend of mine who took an ethnic studies class online last semester, says she developed the confidence to join face-to-face classroom discussions by participating in online discussions.

[17]Some people claim that the quality of distance education is not as high as that of traditional college programs. [18]It is true that quality varies among distance learning programs, just as it varies in traditional face-to-face programs. [19]However, distance learning courses have been earning increasing respect. [20]In 2006, a survey of 2,200 colleges and universities found that 62 percent of academic leaders rated distance learning as equal to or more effective than traditional courses (Allen and Seaman, 2). [21]Furthermore, a review of over 500 reports of research investigating the effectiveness of distance learning versus traditional learning found that distance learning students received slightly better exam scores and grades than traditional students (Allen et al., 402, 408). [22]This may be because distance learning requires more effort by students and distance learning students actually spend more time working independently than students in traditional classrooms.

[23]Distance learning is not for everyone—to succeed, a student must be goal-oriented, able to manage time, and able to solve problems independently. [24]For such students, a distance learning program is a wonderful option, provided that the program suits their needs. [25]Before signing up, students should ask questions about

the instructors' qualifications, the technology, the teaching methods, and the teaching materials. [26]They should ask to see sample lessons and perhaps talk to graduates of the program. [27]Finally, they might want to ask current or prospective employers if the program prepares students with the skills and knowledge required in their workplace. [28]Then, if the program checks out well and is a good match for the student, he or she should click on "Enroll."

Allen, Elaine and Jeff Seaman. *Making the Grade: Online Education in the United States, 2006*. The Sloan Consortium. Nov. 2006. 22 Jan. 2010. <http://www.sloan-c.org/publications/survey/survey06.asp>

Allen, Mike, et al. "Evaluating the Effectiveness of Distance Learning: A Comparison Using Meta Analysis." *Journal of Communication* 54 (2004): 402-420. 22 Jan. 2010. <http://community.nmsu.edu/success/files/Evaluating_effectiveness_DE.pdf>

REVISION CHECKPOINT 2

Organizing and Developing Arguments

Ask yourself if each of your reasons or supporting arguments is well developed. Review the six strategies (*cause-and-effect reasoning, comparison, examples, explanation, facts or statistics,* and *outside sources*), count how many you have used, and ask yourself if you can add more. Make sure that your body paragraphs are both balanced (equally well developed) and cohesive. Finally, if you have used published sources, make sure that you have identified them with correct in-text and end-of-text citations.

Opposing points of view. An **opposing view** is a supporting reason for the side of the argument you oppose. It is not always necessary to present an opposing view in an argumentative essay, but it is a good idea to include an opposing view when you think that your readers are likely to be aware of it. By including an opposing view, you show readers that you have analyzed your topic thoroughly, and by **refuting** the opposing view (proving it to be incorrect by presenting a stronger supporting argument), you strengthen your argument overall. You may also choose to **concede** (admit) that part of the opposing view is correct; in fact, conceding shows that you are fair-minded.

Opposing views, concessions, and refutations must be introduced with signals. Here are some signals you can use.

To Introduce an Opposing View	To Signal a Concession	To Signal a Refutation
Some people say that	Granted,	However,
Proponents of . . . claim that	Indeed,	But (in fact/as a matter of fact/it is a fact that)
Critics of . . . maintain that	It is a fact/true that	Yet (in fact/as a matter of fact/it is a fact that)
A criticism of . . . is that		Nevertheless,

Here is an example of an opposing view and refutation from an essay that expresses the opinion that teenage boys and girls should not be separated in school.

OPPOSING VIEW

[Some people say that teenage boys and girls should study in separate classes.]

REFUTATION

However, such a separation creates an unnatural situation.

Here is the same example with a concession statement.

OPPOSING VIEW

[Some people say that teenage boys and girls should study in separate classes.]

CONCESSION

Granted, all-boy or all-girl classes are easier for teachers to control.

REFUTATION

However, such a separation creates an unnatural situation. When boys and

girls are separated, they do not learn how to get along with each other.

EXERCISE 12

A. *Reread "The Benefits of Community Service" on page 169 and "A New Alternative—Distance Education" on page 174. Put brackets [ ] around clauses and sentences that state opposing views, broken lines under concessions, and solid lines under refutations.*

B. *Compare your answers with a partner's. Then imagine each essay without the opposing view(s). Do the opposing views make these essays stronger? If so, why? Tell a partner what you think.*

If you decide to include an opposing view in your essay, consider the following questions.

1. Where should I put the opposing view?

   If the opposing view relates to one of your supporting arguments, put it in the body paragraph where that supporting argument is presented. If the opposing view relates to your thesis, you can put it in the introduction, in the body of the essay, or in the conclusion. (If you are writing on a computer, you can easily move the opposing view around to evaluate its effect in various parts of your paper.) If your topic is very controversial, it is a good idea to present and refute the opposing view early in your paper so that readers can focus on your argument.

2. Should I **concede** (agree in part) with the opposing view?

   If you feel that the opposing view contains some truth, you should say so. Readers will appreciate your showing them which part of the opposing view you think is correct and which part is not.

3. How should I respond to the opposing view?

   You must **refute** it, or say clearly that you disagree with the opposing view and give one or more strong reasons for your disagreement. The fact that the opposing view appears in your essay without supporting reasons and your refutation appears with reasons strengthens your argument.

EXERCISE 13

The following thesis statement and body paragraphs are from an essay on the topic Should teenagers work? *In the box are three opposing views that readers would likely be aware of. On another piece of paper, revise the body paragraphs. Begin each body paragraph with an opposing view, and make sure a refutation follows it. (Some of the refutations are in the essay already.) When appropriate, add a concession before the refutation.*

You do not need to write out complete body paragraphs. Just write enough to show the opposing view, any concessions you include, and the refutation.

Opposing views

- By working, youth can help their families financially.
- Youth gain valuable experience by working.
- Work teaches youth how the real world operates.

The Effects of Work on Teenagers

1 THESIS: [1]Except in cases of real economic need, high school students should not work for several reasons: Having additional pocket money encourages them to be materialistic, part-time jobs cause them to forfeit valuable extracurricular activities, and work has a negative impact on their performance in school.

2 [2]Work encourages teenagers to become materialistic. [3]Very few young workers actually give their earnings to their parents or save for their own future, but instead spend their earnings on themselves—on cars, clothes, music, and electronic gadgets. [4]Earning and spending money on material possessions distracts teens from much more important matters such as figuring out what their goals in life are and how they will reach those goals. [5]The teenage years should be a time when young people acquire a sense of themselves and learn how to get along in society, not a time for acquiring material possessions.

3   [6]Working students do not have time for extracurricular activities, and if they miss the many programs and clubs that high schools offer, they will never have a second chance to take advantage of them. [7]Students can participate in sports, orchestra, student government, speech club, drama, and many other activities. [8]These extracurricular programs give young people a chance to make friends, learn to cooperate with others, and acquire confidence. [9]A low-level part-time job such as one in a fast-food restaurant does not give teenagers the same quality of learning experience or sense of accomplishment as the extracurricular activities available in high school.

4   [10]The most important problem associated with high school students working is that jobs take time away from study. [11]A high school curriculum is challenging. [12]High school teachers give complex long-term projects which require doing research, writing papers or delivering speeches, and sometimes creating posters or models. [13]Teachers often assign these projects to groups of students who may have to meet after school to complete their assignments. [14]Working students aren't able to collaborate with classmates after school and often cannot manage to complete even short homework assignments on their own. [15]After four or five hours at an after-school job, they return home too tired to study well. [16]If they try to do their homework, they lose valuable sleep and will not be able to concentrate in class the next morning. [17]As a result, their grades are likely to drop, threatening their chances of getting admitted to a good college later on.

> *After you revise the paragraphs, compare your concessions and refutations with your classmates'. Discuss how adding refutations has changed the effectiveness of this essay.*

REVISION CHECKPOINT 3

> **Opposing Points of View**
> Review your essay, asking yourself whether including an opposing view would strengthen your essay. If you have not included an opposing view, but think adding one will improve your essay, add one now. If you have included an opposing view, evaluate its placement and your response to it.

Conclusion. The final paragraph in an argumentative essay is important because readers often recall the last part of a text most clearly. Therefore, in the conclusion writers present what they want readers to remember—whether that is a restatement of the thesis, a summary of the main points, a suggestion, a prediction about the future, or a warning about possible future consequences. Also, argumentative essay conclusions frequently ask the audience to do something—to consider a new point of view or to take action. For example, the essay opposing a college-for-all policy on page 152 concluded by recommending that high school students be encouraged to set goals and that a high school education be a first-class ticket to the future.

EXERCISE 14

Reread the conclusion to "A New Alternative—Distance Education" on pages 175–176. What strategy or strategies (restatement of the thesis, summary of the main points, suggestion, prediction, or warning) does it use? Write your answers in the margin next to the concluding paragraph.

EXERCISE 15

Write a conclusion for the essay "The Effects of Work on Teenagers" on pages 178–179, and then share it with your classmates. As you listen to the conclusions your classmates have written, comment on how they have incorporated summary, predictions, or recommendations to consider a new point of view or take action.

REVISION CHECKPOINT 4

Conclusions

Review the conclusion of your own essay, checking to see that it contains a brief summary of your main points. If your conclusion does not include a prediction or recommendation, ask yourself if it would be improved by adding either one. Make any revisions that are needed.

Language Focus

Modal verbs. Modal verbs, which add meanings such as *possibility* and *recommendation*, are common in argumentative essays. Here are some examples from an essay that argues for physical education in high schools.

Examples	Meaning
Physical education **should** be mandatory for teenagers.	opinion, recommendation, expectation
High school students **must** burn off restless energy.	strong necessity
Physical education **can** take many forms. For example, students **can** play competitive games like soccer, get an aerobic workout by running, do stationary exercises like pushups, or dance to a lively beat.	possibility in general statements
Through physical education, a teenager **may/might** discover a new interest or pastime.	possibility (a prediction with less than 50 percent certainty)
A mandatory physical education program **will** have many benefits.	prediction (100 percent certainty)

 For more on modal verbs, see Appendix IA, page 280.

EXERCISE 16

NOTE
→ You will learn more about modal verbs in the next two sections, which are about conditional statements and qualifiers.

Underline the correct modal verbs to complete this paragraph, and write the meaning of each modal you choose on a line to the right of the paragraph. In some situations, two answers are possible.

Cell Phones—a Problem at School

Elementary, middle, and high schools 1) <u>should</u>/may ban cell phones because they are a distraction and they interfere with learning. First, cell phones distract students from their studies. Students 2) can/must play games, take pictures, and send text messages during class by hiding their phones under their desks and turning off their ring tones. To prevent these activities, teachers 3) can/must walk around peering under students' desks; consequently, they 4) may/should not be able to concentrate fully on their teaching. Second, cell phones at school interfere with learning. Students with cell phones that have Internet access know that information is readily available, so they 5) may/might fail to memorize facts that they 6) should/will learn. Finally, cell phones 7) might/can encourage cheating. Some students 8) should/may try to text someone to get an answer to a question during a quiz. If they are caught, they 9) can/will face a serious punishment, such as suspension. A ban on cell phones at school 10) must/will help students focus on their schoolwork and master the information and skills they need.

1. _opinion, recommendation_

2. _____

3. _____

4. _____

5. _____
6. _____
7. _____
8. _____

9. _____

10. _____

REVISION CHECKPOINT 5

Modal Verbs
Review your own essay, and underline any modal verbs that you have used. Check to see that you have selected the right modals for the meanings you want to express. If you have any questions about the modal verbs in your essay, write a note to your teacher in the margin of your draft.

Conditional statements. Writers of argumentative essays often ask readers to consider possible outcomes. The most common way to do this is to write conditional sentences with *if*.

REAL FUTURE: If the government *provides* more financial aid to students, students *will* not *have* to work.

UNREAL PRESENT OR FUTURE: If the government *provided* more financial aid to students, students *would* not *have* to work.

To choose between the **real future conditional** and the **unreal present or future conditional**, ask, "How likely is this to happen?" If the outcome is possible, use the real future; if the outcome is unlikely or impossible, use the unreal, or **hypothetical**, present or future.

REAL FUTURE: If I ***receive*** financial aid, I **will** not **have to** work. (I am going to apply for financial aid, and I may receive it. It is a real possibility.)

UNREAL PRESENT OR FUTURE: If I ***received*** financial aid, I **would** not **have** to work. (I do not receive financial aid now. It is unlikely or impossible that I will receive it in the future, so this idea is hypothetical.)

NOTE Unreal conditional sentences do not use *was* in the *if* clause. In other words, when you use the *be* verb in the dependent clause in an unreal conditional sentence, you must use *were*, even if the subject is singular.

Notice that an unreal sentence has a past tense verb form, *received,* but it is not a past tense sentence. The past tense form after *if* is a signal that the sentence is unreal.

were
If I ~~was~~ eligible for financial aid, I would not need to work.

were
If Paul ~~was~~ eligible for financial aid, he would not need to work.

 For more on real and unreal conditional sentences, see page 243 in Appendix IA.

Read each opinion and conditional statement that follows it. Decide whether—in your judgment—the conditional should be real or hypothetical, and then fill in the blanks with appropriate verb forms.

1. I think preschool should be mandatory for all four-year-olds. If all four-year-olds ___*attend*___ (attend) preschool, they ___*will be*___ (be) ready to start learning to read in first grade.

   ___✔___ REAL   _____ HYPOTHETICAL

   OR

   I think preschool should be mandatory for all four-year-olds. If all four-year-olds ___*attended*___ (attend) preschool, they ___*would be*___ (be) ready to start learning to read in first grade.

   _____ REAL   ___✔___ HYPOTHETICAL

2. I think teachers should earn higher salaries. If teachers _____ (earn) higher salaries, there _____ (be, *negative*) a shortage of teachers.

   _____ REAL   _____ HYPOTHETICAL

3. I think the punishment for bullying in elementary and middle school should be stronger. If we _____ (have) stronger punishments for bullying, this unacceptable behavior _____ (decrease).

   _____ REAL   _____ HYPOTHETICAL

4. I think homework should be optional in first and second grade. If homework _____ (be) optional for first and second graders, families _____ (have) more time to spend together.

   _____ REAL   _____ HYPOTHETICAL

5. Public school funding in the United States is tied to the amount of tax revenues that are collected in local areas. This means that public school funding varies from one school district to another. I think all public schools should receive equal funding. If all public schools _____ (receive) equal funding, students everywhere _____ (have) the same educational opportunities.

_____ REAL _____ HYPOTHETICAL

6. Hate speech refers to a kind of communication that is intended to hurt or insult certain individuals or groups. I think colleges and universities should prohibit hate speech on campus. If colleges and universities _____ (ban) hate speech, everyone _____ (feel) more welcome on campus.

_____ REAL _____ HYPOTHETICAL

7. I don't think children should be allowed to watch television on school nights. If children _____ (watch, *negative*), they _____ (spend) more time on their homework.

_____ REAL _____ HYPOTHETICAL

Modal verbs are often used in conditional sentences to weaken the sense of certainty. Compare these examples:

REAL FUTURE:

If children do not watch TV on school nights, they **will** spend more time on their homework. (100 percent certainty of this possible result)

If children do not watch TV on school nights, they **may/might** spend more time on their homework. (less than 50 percent certainty of this possible result)

UNREAL PRESENT OR FUTURE:

If children did not watch TV on school nights, they **would** spend more time on their homework. (100 percent certainty of this hypothetical result)

If children did not watch TV on school nights, they **might** spend more time on their homework. (less than 50 percent certainty of this hypothetical result)

Sometimes the *if* clause is omitted when the meaning is clear without it or when it is awkward to include it. Notice that a prepositional phrase (*with . . . / without . . .*) or the adverb *otherwise* can replace an *if* clause.

> Schools should set a no-TV-on-school-nights policy. *With this policy,* students will do more homework and learn more. (*If schools set this policy,* students will learn . . . .)

> Schools should set a no-TV-on-school-nights policy. *Without this policy,* students will not do enough homework . . . . (*If schools do not set this policy,* students will not do enough homework . . . .)

> Schools should set a no-TV-on-school-nights policy. *Otherwise,* students will not do enough homework and will not learn enough. (*If schools do not set this policy,* students will not do enough homework . . .)

REVISION CHECKPOINT 6

Conditional Statements
Review your essay to see if you have used any conditional sentences. If you have any conditional sentences, decide whether you have chosen the correct verb forms to express the meanings you want to express. If you find any mistakes, fix them now, and if you have questions, write a note to your teacher in the margin of your paper.

Qualifiers. Qualifiers are words and phrases that are used to soften the strength of general statements and predictions. For example, you have seen that modal verbs have different meanings; we could say that some modal meanings are stronger, and others are weaker. Look at these examples.

> Schools *must* require homework. (stronger)

> Schools *should* require homework. (weaker)

> If schools require homework, students *will* learn faster. (stronger)

> If schools require homework, students *may* learn faster. (weaker)

Qualifiers can be very useful in argumentative essays, especially when you are expressing a view that is controversial or unpopular. If you express a controversial or unpopular view too strongly, readers who disagree with you will lose confidence in you as a writer.

English has many kinds of qualifiers. Here are some examples of qualifiers in statements from an essay that expresses an opinion about punishment for disruptive children.

Strong Statement	Statement Softened with a Qualifier
Disruptive behavior interferes with everyone's learning. →	Disruptive behavior **can** interfere with everyone's learning. Disruptive behavior **may** interfere with everyone's learning. Disruptive behavior **is likely to** interfere with everyone's learning.
Disruptive children enjoy annoying their teachers. →	Disruptive children **usually/often** enjoy annoying their teachers. Disruptive children **tend to** enjoy annoying their teachers. Disruptive children **seem to** enjoy annoying their teachers. **Many/Some** disruptive children enjoy annoying their teachers.
If a teacher gets annoyed with a disruptive child, he or she will be impatient with other children. →	If a teacher gets annoyed with a disruptive child, he or she **may/might** be impatient with other children. If a teacher gets annoyed with a disruptive child, he or she will **probably** be impatient with other children. If a teacher gets annoyed with a disruptive child, he or she will be **less** patient with other children. If a teacher gets annoyed with a disruptive child, he or she will be **more** impatient with other children.

To further soften a statement, you can use two qualifiers in a sentence.

If a teacher gets annoyed with a disruptive child, he or she **may** be **less** patient with other children.

Here are some unqualified statements from an essay that expresses the view that the school year should be twelve months instead of nine. *On another piece of paper, rewrite each statement, softening it with a qualifier. Each item has several possible answers; use a different qualifier in each sentence.*

1. Children forget what they have learned in the previous year over the three-month summer vacation.

   Children can/may/often/tend to forget what they have learned in the previous year over the three-month summer vacation.

   OR

   Many children forget what they have learned in the previous year over the three-month summer vacation.

2. If we have year-round school, children will learn more.

3. Although children say that they like vacation, they are unhappy when they are bored.

4. For older children, summer vacation is wasted time.

5. Teenagers with nothing to do and no supervision get into trouble during summer vacation.

6. Today mothers and fathers work, and it is difficult for them to find someone to supervise their school-age children during the summer.

7. Several short breaks will be more pleasant than one long break.

REVISION CHECKPOINT 7

Qualifiers

Review your essay, focusing on the strength of your statements. If you find any statements that might seem too strong to readers who disagree with your point of view, revise them by adding qualifiers.

■ FINAL DRAFT

1. Before you write your final draft, look over your essay one last time to decide if you want to make any further changes.

2. Prepare a final draft of your composition. Make sure that you have used capital letters at the beginning of your sentences and periods at the end, and check your spelling.

3. Exchange papers with one or two classmates. Read each other's papers carefully. Turn to page 302 in Appendix II, and fill out the Peer Review Form.

4. Check your paper again and make any necessary corrections. Turn in your paper to your teacher.

■ CHAPTER REVIEW

Look back at what you have accomplished in Chapter 5. Check (✔) what you have learned and what you have used as you have written and revised your composition.

Chapter 5 Topics	Learned	Used
defining, analyzing, and limiting an argumentative topic before writing (pages 162–163)		
writing introductions and thesis statements for argumentative essays that include necessary definitions of key terms and limiting statements (pages 172–173)		
presenting supporting arguments in the topic sentences of body paragraphs with transitions (pages 173–174)		
using various strategies to develop supporting arguments including explanation, cause-and-effect reasoning, examples, facts or statistics, comparison, and outside sources (pages 174–176)		
including opposing views and responding to them with concessions, when appropriate, and refutations (pages 176–178)		
writing conclusions for argumentative essays using summary, suggestion, or a prediction (pages 179–180)		
using conditional sentences to express possible outcomes (pages 182–185)		
using qualifiers to modify general statements and predictions (pages 185–187)		

PART II

Academic Writing Skills

In this second section of *Engaging Writing 2*, you will develop the skills you will need for future academic assignments, such as research papers. You will learn how to include information from articles, books, and other sources in your writing by following the sequence of explanations and completing the exercises.

■ Quoting, Paraphrasing, Citing Sources, and Summarizing

During your time as a student, you will often be asked to read something and then to write about what you have read. Sometimes you will answer information questions about a text (an article, essay, or part of a book). Sometimes you will write a response (an explanation of your thoughts and feelings about what you have read) or a summary (a short statement of the main and supporting ideas in a text). Also, someday you may write a **research paper**, a longer essay that discusses information and ideas from a number of texts on a single topic. No matter which subjects you study in school, you will no doubt find yourself reading texts and writing about them.

For all kinds of reading-writing assignments, you must know the rules that academic writers follow. The first and most important rule is that you must show clearly in your writing which ideas, words, and sentences have come from **sources** (texts you have read) and which are your own. This means you must identify the authors whose ideas and words you refer to in your writing. In addition, you must put the authors' words in quotation marks or paraphrase them, that is, restate the authors' ideas in your own words.

When writers do not make clear which ideas and words are from other sources, they are **plagiarizing. Plagiarism** includes failing to identify the source of information or ideas and using another writer's words without quoting or paraphrasing. Plagiarism is never acceptable, and many colleges and high schools have very strict policies about plagiarism. Students who plagiarize usually receive an "F" on their assignment and sometimes fail the course.

In this part of *Engaging Writing 2*, you will learn how to avoid plagiarism. You will do this by becoming skilled at quoting, paraphrasing, and identifying your sources.

Quoting

If you want to include a complete sentence, several sentences, or part of a sentence from a source in your writing, you must use quotation marks. You must also identify the source of a quotation by giving the author's name. Look at the following source and sentences that contain quotations from the source.

> Innovation is the route to economic growth. Industries are maturing. Products are maturing. Innovation is the creation and transformation of new knowledge into new products, processes, or services that meet market needs. As such, innovation creates new businesses and is the fundamental source of growth in business and industry.
>
> ---
>
> Cohen, Lorraine Yapp. "Top 10 Reasons Why We Need INNOVATION." *American Creativity Association*. 22 Feb. 2010. <http://amcreativityassoc.org/Articles/Cohen-TOP%2010%20 Reasons%20Why%20We%20Need%20INNOVATION.pdf>.

- When you quote a complete sentence, place a comma after the reporting verb that introduces the quotation. The period at the end of the quotation must be inside the quotation marks.

  Lorraine Yapp Cohen wrote, "Innovation is the route to economic growth."

- When you quote more than one sentence, place a comma after the reporting verb that introduces the quotation, mark the boundaries of the sentences inside the quotation with periods and capital letters, and place the final period at the end of the quotation inside the quotation marks.

  Lorraine Yapp Cohen wrote, "Innovation is the creation and transformation of new knowledge into new products, processes, or services that meet market needs. As such, innovation creates new businesses and is the fundamental source of growth in business and industry."

- When you quote part of a sentence, do not place a comma before the quotation or use a capital letter at the beginning of the quotation.

  Lorraine Yapp Cohen wrote (that) "innovation creates new businesses."

The information in the box in small type below Cohen's words identifies the source. This is called a **citation**. (You will learn how to write citations on pages 214–218.) In a citation, the author's last name comes first and is followed by a comma. Compare the citation with the sentences containing the quote. To introduce an author in your writing, give his or her full name—first and last, starting with the first—and do not use a comma. The next time you mention him or her, you may use the last name only. Look at this example:

  Lorraine Yapp Cohen wrote, "Innovation is the route to economic growth." *Cohen* also wrote that innovation is the "transformation of new knowledge into new products."

When you write about a text, you can use either past tense reporting verbs (*wrote, said*) or present tense reporting verbs (*writes, says*). Both tenses are acceptable in most situations. (For more on reporting verbs, see page 219.)

Ellipsis and brackets. When you quote a source in your writing, you cannot change the language inside quotation marks in any way—the words in quotations must be *exactly* the same as those in the source. However, you can modify the text inside quotation marks if you use **ellipsis** or **brackets**. Look at this text and the quotations that follow.

> In terms of using mental energy creatively, perhaps the most fundamental difference between people consists in how much uncommitted attention they have left over to deal with novelty. In too many cases, attention is restricted by external necessity. We cannot expect a man who works two jobs, or a working woman with children, to have much mental energy left over to learn a domain, let alone innovate in it. Einstein is supposed to have written his classic papers on the kitchen table of his small apartment in Berne, while rocking the pram of his baby. But the fact is that there are real limits to how many things a person can attend to at the same time, and when survival needs require all of one's attention, none is left over for being creative.
>
> _____
>
> Csikszentmihaly, Mihaly. *Creativity: Flow and the Psychology of Discovery and Invention.* New York: Harper, 1996.

When you want to remove words from a quotation, show the omission with three spaced dots, known as **ellipsis**.

- If you omit the beginning of a sentence, do not use a comma before the quotation or start the quotation with a capital letter.

    Mihaly Csikszentmihaly wrote ". . . perhaps the most fundamental difference between people consists in how much uncommitted attention they have left over to deal with novelty." (Words from the beginning of the sentence were removed.)

- If you omit parts of a sentence, make sure that the remaining parts make sense on their own.

    Csikszentmihaly wrote, "Einstein is supposed to have written his classic papers . . . while rocking the pram of his baby." (Words from the middle of the sentence were removed.)

- If you omit the end of a sentence, use three spaced dots and a period (four dots).

    Csikszentmihaly wrote, "But the fact is that there are real limits to how many things a person can attend to at the same time. . . ." (Words from the end of the sentence were removed.)

- When you want to add a word or phrase to a quotation or replace a word or phrase in a quotation, use **brackets [ ]**.

> Csikszentmihaly wrote, "In too many cases, [people's] attention is restricted by external necessity." (The word *people's* has been added.)

> Csikszentmihaly wrote ". . . when survival needs require all of one's attention, [nothing] is left over for [creativity]." (*Nothing* replaces *none*, and *creativity* replaces *being creative*.)

EXERCISE 1

Read the text below. Then answer the questions that follow on another piece of paper. Every answer must include a quotation from the text. Use ellipsis or brackets if necessary.

Reading

SERENDIPITY IN SCIENCE
by M. Hayden

[1]In 1856 an eighteen-year-old student, William Perkin, decided to undertake a project on his spring vacation from the Royal College of Chemistry in London. [2]Perkin wanted to find a way to make quinine artificially. [3]At the time, quinine, which was the only treatment for malaria, an often-fatal disease, could only be made from the bark of a tree grown in the East Indies. [4]Perkin began his experiment with aniline, a chemical made from the indigo plant. [5]He then added carbon, hydrogen, and oxygen to the aniline. [6]The result was not quinine, but a mysterious black solid, which Perkin decided to throw away. [7]Later, as he was cleaning up, he noted that the water and the cloth he was using turned a lovely shade of purple. [8]Perkin realized he had discovered the first artificial dye and that it could be manufactured inexpensively. [9]This meant that, for the first time in history, people of average means could afford to wear the color purple.

[10]In 1875, Alfred Nobel, the Swedish chemist and engineer who had invented dynamite in 1867 and who would donate his fortune to the Nobel prizes at the end of his life, accidentally cut his finger one day while working in his laboratory. [11]He applied collodion to the finger, a common treatment at the time. [12]The collodion, a clear liquid, dried to a protective film and kept the wound clean. [13]But the pain in his finger kept Nobel awake that night, and he began to think about a problem he had been trying to solve in his lab, the question of how to produce a safer explosive. [14]The collodion gave Nobel an idea—it might be added to nitroglycerin to produce a more stable and thus less dangerous explosive. [15]Nobel got up at 4:00 a.m., went back to his lab, and within hours developed the first explosive gelatin, gelignite. [16]Gelignite was easier to transport than dynamite and could be shaped to fit into the blasting holes used in mining.

(continued)

[17]In 1928 Alexander Fleming, a Scottish bacteriologist, returned from his vacation to check his laboratory, where he had been investigating a bacterium that caused influenza. [18]As he looked over the dishes containing bacteria samples in his lab, he saw that one of them had become moldy. [19]Upon close inspection, Fleming saw that the mold appeared to have killed the bacteria around it. [20]Fleming did not discard the dish with the mold, but instead tested its ability to kill other kinds of bacteria. [21]He found that the mold produced a substance that destroyed various kinds of bacteria responsible for many infections in humans and animals. [22]Fleming named the substance *penicillin* and expressed wonder at his good fortune when he said, "There are thousands of different molds and there are thousands of different bacteria, and that chance put the mold in the right spot at the right time was like winning [the lottery]" (Roberts 162).

[23]Perkin, Nobel, and Fleming benefited from happy accidents, but their discoveries were not purely accidental. [24]Their discoveries are examples of *serendipity*, which means the wise use of fortuitous accidents. [25]Serendipity has played a role in many important scientific achievements including the discovery of the x-ray, insulin, and DNA. [26]For serendipity to play a role in scientific discovery, researchers must be keenly observant, open to multiple possibilities, and curious about the unexpected. [27]If Perkin had not noted the color of the substance as he cleaned up after his experiment, he would not have discovered an artificial dye. [28]If Nobel had not permitted himself to ask the question *Can collodion be used in explosives?* he would not have invented gelignite. [29]If Fleming had not been curious about the mold in one of his dishes, he would not have discovered the antibiotic which has relieved so much human suffering.

Source: Roberts, Royston M. *Serendipity: Accidental Discoveries in Science.* New York: Wiley, 1989.

TIP

When answering comprehension questions, you can use some of the words in the question in your answer. For example, begin the answer to number 1 this way: Perkin intended to . . .

1. What did William Perkin intend to do on his spring vacation?
2. When did Perkin become aware that he had made a valuable discovery?
3. Why did Alfred Nobel put collodion on his finger?
4. If Nobel had not cut his finger, would he have discovered gelignite?
5. What did Alexander Fleming infer when he saw the moldy dish?
6. Why was the discovery of penicillin significant?
7. What does *serendipity* mean?
8. According to Hayden, what must scientists do in order to take advantage of lucky accidents?

Quotations within quotations. When you want to quote a sentence that already contains a quotation, place single quotation marks around the existing quotation. This quote is from the text in Exercise 1.

> Hayden wrote, "Fleming named the substance penicillin and expressed wonder at his good fortune when he said, 'There are thousands of different molds and there are thousands of different bacteria, and that chance put the mold in the right spot at the right time was like winning [the lottery]'" (Roberts 162).

EXERCISE 2

Read the passages and their citations. Then, on another piece of paper, write one sentence quoting each passage. Each of your sentences must contain a quotation within a quotation. The first two have been done for you.

1.
> Alfred Nobel hoped by the [prizes] from his huge fortune to accomplish what he had not been able to do in his lifetime: to encourage what would have "the greatest benefit" to mankind, especially peace and "fraternity between nations."
>
> Roberts, Royston M. *Serendipity: Accidental Discoveries in Science.* New York: Wiley, 1989.

Royston Roberts wrote, "Alfred Nobel hoped by the [prizes] from his huge fortune to accomplish what he had not been able to do in his lifetime: to encourage what would have 'the greatest benefit' to mankind, especially peace and 'fraternity between nations.'"

2.
> [In 1949 Alexander Fleming made] one of his best speeches: "The research-worker is familiar with disappointment—the weary months spent following the wrong road, the many failures. But even failures have their uses, for, properly analysed, they may lead him to success."
>
> Maurois, André. *The Life of Sir Alexander Fleming: Discoverer of Penicillin.* New York: Dutton, 1959.

André Maurois wrote, "[In 1949 Alexander Fleming made] one of his best speeches: 'The research-worker is familiar with disappointment—the weary months spent following the wrong road, the many failures. But even failures have their uses, for, properly analysed, they may lead him to success.'"

3.

> The person who sees only what is expected and discards unexpected results as "wrong" will make no discoveries.
>
> Roberts, Royston M. *Serendipity: Accidental Discoveries in Science.* New York: Wiley, 1989.

4.

> Pasteur, who made breakthroughs in chemistry, microbiology, and medicine . . . [said], "In the fields of observation, chance favors only the prepared mind."
>
> Roberts, Royston M. *Serendipity: Accidental Discoveries in Science.* New York: Wiley, 1989.

 For more on quotations, see Appendix IB, pages 294–295.

Responding to a quotation. As a student, you will sometimes be asked to respond to texts in writing. In a written response, you can quote a part of the text and write any thoughts or feelings this passage has triggered in your mind, including

- your opinion about what the author is saying in the quotation.
- what the quotation made you realize or feel.
- a personal experience that the quotation reminded you of.
- an inference (a guess about something that is not completely explained in the text but that you can imagine based on evidence in the text).
- a question that the quotation raised in your mind.

EXERCISE 3

Read the two response paragraphs, and notice that, though they begin with the same quotation, they differ in the way they address the quotation. On the line below each paragraph, identify the writers' strategies, which may include **opinion, realization, feeling, personal experience, inference,** *or* **question**.

1.

> Einstein said, "It is not so very important for a person to learn facts. For that he does not really need college. He can learn them from books. The value of an education in a liberal arts college is not the learning of many facts, but the training of the mind to think something that cannot be learned from textbooks." I agree with Einstein that the most important thing we learn in college is how to think. When I participate in a classroom discussion or write an essay on a controversial topic, I am becoming an independent thinker. However, I can't learn to think for myself without knowing facts. Before I take a position, I must learn the facts of an issue. For example, before I wrote about a ballot measure to increase cigarette taxes, I needed to know the facts about the health effects of smoking. When my sociology class debated surrogate parenting last semester, I was able to express my opinion because I understood the scientific facts as well as the social issues. College has given me opportunities to learn facts and to form and express my own opinions.
>
> Quoted in Frank, Philip. *Einstein: His Life and Times.* Cambridge: DaCapo, 2002.

2.

> Einstein said, "It is not so very important for a person to learn facts. For that he does not really need college. He can learn them from books. The value of an education in a liberal arts college is not the learning of many facts, but the training of the mind to think something that cannot be learned from textbooks." This statement made me question the importance of factual information. I think that to the average person and the average student, facts are important. When we learn facts, we feel we have something solid to hang onto. We feel that we are acquiring the knowledge that the most powerful people in our society possess, and, by doing so, we are becoming more powerful ourselves. The role of a pioneering scientist like Einstein is to question the facts. Einstein's theory of relativity challenged the facts upon which the science of his day was built. Yet in order to challenge the scientific knowledge of his times, Einstein had to have studied that body of factual knowledge. Therefore, I wonder why Einstein wanted to question the importance of learning facts in college.

> Quoted in Frank, Philip. *Einstein: His Life and Times*. DaCapo, 2002.

EXERCISE 4

Read one of the chapter-opening readings in Part I of this book, and select a statement in that text that you would like to respond to. On another piece of paper, start a paragraph with a quotation from the text, and complete the paragraph using one or more of the response strategies listed on page 196.

- Keep in mind that you must identify the author in the first sentence of your paragraph. If you wish, you may include the title of the text as well. Also, in place of a reporting verb such as *say* or *write*, you can use the preposition *according to*.

   Judy Patacsil says/said/writes/wrote, "The first generation of Filipino Americans . . . attempted to remain close-knit within their own ethnic group."

   In "*Kapwa*—Our Shared Identity—and the Influence of Role Models," Judy Patacsil says/said/writes/wrote, "The first generation of Filipino Americans . . . attempted to remain close-knit within their own ethnic group."

   According to Judy Patacsil, "The first generation of Filipino Americans . . . attempted to remain close-knit within their own ethnic group."

   According to Judy Patacsil in "*Kapwa*—Our Shared Identity—and the Influence of Role Models," "The first generation of Filipino Americans . . . attempted to remain close-knit within their own ethnic group."

- "*Kapwa*—Our Shared Identity—and the Influence of Role Models" is in quotation marks because it is the title of an essay within a book.

Put quotations around parts of books (chapter titles or titles of stories or essays) and parts of newspapers or magazines (titles of articles and essays). Underline or italicize the title of a complete publication, such as the name of a book, newspaper, magazine, or website.

> In <u>Engaging Writing 2</u>, Judy Patacsil says/said/writes/wrote, "The first generation of Filipino Americans . . . attempted to remain close-knit within their own ethnic group."

- As you write a response paragraph, focus on exploring ideas. Then, after you finish writing, check to make sure that the paragraph makes sense and that the ideas flow in a logical, connected way.

Paraphrasing

Paraphrasing, or changing the vocabulary and grammar of a statement while keeping the original meaning, is an essential writing skill that you will use in a wide range of assignments in all your academic classes.

Why do I need to paraphrase? First and most importantly, you must avoid plagiarism, or copying words and ideas from sources into your writing without using quotation marks or giving credit to the author. In addition, you should avoid using too many quotations in your writing. Writing that contains too many quotations is hard to read and leaves readers with the impression that the writer didn't do his or her own thinking.

How can I learn to paraphrase? Learning to paraphrase well takes practice. However, you already know the fundamentals of paraphrasing. Paraphrasing is what you do when you want to repeat what someone said but you can't remember the person's exact words. You focus on the meaning of the statement, and express it in your own words. As a first step to learning the skill of paraphrasing, do the following oral exercise.

EXERCISE 5

Work with a partner. One of you will take the part of Speaker A and the other will take the part of Speaker B. First, Speaker B will close his or her book and listen as Speaker A reads aloud a popular saying (an expression of common wisdom). After listening, Speaker B will paraphrase the saying (repeat the idea in his or her own words). Switch roles after Speaker A has read aloud the first five sayings and Speaker B has paraphrased them.

> Speaker A: "A chain is only as strong as its weakest link."

> Speaker B: A weak or incapable person in a group weakens the whole group, or an inefficient part of an organization makes the whole organization inefficient.

Speaker B: "It's better to light a candle than curse the darkness."

Speaker A: You shouldn't complain when you have a problem. You should just try to solve it.

Set 1: Speaker A

1. "Honesty is the best policy."
2. "A leopard cannot change its spots."
3. "Every dark cloud has a silver lining."
4. "Tomorrow is another day."
5. "A house divided against itself cannot stand."
6. "The pen is mightier than the sword."

Set 2: Speaker B

1. "A fool and his money are soon parted."
2. "Necessity is the mother of invention."
3. "A picture is worth a thousand words."
4. "Absence makes the heart grow fonder."
5. "Genius is 1 percent inspiration and 99 percent perspiration."
6. "The child is father to the man."

Paraphrasing strategies. To do Exercise 5, you had to figure out the basic meaning of each saying and then put it in your own words. You probably did this quickly without analyzing the grammar or vocabulary of the sentence. This is the simplest and most direct way to paraphrase, and it often works well. However, when you need to paraphrase a longer, more complicated statement from your reading, you will have to analyze the grammar and vocabulary and then change the statement one part at a time. Here are some strategies you can use.

Note: To paraphrase successfully, you need to change a sentence as many ways as possible. However, to show each strategy clearly, we have presented it by itself. Please be aware, though, that the examples you will see here are not good paraphrases. In fact, they may be examples of plagiarism because they contain only one paraphrasing strategy.

Ways to Paraphrase

1. Use synonyms or synonymous phrases.

   ORIGINAL: "*Parents* *frequently* *remark* . . ."

   Mothers and fathers often say . . .

2. Change the form of words.

> ORIGINAL: "*A physically fit person feels good. . . .*"

> Physical fitness produces good feelings . . .

3. Change the subject of the sentence.
   - Make a singular subject plural or a plural subject singular.

   > ORIGINAL: "*An individual is . . .*"

   > Individuals are . . .

   - Change the pronoun point of view (*we, you, they, he/she*) to another pronoun point of view.

   > ORIGINAL: "*We have to be responsible for ourselves. . . .*"

   > Citizens have to be responsible for themselves. . . .

   - Make an active sentence passive or a passive sentence active.

   > ORIGINAL: "*Newspapers report stories . . .*"

   > Stories are reported by newspapers . . .

4. Change the logical connectors (coordinating conjunctions, subordinating conjunctions, and transition words).

   > ORIGINAL: "*The answer is wrong. Therefore we must rework the problem.*"

   > The answer is wrong, so we must rework the problem.

   > Because the answer is wrong, we must rework the problem.

5. Move parts of the sentence (adverb phrases, adverb clauses).

   > ORIGINAL: "*The law was signed in 2007.*"

   > In 2007, the law was signed.

   > ORIGINAL: "*By marching in the streets, people protested the law.*"

   > People protested the law by marching in the streets.

   > ORIGINAL: "*People protested because the law was unfair.*"

   > Because the law was unfair, people protested.

6. Combine short sentences or divide long sentences.

> ORIGINAL: *"The building withstood the earthquake. That is surprising."*
>
> It is surprising that the building withstood the earthquake.

> ORIGINAL: *"With the cold weather months ahead, many people are concerned that individuals on fixed incomes will not be able to afford the higher heating bills and thus will have to choose between buying food and heating their homes."*
>
> Because the cold weather months are ahead, many people are concerned about higher heating bills. Individuals on fixed incomes will not be able to afford the higher bills. As a result, they will have to choose between buying food and heating their homes.

7. Omit any unnecessary words that do not contribute to the meaning.

> ORIGINAL: *"Mr. Smith has a physical fitness routine which varies with the days of the week."*
>
> Mr. Smith's physical fitness routine varies with the days of the week.

EXERCISE 6

Review the list of ways to paraphrase on pages 199–201, and identify the strategies used in each paraphrase by writing the number(s) of the strategy or strategies used.

1.
> Scientists have found that the mere act of smiling can generate positive feelings within us, at least if the smile is not forced.
>
> Ehrenreich, Barbara. *Bright-Sided: How the Relentless Promotion of Positive Thinking Has Undermined America.* New York: Metropolitan, 2009.

Paraphrase: Barbara Ehrenreich wrote that science has shown that smiling makes people feel happier as long as their smiles are genuine.

Strategies: _____ 1, 2, 3, 4, 7 _____

2.
> Happiness lies, first of all, in health.
>
> Curtis, George William. *Lotus-Eating: A Summer Book.* New York: Harper, 1852. 24 Feb. 2010 <http://www.archive.org/details/lotuseatingsumme00curtrich>.

Paraphrase: George William Curtis wrote that the first condition for happiness is good health.

Strategies: _____ 3, 5 _____

3.
> [1]If we really know how to live, what better way to start the day than with a smile? [2]Our smile affirms our awareness and determination to live in peace and joy.
>
> ---
>
> Nhat Hanh, Thich. *Peace Is Every Step: The Path of Mindfulness in Everyday Life.* New York: Bantam, 1991.

Paraphrase: Thich Nhat Hanh wrote that to live well, one should smile upon getting out of bed. This act shows that one is aware and committed to living a life filled with peace and happiness.

Strategies: _____

4.
> [1]It is curious to observe what different ideals of happiness people cherish, and in what singular places they look for this well-spring of their life. [2]Many look for it in the hoarding of riches, some in the pride of power, and others in the achievements of art and literature; a few seek it in the exploration of their own minds, or in search for knowledge.
>
> ---
>
> Keller, Helen. "Optimism." 1903. 22 Feb. 2010. <.http://www.afb.org/Section.asp?SectionID =1&TopicID=193&SubTopicID=22&DocumentID=1208>.

Paraphrase: Helen Keller wrote that the human quest for happiness is fascinating. People value different things and search for happiness in different areas of their lives: Many seek happiness in money, some look for it in power, and others pursue it in the arts. Lastly, a few people try to find happiness through self-understanding and education.

Strategies: _____

5.
> [1]The majority of people in the world, across vast continents and cultures, profess that being happy is one of their most cherished goals in life—for themselves and, above all, for their children. [2]What's more, happiness offers myriad rewards, not just for the happy person but for his or her family, workplace, community, nation, and society. [3]Working on how to become happier, the research suggests, will not only make a person *feel* better but will also boost his or her energy, creativity, and immune system, foster better relationships, fuel higher productivity at work, and even lead to a longer life.
>
> ---
>
> Lyubomirsky, Sonja. *The How of Happiness: A Scientific Approach to Getting the Life You Want.* New York: Penguin, 2008.

Paraphrase: Sonja Lyubomirsky writes that most people in the world want to be happy for their own sake and, even more, for their children. Happiness yields many rewards—not just to happy individuals, but to those surrounding them. Research indicates that when people try to be happier, they not only feel better but become more energetic, creative, and resistant to disease. Furthermore, they have better relationships, work more efficiently, and live longer.

Strategies: _____

6.

> [1]Within the first nine months, before babies can walk or talk or even crawl, they can tell the difference between expressions of happiness and sadness and anger, and even can recognize that a happy-looking face, a face with a smile and crinkling eyes, goes with the chirp of a happy tone of voice. [2]You can show them two films, side by side, one of a face with a happy expression and one of a face with a sad expression. [3]If you turn on a sound track playing either a happy or a sad voice, babies will look longer at the face displaying the emotional expression that matches the emotion they hear.
>
> ---
>
> Gopnik, Alison, Andrew N. Meltzoff, and Patricia K. Kuhl. *The Scientist in the Crib: Minds, Brains, and How Children Learn.* New York: Morrow, 1999.

Paraphrase: Gopnik, Meltzoff, and Kuhl wrote that babies less than nine months old are able to distinguish between happy, sad, and angry faces. Moreover, when they are shown a film of a happy face and a sad face side by side and they hear either a happy or a sad voice, they can match the emotion of the voice with the appropriate facial expression. Babies look longer at a face that matches the kind of voice they hear.

Strategies: _____

Exercise 7

Using the strategies listed on pages 199–201, write a paraphrase for each of these statements on another piece of paper. In each paraphrase, use as many strategies as you can. Then write the numbers of the strategies you used in each paraphrase.

1. The performance lasted only for a short duration, so the viewers were left hungry for further entertainment. Long after the curtain fell, they remained in their seats applauding.

   The show did not last long; therefore, the audience wanted to be entertained more. They stayed in their chairs for a long time and continued to clap after the curtain came down.

   Strategies: _____1, 2, 3, 4, 7_____

2. The documents were delivered by the clerk before this morning's meeting started. This was fortunate.

3. We can prevent illness by washing our hands regularly during the flu season.

4. Pedro reserved a seat on a flight to Quito for November 16; however, he was forced to change the booking due to a delay in the processing of his visa. He did not travel until December 9.

5. A friend with loyalty is worth keeping, my grandmother told me again and again.

6. As employees, you must adhere to the guidelines that are provided by authorities. Should you fail to heed regulations, you could lose your positions.

7. Fatigue and lack of energy led to Karl's poor performance in the footrace. Karl had neglected to eat a nutritious meal and had visited a disco instead of going to sleep early the night before the competition.

8. In the early spring of 2009, precipitation was lighter than normal. Consequently, the state charged farmers more for water. A majority of farmers opted not to cultivate their fields that year.

9. When Vendo Corporation's annual earnings fell by 4 percent in 2007, the board replaced the CEO Reed Harrison, eliminated its home furnishings division, and opened new facilities for the manufacture of fine garments and leather goods.

10. The election of a new head of state had a significant impact on the citizenry: People started thinking more optimistically and began to have faith that problems could be solved by government.

Now that you have seen some paraphrases and done some paraphrasing yourself, you may have some questions, such as these:

Do I have to change every word in a paraphrase? No. You should not change a word or phrase if it significantly changes the meaning of the original statement. Here are some situations in which you should avoid or be cautious about word changes.

- Do not alter facts or numbers, and don't change the proper names of people and places.
- Be cautious about changing key terms. For instance, some of the statements in Exercise 6 are about happiness. While the noun *happiness* does have synonyms (*contentment, satisfaction, joy, bliss*), none of these synonyms have exactly the same meaning as *happiness*. Do not replace a key term if doing so changes the meaning of a passage.
- Do not change technical terms. Technical terms have specific definitions and often have no synonyms. When you are writing a paper in a subject with technical language, learn the meanings of terms so that you can use them accurately. For example, if, in a paper for an environmental studies class, you paraphrased "the *climate* of Hawaii" as "the *weather* of Hawaii," you would be wrong—although we sometimes use the terms *climate* and *weather* interchangeably in casual speech and writing, the technical meanings of these words are different.

What distinguishes acceptable paraphrasing from plagiarism? A paraphrase is acceptable if the writer has used more than one of the strategies listed on pages 199–201 and has changed everything that can be changed without altering the meaning of the original statement. Plagiarism involves 1) failing to change words, phrases, and clauses that can be changed; 2) omitting necessary information; or 3) changing information in the original text.

Can I add information or ideas to a paraphrase? No. A paraphrase must faithfully represent the information and ideas of the original source text.

Do I always have to identify the source? Yes. You must always make clear which information and ideas come from sources and which are your own. You will learn more about how to do this in Integrating Source Material in Body Paragraphs on page 211 and Citing Sources on page 214.

EXERCISE 8

A. *Read each statement from a source and its restatement. Some of the restatements are acceptable paraphrases and some are not. Decide whether each restatement is an acceptable paraphrase. (Remember that an acceptable paraphrase must identify the source.) If you identify plagiarism, underline the words or phrases in the restatement that are problematic.*

1.
   > Nothing matters more to a child than a place to call home.
   >
   > Donald, Brenda. "Commentary—Brenda Donald: Mission Possible for Maryland: 1000 New Foster Parents by 2010." *examiner.com* 5 Feb. 2008. 26 Feb. 2010. <http://www.examiner.com/a-1201059~Brenda_Donald__Mission_possible_for_Maryland__1_000_new_foster_parents_by_2010.html>.

   Restatement: According to Brenda Donald, the most important thing in a child's life is <u>a place to call home</u>.

   ☐ Acceptable Paraphrase   ☑ Unacceptable

2.
   > . . . love and hate are two aspects of the same human capacity to react to other human beings in terms of experience. The infant whose world is warm, giving, and reliable responds with love that echoes the love he has received. But the infant who is continually hungry, cold, and neglected will come to hate those who hurt him and do not attend to his needs.
   >
   > Mead, Margaret. *Margaret Mead: Some Personal Views.* New York: Walker, 1979.

   Restatement: Margaret Mead said that human beings are capable of both love and hate. Love and hate come from the same source—the ability to respond to others based on experience. When children are raised by caring, responsible adults, they respond by loving. When children lack the care of adults and suffer neglect, they respond by hating.

   ☑ Acceptable Paraphrase   ☐ Unacceptable

3.

> Effective parenting centers around love that is not permissive, that doesn't tolerate disrespect, and that is powerful enough to allow kids to make mistakes and permit them to live with the consequences of those mistakes.
>
> Cline, Foster and Jim Fay. *Parenting with Love and Logic: Teaching Children Responsibility.* Colorado Springs: Piñon, 2006.

Restatement: Parents who are successful with their children are not permissive, don't tolerate disrespect, and are able to permit their children to make mistakes and experience the outcomes of their mistakes.

❑ Acceptable Paraphrase   ❑ Unacceptable

4.

> Human infants differ from the young of other species in their long period of dependency on adults. Young children cannot fend for themselves—they need years of adult care and supervision to survive. But parents want more for their children than just to survive. Parents want children to grow up to be healthy, happy, successful, and decent members of society.
>
> Waldfogel, Jane. *What Children Need.* Cambridge: Harvard, 2006.

Restatement: According to Jane Waldfogel, unlike other species, human young depend for their survival on adults. For a very long time, babies and young children require adults to watch over them and tend to their needs. At the same time, parents expect their children to thrive, not just survive: They hope their children will have health and happiness, achieve success, and live moral lives.

❑ Acceptable Paraphrase   ❑ Unacceptable

5.

> We grow morally as a consequence of learning how to be with others, how to behave in the world, a learning prompted by taking to heart what we have seen and heard. The child is a witness; the child is an ever-attentive witness of grown-up morality—or the lack thereof; the child looks and looks for cues as to how one ought to behave, and finds them galore as we parents and teachers go about our lives. . . .
>
> Coles, Robert. *The Moral Intelligence of Children.* New York: Random, 1997.

Restatement: Children learn morality by watching adults. As they observe, they learn how to relate to people and how to behave from their adult models.

❑ Acceptable Paraphrase   ❑ Unacceptable

6.

> Parents have the primary responsibility for instilling an ethic of hard work and educational achievement in their children.
>
> ---
>
> Obama, Barack. *The Audacity of Hope*. New York: Crown, 2006

Restatement: According to Barack Obama in <u>The Audacity of Hope</u>, parents have a fundamental duty. That is, they must teach their kids the importance of being diligent and succeeding in school.

❑ **Acceptable Paraphrase**   ❑ **Unacceptable**

7.

> Children who are brought up without strong bonds of family love, consistent discipline, and models of moral behavior become adults who are fearful, insecure, distrustful, and self-centered—the very traits intolerance thrives upon. Children who are sure of their parents' love, who have had consistent guidance in moral issues, and who have witnessed the principles of tolerance in action in their own families are likely to become open-minded and compassionate adults.
>
> ---
>
> Bullard, Sara. *Teaching Tolerance: Raising Open-Minded, Empathetic Children*. New York: Doubleday, 1996.

Restatement: Sara Bullard writes that kids who grow up in homes that do not offer love, guidance in how to behave, or good adult models do not develop confidence or empathy as they reach adulthood. Thus, they are likely to become intolerant adults. By comparison, kids who grow up in loving homes where adults provide discipline and model tolerance usually mature into tolerant, caring adults.

❑ **Acceptable Paraphrase**   ❑ **Unacceptable**

B. *Compare your answers with a partner's. Identify the reasons that some restatements are not acceptable paraphrases. If you do not agree about a particular item, discuss it with your teacher and classmates.*

EXERCISE 9

A. *Using the strategies listed on pages 199–201, paraphrase each of these statements on another piece of paper.*

1.
> It is quite obvious that healthy people are happier than unhealthy people. What is now becoming increasingly evident through study is that the reverse is also true: happy people are healthier than unhappy people. It appears that happiness, which simply means having happy thoughts most of the time, causes biochemical changes in the brain that in turn have profoundly beneficial effects on the body's physiology.
>
> Chopra, Deepak. *Creating Health: How to Wake Up the Body's Intelligence.* Boston: Houghton Mifflin, 1987.

Deepak Chopra wrote that we all recognize that people with good health are happier than those whose health is not as good. Research is revealing that the opposite is true as well: Happy individuals enjoy better health than unhappy individuals. Happiness, or the quality of thinking positively most of the time, probably stimulates biochemical reactions in the brain that protect one's physical health.

2.
> Mind and body are inextricably woven together. Every primary physician knows that. Studies show that probably half of the visits to us in the office are for things related to mind issues rather than body issues. We'd better be educated in both if we're going to serve those patients well.
>
> Thomas Delbanco, M.D., quoted in Bill Moyers, *Healing and the Mind.* New York: Doubleday, 1993.

3.
> Your health is bound to be affected if, day after day, you say the opposite of what you feel, if you grovel before what you dislike, and rejoice at what brings you nothing but misfortune.
>
> Pasternak, Boris. *Doctor Zhivago.* New York: Pantheon, 1958

4.
> Given the opportunity, most pet owners will rave about the joys of sharing their homes with an animal. . . . But they may not realize that, beyond pleasure, their nonhuman companions could help to improve their mental and physical health and even extend their lives.
>
> Brody, Jane E. "Owning a Pet Can Have Therapeutic Value." *New York Times* 11 Aug. 1982. 20 Feb. 2010. <http://www.nytimes.com/1982/08/11/garden/owning-a-pet-can-have-therapeutic-value.html?&pagewanted=2>.

5.

> The truth is that the more researchers understand about the ingredients found in fruits, vegetables, beans and herbs, the more impressed they are with the power of those compounds to retard the bodily breakdown that results in cancer and other chronic diseases.
>
> ───────────────
> Brody, Jane E. *The New York Times Book of Health: How to Feel Fitter, Eat Better, and Live Longer*. New York: New York Times, 1997.

6.

> If you follow these four precepts—eat less, move more, eat lots of fruits and vegetables, and go easy on junk foods—the question of what to eat becomes much easier to answer.
>
> ───────────────
> Nestle, Marion. *What to Eat*. New York: North Point, 2006.

7.

> Health is not the absence of disease. It's the capacity to thrive.
>
> ───────────────
> Fawcett, Jeffry and Layna Burman. *Too Much Medicine, Not Enough Health*. Berkeley: Your Own Health and Fitness, 2009.

B. *Compare your paraphrases with a partner's. Notice that two paraphrases can have quite different vocabulary and grammar and still express the same meaning. If you have questions about the best way to paraphrase a particular word, phrase, or clause, discuss it with your classmates and teacher.*

Combining paraphrases and quotations. Occasionally you will find that it is not possible or not advisable to try to paraphrase every part of every passage. Sometimes you cannot find synonyms, or you cannot find a way to change the grammar. Sometimes you may be able to paraphrase, but you find that a paraphrase is less effective than the original text, perhaps because the writer used expressive language. In situations such as these, you should select the parts of the passage that you are able to paraphrase, paraphrase them as well as you can, and put the remainder of the passage in quotations. This is called a **partial paraphrase**.

In this passage, the parts that cannot be paraphrased effectively are underlined. In the partial paraphrase that follows, you will see that those parts are in quotation marks.

> . . . early experiences with school not only create the foundations on which all [a child's] later educational experiences rest, but to a considerable degree influence how he comes to think of himself in relation to the wider world. These first experiences with learning in school are often decisive in forming the child's view of himself as part of society; depending on them, either he may <u>feel welcomed and well served</u> by it, and conclude that he will be successful within it, or he may feel that since this institution supposedly created for him is <u>at best</u> <u>indifferent to his needs and at worst inimical</u>, then the same is probably true for the rest of society and its institutions. If this happens, the child feels <u>defeated by society from an early age.</u>
>
> ───────────────
> Bettelheim, Bruno and Karen Zelan. *On Learning to Read: The Child's Fascination with Meaning*. New York: Knopf, 1982.

Partial Paraphrase: According to Bruno Bettelheim and Karen Zelan, the early years of school are critical because they set the foundation for the rest of children's education and influence the way children see themselves within society. As a result of these early experiences, children will either "feel welcomed and well served" and grow to believe that they will succeed in school, or they will feel that school is "at best indifferent to [their] needs and at worst inimical." If children reach this negative conclusion, they will feel "defeated by society from an early age."

EXERCISE 10

Write a partial paraphrase of each passage. First, put parentheses ( ) around the parts of the passage that you can paraphrase and paraphrase them. Then underline the parts of the passage that you want to quote directly. Next, fit your paraphrases together with the parts of the passage that you want to quote. Check your sentences to make sure that the paraphrases and the quotes work together grammatically. Finally, write your partial paraphrases on another piece of paper.

1. Possibly the most influential of [the] early experiences for the child's future academic career is his encounter with his teacher. Through [him or] her, [the child] encounters the educational system. If things go well, the child learns to cope adequately with academic demands and derives satisfaction from being able to do so. If things go badly, [the child] becomes suspicious of the teacher's and the system's purposes. [The child] then closes his mind to the teacher's efforts and either learns to beat the system, withdraws into himself, or becomes a little rebel.

   Bettelheim, Bruno and Karen Zelan. *On Learning to Read: The Child's Fascination with Meaning*. New York: Knopf, 1982.

2. Throughout history, education has been at the heart of a bargain this nation makes with its citizens: If you work hard and take responsibility, you'll have a chance for a better life. And in a world where knowledge determines value in the job market, where a child in Los Angeles has to compete not just with a child in Boston but also with millions of children in Bangalore and Beijing, too many of America's schools are not holding up their end of the bargain.

   Obama, Barack. *The Audacity of Hope*. New York: Crown, 2006

3.

> Strong parenting is the essential ingredient in a child's success at school. The benefits provided by parents who are involved in their children's lives go beyond merely ensuring their kids do the homework. Carolyn Hoxby of Harvard, for instance, has found compelling evidence that it is the role of the parents and their ability to influence who [their children] associate with that is one of the most powerful factors in [the] children's academic success.
>
> ───────────────────────
> LeGault, Michael R. *Th!nk!: Why Crucial Decisions Can't Be Made in the Blink of an Eye*. New York: Threshold, 2006.

Integrating source material in body paragraphs. Sometimes you will want to use sources to develop ideas in an essay. When you use source material in an essay, remember that the thesis and main supporting ideas must be your own. This means that you will have to gather information about your topic and then think deeply about it until you know what you want to say. When you have arrived at a thesis and decided on your major supporting points, you can collect passages from your sources to develop your points. To incorporate source material in body paragraphs of an essay, follow these guidelines.

- Use quotations or paraphrases from sources only on the third level of your essay—that is, as support within the body paragraphs.
- Do not simply dump a quotation or paraphrase into the middle of a paragraph—it must be connected to the sentences before and after it. To make sure that a quotation or paraphrase is well integrated into a paragraph, first check to make sure that the ideas in the quotation or paraphrase relate to the ideas in the sentences before and after it. Revise your sentences if necessary. Finally, look for cohesion strategies such as repeated words, pronouns, and transitions that make the connection between the quotation or paraphrase and the rest of the paragraph clear. (See pages 135–139.)

EXERCISE 11

In this exercise, you will work with three body paragraphs from an essay about Dr. Martin Luther King, Jr. Here is the thesis of the essay.

> Martin Luther King, Jr. is a true hero because he introduced the principle of non-violence to the United States, set an example of unselfishness, and showed an ability to love to an extraordinary degree.

A. *In the first body paragraph on page 212, underline the sentences that contain quotations. Look for cohesion signals (repeated and related words and phrases, word forms, pronouns, and pointing words like **this** and **that***) *in the sentences before and after each quotation. Circle any words or phrases that serve to connect the quotations to the rest of the paragraph.*

First Body Paragraph

[1]First of all, Martin Luther King, Jr. brought Gandhi's principle of non-violence to the United States and showed Americans how it could work. [2]King studied Gandhi's ideas about using non-violent action to end injustice, and he knew that Gandhi's campaign had succeeded in winning India's independence from Britain. [3]Therefore, King asked his followers to avoid the use of violence, even when facing police dogs and fire hoses. [4]In 1963 in Birmingham, Alabama, he said to them, "The reason I can't follow the old eye-for-an-eye philosophy is that it ends up leaving everybody blind" (cited in Carson, 209). [5]King's strategy worked. [6]Though Birmingham had been the scene of much violence against blacks and in particular against the civil rights movement, on May 5, 1963, the police backed away from the protesters. [7]King said afterward, "I saw there, I felt there, for the first time, the pride and the *power* of non-violence" (Washington, 349). [8]The public took notice, and, as a result of the protest, restaurant owners in Birmingham agreed to seat blacks, and business owners in Birmingham agreed to hire more blacks.

*B. Below you will see two groups of sentences which make up the second and third body paragraphs of the essay. The sentences in each group are in scrambled order. The topic sentence in each group is marked **TS**. Read each group, and underline the sentences that contain quotations. Next, look for logical connections between the remaining sentences, and circle all the cohesion signals. Finally, assign a sequence to the remaining sentences, starting with number **2**.*

Second Body Paragraph

_____ a. He was jailed seventeen times and received many death threats, so he was aware of his vulnerability.

_____ b. Over those years, he saw his family infrequently and earned little to support them.

_____ c. King, a private citizen who never held elected office, gave his life to make our society better.

_____ d. Alex Ayres wrote that King once startled people who were praying in church with him when he suddenly cried out, "'Lord, I hope no one will have to die as a result of our struggle for freedom in Montgomery. But if anyone has to die, let it be me!'" (200).

_**TS**_   e. Martin Luther King, Jr. also set an example of unselfishness for the American people.

_____   f. Surely King must have been frightened often, but he strongly believed that it was his duty to fight injustice; in fact, he could not have lived with himself if he had not fulfilled that duty.

_____   g. For thirteen years, he traveled through the southern states and to Washington D.C., St. Augustine, Los Angeles, Chicago, and New York, organizing protests and speaking out against racial injustice.

Third Body Paragraph

_____   a. King wrote, "Forgiveness does not mean ignoring what has been done or putting a false label on an evil act. It means, rather, that the evil act no longer remains a barrier to the relationship" (35).

_**TS**_   b. King showed an ability to love to an extraordinary degree because he saw the humanity in everyone.

_____   c. Also, King realized that because he believed in universal brotherhood, he had to forgive his enemies.

_____   d. In one of his sermons, King said, "The good neighbor looks beyond the external accidents and discerns those inner qualities that make all men human and, therefore, brothers" (19).

_____   e. King was able to love his enemies because he saw their humanity and was able to forgive them.

Ayres, Alex. *The Wisdom of Martin Luther King, Jr.: An A-to-Z Guide to the Ideas and Ideals of the Great Civil Rights Leader.* New York: Meridian, 1993.

Carson, Clayborne, ed. *The Autobiography of Martin Luther King, Jr.* New York: Warner Books, Inc., 1998.

King, Martin Luther. *Strength to Love.* New York: Harper, 1963.

Washington, James Melvin, ed. *Testament of Hope: The Essential Writings of Martin Luther King, Jr.* San Francisco: Harper, 1986.

Citing Sources

Giving a **citation** means identifying the source of your information. Whenever you use outside sources—whether you are quoting or paraphrasing a single sentence or summarizing an entire book—you need to identify the source of your information and give credit to the author. You do this with **in-text** and **end-of-text citations** and **text references.**

You will need to use **in-text** and **end-of-text** citations together. Look at this example.

IN-TEXT CITATION

> Cory Meacham wrote, "Tigers are a wonder. It doesn't matter what language we use to explain that" (223). A tiger can weigh up to 800 pounds (363 kilograms), and yet move through forest or tall grass almost soundlessly. The tiger's stripes, while very noticeable in open areas, make the animal almost invisible in dense vegetation. When hunting, tigers will seek out the largest prey they can find as they need to consume about 35 pounds (16 kilograms) of meat per day. Tigers hunt and live alone, marking and defending their own territories, yet they communicate with one another over long distances, making some sounds so low that they are inaudible to humans.

END-OF-TEXT CITATION

Meacham, Cory. *How the Tiger Lost Its Stripes: An Exploration into the Endangerment of a Species.* New York: Harcourt, 1997.

The in-text citation "(223)" is the page number from the source. Place it in the sentence that contains the quote or paraphrase. The end-of-text citation is the line that identifies the author, title, place of publication, publisher, and date of publication. Place this line at the end of a paper.

There are two main styles for citations, MLA (Modern Language Association) and APA (American Psychological Association). MLA style is used in business, literature, history, and related subjects. APA style is used in social science. The Meacham citations above and most of the other citations you have seen in this book are in MLA style.

The MLA and APA styles are briefly described below. For more details about these styles, refer to an English handbook or the *MLA Handbook for Writers of Research Papers* and the *Publication Manual of the American Psychological Association*.

NOTE
Do not mix citation styles. Ask your teacher which style you should use in an assignment, and use only that one style.

In-text citations. An in-text citation in your paper alerts readers that the information in a sentence is from an outside source, and it directs them to your end-of-text citations. Use in-text citations wherever you include words, ideas, or facts from an outside source in your writing.

MLA style in-text citations. Write *page numbers* in parentheses at the end of the sentence in which the information from the source appears. If you don't mention the author in the sentence, include his or her name with the page numbers.

DIRECT QUOTATION

Cory Meacham writes, "Tigers, though they do not purr, make a delightful array of endearing noises" (250).

PARAPHRASE

Cory Meacham writes that tigers produce a great variety of wonderful sounds, but they do not purr (250).

Tigers produce a great variety of wonderful sounds, but they do not purr (Meacham, 250).

APA style in-text citations. Write *the year of publication* in parentheses after the author's name in the sentence in which the information from the source appears. If you don't mention the author in the sentence, include his or her name in the parentheses and place the citation at the end of the sentence.

DIRECT QUOTATION

Cory Meacham (1997) writes, "Tigers, though they do not purr, make a delightful array of endearing noises" (250).

PARAPHRASE

Cory Meacham (1997) writes that tigers produce a great variety of wonderful sounds, but they do not purr.

Tigers produce a great variety of wonderful sounds, but they do not purr (Meacham, 1997).

End-of-text citations. Your in-text citations must match your end-of-text citations, or list of works. That is, for every in-text citation in your writing, you must include a complete reference to a book, magazine, or website in your end-of-text citations. In addition, your end-of-text citations must include some sources that you do not cite in in-text citations. That is because you must include in your end-of-text citations any source which you have summarized in your writing or which you have used for background information about the topic you are discussing.

Each style (MLA or APA) distinguishes between books, periodicals (magazines), and online sources in various ways. Look at the following examples.

MLA style end-of-text citations.

MLA BOOK CITATION

Matthiessen, Peter. *Tigers in the Snow*. New York: North Point, 2000.

MLA PERIODICAL CITATION

Brooke, Michael. "Birds in Decline around the Globe." *New Scientist* 13 March 2004: 14-15.

MLA ONLINE CITATION

"Welcome to CITES." *The Convention on International Trade in Endangered Species of Wild Flora and Fauna*. 2 July 2004. 6 July 2004. < http://www.cites.org/>.

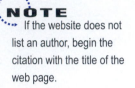

NOTE If the website does not list an author, begin the citation with the title of the web page.

Form and Dating of MLA End-of-Text Citations
- **Underline** or **italicize** the titles of books, periodicals, and websites.
- Put **quotation marks** around titles of parts of books, articles from periodicals, or individual web pages on a website.
- Put **periods** after authors' names, after titles, after dates in website citations, and at the end of citations.
- Internet citations have two **dates**. The first is the date when the site was created or updated. The second is the date you accessed it.

APA style end-of-text citations.

APA BOOK CITATION

Matthiessen, P. (2000). *Tigers in the snow*. New York: North Point.

APA PERIODICAL CITATION

Brooke, Michael. (2004, March 13). Birds in decline around the globe. *New Scientist*, 181(2438), 14-15.

APA ONLINE CITATION

Welcome to CITES. (2004, 2 July). *The Convention on International Trade in Endangered Species of Wild Flora and Fauna*. Retrieved July 6, 2004, from http://www.cites.org/

Form and Dating of APA End-of-Text Citations

- **Italicize** titles of books, periodicals, and websites. If you handwrite your paper, **underline** the titles.
- In titles, use capital letters *only* for the first word or the first word after a colon. Do *not* use *any* quotation marks.
- Put **periods** after dates of book or periodical publication or website creation/updating, after titles, and at the end of citations, except after a URL.
- Put **dates** after the authors' names, or, if there is no author's name, after the title. In online citations, put *Retrieved* and the date of access followed by *from* and the URL, or Internet address, at the end of the citation.
- Put the **volume number** after the name of the periodical and then the issue number, if available, in parenthesis.

EXERCISE 12

A. *On another piece of paper, copy the following statements, and add in-text citations to each one. Use either MLA or APA style, but do not mix styles. Refer to the chart on page 218 for dates for APA citations.*

1. According to Scott Ian Barry, wolves interpret the direct gaze of a human or an animal as threatening. (The information appears on page 6 of the book.)

2. Douglas Chadwick writes, "Wolves, when you get down to it, are a lot like us. They are powerful, aggressive, territorial, and predatory. They are smart, curious, cooperative, loyal, and adaptable." (This statement appears on page 38 of the magazine.)

3. L. David Mech reports, ". . . wolves really have never been hunted or seriously pursued in most of the High Arctic, [unlike] their counterparts throughout the rest of the northern hemisphere. This makes them mostly unafraid of any human beings they do run into." (This statement appears on page 1, the first and only page of the website.)

B. On another piece of paper, use the same style you used in Exercise 12A (MLA or APA) to create an end-of-text citation list. Use the information in the chart that follows.

- Alphabetize the list according to the authors' last names.
- If you use MLA, put the title "Works Cited" in the center at the top of the page. If you use APA, put the title "References" in the center at the top of the page.
- You may handwrite the list, but typing is preferable because typing allows you to show italics.

Type of Publication	book	magazine article	online article
Author(s) (first name first)	Scott Ian Barry	Douglas H. Chadwick	L. David Mech
Title of Work	Wolf Empire: An Intimate Portrait of a Species	Wolf Wars	Arctic Wolves and Their Prey
Title of Publication/Title of Website	---------	National Geographic	National Oceanic and Atmospheric Administration: Arctic Theme Page
Place of Publication	New York	---------	---------
Publishing Company	Lyons Press	---------	---------
Other	date of publication: 2007	date of publication: March 2010 volume: 217 number: 3 pages 34-55	date of access: 3/8/2010 date of publication: 5/30/2007 web address: http://www.arctic.noaa. gov/essay_mech.html

Reporting verbs. Reporting verbs, which are shown in the chart that follows, vary in meaning. For example, the verbs *say* or *write* express a neutral attitude. In contrast, verbs like *argue, assert, claim, contend,* and *maintain* indicate that there are two opposing opinions and that there may be a strong challenge to the argument in the text reference.

> John Smith *contends* that many animal species are endangered. However, he does not offer solid scientific evidence to support this view.

Here are the common reporting verbs. Check your dictionary to learn about the differences in their meanings.

Reporting Verbs			
Neutral Verbs		**Verbs That Indicate Persuasion**	
discuss	report	argue	maintain
explain	say	assert	recommend
observe	state	claim	remind
present	tell	contend	suggest
point out	write	encourage	urge
relate			

Grammar Notes

1. In text references, reporting verbs are used in either the present or the past tense with little difference in meaning. However, if you use a past tense reporting verb, you must make sure that any verbs that follow it agree in tense. (For more information about verb tense in noun clauses, see Appendix IA, page 258.)

2. Verbs differ in terms of what patterns may follow them. Most of the verbs in the chart are followed by a noun clause:

> NOUN CLAUSE
> John Smith *explains* that the world's fish supplies are dwindling.

The verbs *tell, encourage, remind,* and *urge* require an indirect object.

> I. O.
> John Smith *tells* readers that the world's fish supplies are dwindling.

> I. O.
> John Smith *urges* readers to avoid buying fish species that are endangered.

To learn what sentence patterns may be used with a particular verb, check your dictionary.

Summarizing

Finding and presenting the main and supporting ideas of a whole article or section of a text is called **summarizing**. In general, summaries contain broad concepts and explain relationships between ideas but include very few supporting details such as facts or statistics. They can vary in length from one sentence to a paragraph or more. If you are writing a paper for school and want to include a summary of an article in it, you should keep the summary short—probably no more than two or three sentences. But if you have an assignment to write a summary of an article or a section of a textbook, you will need to write a longer, more complete summary. A complete summary of a section from a textbook might be one paragraph in which each sentence summarizes a paragraph in the original text. Follow these four steps to write a summary of any length.

How to Summarize

1. *Read carefully*. Read the selection once to get a general idea of what it is about and to determine what the author's purpose is. Ask yourself if the author is trying to persuade or inform and what his or her main message is. You do not have to understand all the vocabulary in the reading in order to summarize it, but if an unfamiliar word relates to a main or supporting idea in the text, you must find out what it means.

2. *Locate the main and supporting points*. Read the text again, and underline the words, phrases, clauses, and sentences that contain the main and supporting points. (Summarizing steps 3 and 4 will appear on pages 222 and 223.)

Different kinds of writing have different types of organization. Academic writing is highly organized, so if you are summarizing an excerpt from a textbook or an academic journal, you will probably find the main and supporting points easily: The main idea will be stated near the beginning, and most of the supporting points will be in the topic sentences of body paragraphs. A summary statement may be included near the end.

On the other hand, if you are summarizing an article from a newspaper, a popular magazine, or the Internet, you will see that the organization is looser. The main idea may appear anywhere in the article, and the paragraphs may be very short and may lack topic sentences. In such writing, look for signals that tell you what the writer wants to emphasize, such as a carefully developed description or explanation, an attention-getting quotation, a short one-sentence paragraph after a longer paragraph, or transition signals such as *major*, *main*, *largest*, and *above all*.

In the following article, words, phrases, clauses, and sentences containing the main and supporting ideas have been underlined.

THE RAINFOREST IN YOUR CUP

1   If you drank coffee this morning, you are most likely responsible for clearing a patch of <u>rainforest</u> about the size of your coffee mug. That's the amount of forest, in Latin America at least, that <u>is cleared for firewood to dry the beans required for a cup of coffee</u>. And if you drink a cup every morning, that adds up to a lot of forest: Each year in Latin America, about 65 square kilometers (16,000 acres) are cut to fuel coffee drying, according to the Mesoamerican Development Institute. This loss of forest is occurring despite the fact that in recent years coffee growers have adopted new production methods which are better for the environment.

2   All coffee beans—whether they are grown with new environment-friendly or with conventional methods—still need to be dried after the berries are picked. And currently that's being done with tons of firewood and diesel fuel.

3   "<u>The largest threat to forests right now</u> is not shade-coffee plantations being cleared and converted to technified plantations," <u>said Raul Raudales, an energy engineer</u> who has been working to develop forest-friendly technologies. "The biggest impact on forests <u>is the use of firewood to dry the coffee</u>." Coffee is the second largest traded commodity worldwide. So the amount of forest cleared to dry millions of coffee berries each year is large.

4   <u>Raudales and his team have developed</u> an efficient alternative to the massive blast-furnace dryers that are used to dry coffee all over the world. His company, Solar Trade, builds <u>a solar coffee dryer which uses</u> a high-tech heating chamber kept hot by <u>solar heaters and</u> super-efficient fans to dry the coffee beans. On rainy days or at night, the dryers get their heat from burning the <u>husks of previously dried coffee berries</u>.

5   Right now there are three solar dryers in operation, two in Costa Rica and one in Nicaragua. There is already some demand in Europe for the solar-dried coffee. "We call it 'Cafe Solar,'" said Richard Trubey, the company's vice president for marketing. "We are promoting the benefits of preserving the forest by not burning it to dry coffee."

6   The design for the conventional industrial dryers that are in widespread use hasn't changed in the last 80 years. <u>The old-style dryers heat the coffee with firewood and diesel fuel</u>. Large horsepower fans blow the hot air through the wet coffee beans, requiring large amounts of electricity.

7   "So the energy consumption each year at a facility that handles 10,000 sacks of coffee—which is small, there are many others that produce twenty times that—costs about $20,000 for electricity and firewood," said Raudales. "For the solar dryer, those costs are about $1,700." <u>In many parts of Latin America electricity prices have been rising rapidly in the past decade</u>, increasing by about 20 percent a year.

(continued)

8   Solar Trade estimates that the efficiency savings would easily cover a company's cost of changing to solar within seven to eight years. "<u>It makes sense for</u> these <u>companies to change right now</u>, whether they have newer or older equipment, simply <u>because the conventional systems require a tremendous amount of energy and money to operate</u>," said Trubey. (WRI Features)

Adapted from Runyan, C. (2004, January). The rainforest in your cup. *World Resources Institute.* Retrieved July 6, 2004, from http://pubs.wri.org/pubs_content_text.cfm?ContentID=2368

3. *Paraphrase*. Once you have underlined the main idea and the supporting points, you can paraphrase what you have marked. (For more information about how to paraphrase, see pages 199–201). Look at the paraphrases below.

. . . <u>rainforest</u> . . . <u>is cleared for firewood to dry the beans required for a cup of coffee</u>.

People are cutting down rainforests to get firewood to dry coffee beans.

<u>The largest threat to forests right now</u> . . . <u>said Raul Raudales, an energy engineer</u> . . . <u>is the use of firewood to dry the coffee</u>.

Energy engineer Raul Raudales says cutting firewood causes the most damage to rainforests.

<u>Raudales and his team have developed</u> . . . <u>a solar coffee dryer which uses</u> . . . <u>solar heaters and</u> . . . <u>husks of previously dried coffee berries</u> . . . .

Raul Raudales and his partners have created a solar-powered coffee dryer that runs on sunlight and the skins of previously dried berries.

<u>The old-style dryers heat the coffee with firewood and diesel fuel</u>.

The traditional dryers burn firewood and diesel fuel to dry coffee.

In many parts of Latin America electricity prices have been rising rapidly in the past decade . . . .

Much of Latin America has experienced rising energy costs over the last ten years.

It makes sense for . . . companies to change right now . . . because the conventional systems require a tremendous amount of energy and money to operate. . . .

Due to the very large amount of energy and money required by conventional coffee-drying methods, solar coffee dryers offer a sensible alternative to companies right now.

4. *Write a paragraph*. When you have finished paraphrasing, combine the paraphrases in a paragraph. Include a text reference (the author's name, the in-text citation, and, if you wish, the name of the article or publication) in the first sentence. If your summary will be more than three sentences long, begin with a topic sentence that introduces the general idea of the reading. If you find that there are information gaps in your paragraph, reread the text, looking for information to paraphrase in order to fill in the gaps. After you have finished writing, check your paragraph for cohesion, and revise if necessary. Be sure to include an end-of-text citation.

Curtis Runyan (2004) reports in WRI Features that people are cutting down rainforests to get firewood to dry coffee beans. He quotes energy engineer Raul Raudales, who says that harvesting trees for firewood causes more damage to rainforests than any other aspect of coffee production. Raudales and his partners have created a solar-powered coffee dryer that runs on sunlight and the skins of previously dried berries. The traditional dryers burn firewood and diesel fuel to dry coffee. Due to the rising energy prices in much of Latin America and the very large amount of energy required by conventional coffee-drying methods, solar coffee dryers offer a sensible alternative right now.

Adapted from Runyan, C. (2004, January). The rainforest in your cup. World Resources Institute. Retrieved July 6, 2004, from http://pubs.wri.org/pubs_content_text.cfm?ContentID=2368

A. *Summarize the two readings below. The first one is from a college textbook and the second one is an editorial (argumentative essay written for a newspaper). Follow the four summarizing steps and include in-text and end-of-text citations. Use the APA style.*

1.

THE ECOLOGICAL CAPITAL OF BRAZIL
by Daniel Botkin and Edward Keller

1   In 1950, the city of Curitiba in Brazil had 300,000 inhabitants; but, by 1990 the population had grown to 2.3 million . . . making it the tenth largest city in Brazil. . . . The growth of Curitiba resulted primarily from migration of rural people displaced by mechanization of agriculture. The newcomers lived in squatter huts at the edge of the city in conditions of great poverty, poor sanitation, and frequent flooding caused by conversion of rivers and streams into artificial canals. By 1970, Curitiba was well on the way to becoming an example of environmental degradation and social decay. The story of how Curitiba turned itself from an urban disaster into a model of planning and sustainability by 1995 illustrates that cities can be designed in harmony with people and the environment [1,2].

2   Much of the credit for the transformation of Curitiba goes to its three-time mayor, Jaime Lerner, who believed a workable transportation system was the key to making Curitiba an integrated city where people could live as well as work. Rather than a more expensive underground rail system, Lerner spearheaded development of a bus system with five major axes, each containing lanes dedicated to express buses . . . with others carrying local traffic and high-speed automobile traffic. Forty-nine blocks of the historic center of Curitiba were reserved for pedestrians. Tubular bus stations were built in which passengers paid fares before boarding, an arrangement that avoids long delays caused by collecting fares after boarding. Circular routes and smaller feeder routes between the major axes maintain vital connections between the central city and outlying areas. As a result, more than 1.3 million passengers ride buses each day. Although Curitiba has the second highest per capita number of cars in Brazil, it uses 30% less gas than eight comparable Brazilian cities, and its air pollution is among the lowest in the country.[2,3]

3   To solve its serious garbage problem, Curitiba required each household to sort recyclables from garbage. As a result, two-thirds of the garbage, more than 100 tons a day, is recycled, with 70% of the population participating. Where streets are too narrow to allow access by garbage trucks, residents are encouraged to bring garbage bags to the trucks. They are reimbursed with bus tokens, surplus food, or school notebooks.

4   Through a low-cost housing program, 40,000 new homes were built, many placed so that residents have easy access to job sites. The city also embarked on a program to increase the amount of green space. Artificial drainage channels were replaced with natural drainage, reducing the need for expensive flood control. Some areas, including those around the river basins, were set aside for parks. In 1970, Curitiba had only 0.5 m^2 of green area per capita; by 1990, the area had increased to 50 m^2 for each inhabitant. The accomplishments of Curitiba have led some to call it the "ecological capital of Brazil" and to hope that it is also the "city of the future."[2, 4]

[1]Dobbs, F. 1995. *Curitiba: City of the future?* Video. World Bank.

[2]Hunt, J. 1994 (April). Curitiba. *Metropolis Magazine*.

[3]Rabinovitch, J. 1997. *Integrated transportation and land use channel Curitiba's growth*. Washington, D.C.: World Resources Institute.

[4]Rabinovitch, J. and J. Leitman. 1996 (March). Urban planning in Curitiba. *Scientific American*, pp. 45-53.

Botkin, D. B., & Keller, E. A. (2003). The ecological capital of Brazil. In *Environmental science: Earth as a living planet* (pp. 576-577). Hoboken, NJ: Wiley.

2.   **THE DEATH OF THE WORLD'S CORAL REEFS**
                              by Joshua Reichert

1   Bigger than anything ever built, Australia's Great Barrier Reef is about 92,000 square miles in size. Like all reefs, it's the product of trillions of tiny animals, no bigger than ants, building the reefs as they secrete limestone.

2   Generations of new corals grow on top of the skeletons of previous generations, building up the reefs at the rate of about 1 inch per year. Coral colonies can live for thousands of years, and at some Pacific atolls, the skeletons of dead coral stretch nearly a mile below the living reef.

3   One would think that creatures capable of such architectural feats would be impervious to human activity.

4   Yet, one fifth of the world's reefs have already been lost, and those remaining are under stress from pollution, sedimentation, destructive fishing practices and global climate change.

5   Reefs have existed on Earth for millions of years, but unless strong action is taken to protect them, more than half of the world's shallow reefs could be gone in the next few decades.

6   The world's reefs are being threatened in a variety of ways. Each year, new coral diseases are identified which many scientists

(continued)

believe are linked to human activity.

7   Sediment, pesticides and pollution from human activities damage coral reefs when transported by rivers into coastal waters. Excessive nutrients in seawater, caused by wastewater discharges from sources that include hotels and resorts, agriculture, golf courses and sewage treatment plants, promote algal growth on coral, blocking sunlight and stunting coral growth.

8   In some parts of the world, destructive fishing practices, including the uses of sodium cyanide and explosives, are seriously damaging coral communities and the fish that live in them.

9   The biggest threat to the world's coral reefs, however, is global warming.

10   Reefs need the right balance of sunlight, temperature, nutrients, and salinity to survive. Most shallow water reefs exist within a narrow temperature range.

11   Increases of less than 2 degrees Fahrenheit can have a devastating effect on these tiny organisms, causing them to expel the symbiotic microalgae that provide them with food. The corals turn white and eventually die— a process called bleaching.

12   By the end of the 21st century, the Earth's temperature is expected to rise by as much as 11.5 degrees Fahrenheit. This is more of an increase than has occurred since the last Ice Age. Many scientists believe that the resulting rise in ocean temperature will be fatal to many reefs.

13   Why should we care?

14   For one, because reefs harbor at least one quarter of all marine life. About 10 percent of the world's fisheries come from reefs, and much of this feeds protein-starved people in underdeveloped countries. Because they harbor so much biodiversity, reefs, like tropical rain forests, also offer excellent prospects for new medicines and natural compounds that can benefit humanity.

15   For example, Australian scientists have developed a highly effective sunscreen from substances that corals use to protect themselves from ultraviolet light.

16   The beauty of coral reefs draws millions of tourists each year, generating revenue for the countries where they are located, many of them impoverished.

17   Finally, reefs provide a natural seawall that protects many coastal populations from tides, storm surges and hurricanes.

18   What can be done to save the world's coral reefs?

19   First, we must curb global warming. As the world's second largest emitter of greenhouse gases, the United States must exercise leadership on this issue . . .

20   Second, because the United States is the No. 1 importer of coral-reef fish, Americans must ensure that tropical fish are

collected in ecologically sound and sustainable ways.

21   Although the United States and many other countries forbid using cyanide and explosives to stun fish, these methods are still widely practiced in the South Pacific and Southeast Asia.

22   In 2008 a federal Coral Reef Conservation Program-sponsored working group strongly recommended US legislation to address this trade.

23   Like many of the planet's living creations, reefs can recover if given some encouragement. But unless action is taken soon, the next generation may never have the chance to experience first hand one of the world's most marvelous feats of nature.

Reichert, J. (2001, July 20, updated June 18, 2010). The death of the world's coral reefs [Editorial]. *The San Francisco Chronicle*, p. A25.

B. With a partner or small group, compare the parts of each article you identified as the main and supporting points, and tell how you found the main and supporting arguments in each reading. Finally, read your summaries to each other. If you do not agree on the main and supporting points, discuss this question with other classmates and your teacher.

Appendix IA: Grammar

■ 1. Adjective Clauses

When writing, you can use adjective clauses to describe or define nouns and to create longer, more sophisticated sentences. An adjective clause begins with a **relative pronoun** (*who, which, that, whose, where,* or *when*). The relative pronoun refers back to the noun or pronoun that the clause modifies.

> I have a friend ***who*** *can play the drums*.

> This is the highway ***that*** *goes to New York*.

Who, which, and that. Use the relative pronouns **who** to refer to people and **which** to refer to things. Use **that** to refer to either people or things.

> I know a man ***who/that*** *speaks Russian*.

> I photographed a building ***which/that*** *is 500 years old*.

Sometimes the relative pronoun is the subject (**S**) of the adjective clause.

> You know the people ***who*** *are coming to visit*.

> I own a car ***that*** *can carry five passengers*.

Sometimes the relative pronoun is the direct object (**O**) of the verb in the adjective clause.

> The people ***who*** *I called* are coming to visit.

> The car ***that*** *I own* can carry five passengers.

Whom. Use **whom** to refer to people. *Whom* is always in the object position in an adjective clause. *Whom* is formal, so it is most often used in writing.

> The people ***whom*** *I called* are coming to visit.

In less formal English, no pronoun (**Ø**) is often used when the relative pronoun is an object in the adjective clause.

> The people (***Ø***) *I called* are coming to visit.

> The car (***Ø***) *I own* can carry five passengers.

All of the adjective clauses discussed so far can be formed more than one way. However, **which** is seldom used as the object of the verb in the adjective clause.

SUBJECT CLAUSE MODIFYING A PERSON
The boy **who/that** *won the prize* was delighted.

SUBJECT CLAUSE MODIFYING A THING
The plane **which/that** *arrived at 5:00* was full.

OBJECT CLAUSE MODIFYING A PERSON
The teacher **who/that/Ø** *I wanted to see* was busy.

OBJECT CLAUSE MODIFYING A THING
The dictionary **that/Ø/(which)** *I bought* is useful.

The relative pronoun (**who**, **which**, etc.) can also be the object of a preposition (**OP**) in the adjective clause.

This is the friend **who/that/Ø** *I eat lunch* **with**.

When a preposition comes at the beginning of the adjective clause, you must use **whom** or **which**.

This is the friend **with whom** *I eat lunch*.

Here is the address **to which** *you should send the letter*.

When a preposition is at the end of the adjective clause, you can omit the relative pronoun (**Ø**).

I contacted the customer **who/whom/that/Ø** *you told me about*.

Here is the address **that/Ø/(which)** *you should send the package to*.

Whose. The relative pronoun **whose** is a possessive in an adjective clause. *Whose* can represent *his, her, its, their, Mario's, the company's*, etc. *Whose* follows a noun that refers to either a person or a thing.

This is the girl. ~~Her~~ *mother brought the cake.*
(whose)

A building is pleasant to be in. ~~Its rooms are bright~~.
(whose rooms are bright)

Where and when. In adjective clauses, **where** and **when** represent adverbs. Use **where** to replace a prepositional phrase of location (*in that building, at the corner*) or the adverbs *there* or *here*.

That is the building. ~~I work in that building~~.
(where I work.)

I went to a park. ~~Lots~~ of children were playing ~~there~~.
(where lots)

Use **when** to replace a prepositional phrase of time (*on that day, at the moment, in the nineteenth century*) or the adverb *then*.

Can you remember the day? ~~You~~ were interviewed? ~~on that day~~.
(when you)

Where and **when** can be replaced by **that** or **Ø**. If **that** or **Ø** replaces **where**, a preposition must be in the adjective clause.

> This is the building ***that/Ø*** *I work **in***.
> Can you remember the day ***that/Ø*** *you were interviewed*?

1a. Position of Adjective Clauses

An adjective clause should come as close as possible to the noun it modifies. In most cases, it immediately follows the noun.

> The books ***that*** *the school is giving away* are in the library storeroom.

However, sometimes a prepositional phrase comes between the noun and the adjective clause that modifies it.

> The boxes of books ***that*** *the school is giving away* are in the library storeroom.

1b. Use of Commas with Adjective Clauses

RULE 1 Some adjective clauses have commas, and others do not. An adjective clause that provides information which is *essential* to define the noun or pronoun does not have commas. It is called a **restrictive clause**.

> The man *who always wears green neckties* is a banker.

An adjective clause that provides *additional* information which is not essential to define the noun or pronoun has commas. It is called a **non-restrictive clause**.

> Antonio, *who always wears green neckties*, is a banker.
> My wife, *who is an artist*, has three paintings in that art gallery.

An adjective clause that modifies either a proper noun (*Antonio*) or a noun that refers to someone or something that is unique (*my wife*) is always non-restrictive and always has commas.

RULE 2 Adjective clauses after indefinite pronouns (*no one, anyone, something*) do not have commas.

> The police are looking for someone *who saw the accident*.
> I could not find anything *that I wanted to eat* on the menu.

RULE 3 Adjective clauses made with expressions of quantity (*one of, some of, all of*) always have commas and use only the relative pronouns **whom**, **which**, or **whose**.

> The bride and groom greeted the guests, ***several of whom*** had traveled long distances to come to the wedding.

> Last year the organization received a sum of money, ***much of which*** has already been spent.

Other nouns can be combined with **of which** to introduce an adjective clause.

> I brought the contract, ***the last page of which*** *you must sign.*

> The instructor gave us a homework assignment, ***the purpose of which*** *was to review verb tense.*

1c. Common Errors in Adjective Clauses

Avoid the following common errors made with adjective clauses.

ERROR 1 The verb in the adjective clause does not agree in number with the noun in the main clause. This problem can only occur when the pronoun is the subject of the adjective clause, and it is most likely to occur when there is a prepositional phrase between the noun and the adjective clause.

> We have contacted the manufacturers of this product who ~~is~~ ^{are} sending us a new catalogue.

ERROR 2 There is incorrect repetition of a pronoun, a preposition, or other words in an adjective clause.

> The groups of people that the advertising consultant has talked to ~~them~~ agree that the product is very useful.

> The chapter of the math textbook with which I had the most difficulty ~~with~~ was the one about graphs.

> The pronunciation class is at 8:00 A.M. in the morning when I'm too sleepy. ~~at 8:00 A.M.~~

ERROR 3 The relative pronoun *where* is used incorrectly. *Where* can only be used to introduce an adjective clause after a noun that refers to a location.

> That is the episode of the TV show ~~where~~ ^{in which} Harry Lam appears.

> Computer hacking is the kind of crime ~~where~~ ^{for which} it is difficult to prepare a legal case.

ERROR 4 Commas are used incorrectly. Sometimes commas are not placed where they are needed. In the sentence below, the adjective clause is non-restrictive because the noun phrase, *my oldest brother,* is unique.

> My oldest brother, who is 33, has two children.

Sometimes commas are placed where they are not needed. In the sentence below, the adjective clause *who looks like me* is restrictive because it is needed to identify the noun *child*.

> The child, who looks like me, is the older one.

EXERCISE 1

As you read the following passage, find and underline the <u>eleven</u> adjective clauses. Then correct the <u>nine</u> adjective clause errors. The first one has been done for you.

are

[1]Fireflies, <u>which ~~is~~ actually not flies but beetles</u>, are known for their unusual ability to produce flashing lights. [2]Fireflies have light-producing organs in their bodies in which a chemical reaction takes place in them. [3]This process is so energy efficient that almost 100 percent of the chemical energy the firefly produces is converted to light.

[4]Adult fireflies produce light to attract mates. [5]Each species of firefly can be distinguished by the color, brightness, length, and duration of its flashing lights. [6]In addition, in most species, males produce a brighter light than females. [7]When a female sees the particular kind of flashing that are produced by a male of her species, she flashes back in response. [8]The pair will continue their dialogue of flashes until they locate each other and mate.

[9]In some species of fireflies, the males gather in groups where they all flash simultaneously. [10]A group may gather in a single tree which lights up with their rhythmically flashing signals. [11]A female is attracted to a male whose his light is the brightest in the group. [12]Biologist John Buck who studied synchronous flashing in fireflies for over forty years found that in order to flash synchronously, male fireflies must be close enough to one another to see each other. [13]A male firefly looks for another male where is close to him, registers the rhythm at which that male is flashing at, and begins flashing synchronously.

[14]Of the more than 2,000 known species of fireflies in the world, fewer than 100 flash synchronously, and most of those inhabit swamps which has dense vegetation. [15]Scientists think that synchronous flashing must give a firefly species an advantage in this type of environment. [16]They think that a female firefly is more likely to find a mate if she can locate him easily, and the flashing of a synchronized group is easier to find than the light of a lone male.

1d. Reducing Adjective Clauses to Adjective Phrases

Adjective clauses that begin with *who, which*, or *that* and a form of the verb *to be* can be reduced, or shortened. By reducing adjective clauses to adjective phrases, you can make your writing more concise. That is, you can present more information in fewer words.

> The money ~~that is~~ on the table is mine.

An adjective clause that contains a progressive verb can be reduced to an *-ing* participial phrase.

> The companies ~~that are~~ selling software are doing well.

An adjective clause that contains a passive verb can be reduced to an *-ed* participial phrase.

> The songs ~~that have been~~ recorded in the last five years are frequently played on the radio.

When reduction of an adjective clause leaves a single adjective, the adjective moves in front of the noun it modifies.

> The dictionary ~~which is~~ red is José's.

When an adjective clause has commas, its reduced form also has commas.

> Genghis Kahn, ~~who was~~ a Mongol emperor from 1206 to 1227, conquered most of Asia.

Subject-type adjective clauses containing verbs other than *be* can sometimes be reduced to *-ing* participial phrases.

> The teacher told us to refer to the chart ~~that shows~~ showing the chemical elements.

Adjective clauses containing the verb *have* can be changed to phrases containing the preposition *with*.

> The man ~~who has~~ with a moustache is the finance minister.

EXERCISE 2

The following passage contains seventeen adjective clauses, <u>sixteen</u> of which can be reduced to adjective phrases. Change the adjective clauses that allow reduction, and notice the effect on the passage. The first one has been done for you.

[1]Calcium, ~~which is~~ a soft whitish chemical element, is the fifth most abundant element in the Earth's crust. [2]Calcium does not occur by itself in nature, but in compounds with other elements. [3]Calcium's most common compounds, which are calcium carbonate, calcium sulfate, and calcium

fluoride, are found in limestone, gypsum, and other rocks and minerals. [4]These compounds have many uses which are important.

[5]Classroom chalk, which is a very soft, fine-grained white limestone, is pure calcium carbonate. [6]It is also an ingredient that is in toothpastes and some stomach medicines, as well as in rubber and paint.

[7]Harder varieties of limestone are used as cut stone in building construction and in the manufacture of mortar and cement. [8]When limestone is heated, it becomes lime, or calcium oxide. [9]Lime is used as a fertilizer, and it has many industrial applications, which include the production of steel, leather tanning, and petroleum refining.

[10]The mineral gypsum, which is soft and whitish-yellow, can be processed to yield calcium sulfate, which is a compound which is used in making cement and plaster. [11]When gypsum is heated, it becomes plaster of Paris, which is a material which is used for all kinds of molds as well as casts which are for broken arms and legs.

[12]Plaster of Paris is named for a gypsum mine which is in France. [13]Calcium sulfate is also used in a wide variety of products which range from fertilizer to candy.

[14]Fluorite, which is a mineral that is found in veins in granite and other rocks, consists of calcium fluoride. [15]Calcium fluoride is important in the production of aluminum, steel, and glass. [16]It is also added to water supplies in small amounts to prevent tooth decay.

[17]Although we don't see calcium in the world around us, it is present in many of the things we use every day.

■ 2. Adjectives and Noun Modifiers

Adjectives are words such as *big* or *expensive* that describe nouns. By selecting and using appropriate adjectives, you can make your writing more descriptive and informative. Adjectives are placed either before a noun or after the verb *be* or a linking verb like *appear* or *seem*. When adjectives are placed before a noun, they must be in the order shown in the following chart.

A noun can have the same function as an adjective. That is, it can modify another noun. A noun that modifies another noun is called a **noun modifier**. A noun modifier, as you see in the chart, is placed directly before the noun it modifies.

Article, Number, Quantity, or Possessive Noun	General	Size	Shape	Age	Color	Nationality	Participial Adjective	Noun Modifier	Noun
an	excellent	pocket-sized						college	dictionary
three/some	unusual		square		green	Turkish			rugs
Mrs. Lee's	elegant, expensive			antique			carved	wood	furniture

Note that when two general adjectives are placed before a noun, either a comma or the conjunction *and* may be placed between them.

> Mrs. Lee has some elegant, expensive antique carved wood furniture.

> Mrs. Lee has some elegant **and** expensive antique carved wood furniture.

Note that noun modifiers, unlike nouns, are not plural.

> INCORRECT: This is a keys chain.

> CORRECT: This is a key chain.

> CORRECT: This is a chain for keys.

Also note that noun modifiers that contain numbers have hyphens.

> a four-room apartment

> a five-story apartment building

> a twenty-year-old building

EXERCISE 3

As you read the paragraph, find and correct <u>eleven</u> errors in the order of the adjectives and noun modifiers. Use the chart on page 236 as a guide. The first one has been done for you.

¹As you step through the doorway, you notice the peacefulness of this quiet, dark reading room. ²Each wall is covered with shelves that hold hundreds of books. ³A red wool ~~soft~~ ^soft^ carpet covers the floor. ⁴Two glass wide doors bring in bright sunlight and give a view of a garden where beautiful pink large roses and blue tiny forget-me-nots are in bloom. ⁵In the middle of the reading room are two upholstered comfortable chairs and a wood polished round table that holds a glass fine green lamp. ⁶Two thick volumes—a Russian nineteenth-century novel and a history of the War of 1812—are on one side of the table. ⁷On the other side are a Mexican twentieth-century well-known novel and a history of Mexico. ⁸A yellow tiger-striped big cat sleeps in one of the chairs and a skinny black little cat sleeps in the other. ⁹The reading room is a calm, restful place to escape from the busy world outside.

2a. Participial Adjectives

Present participles and past participles are often used as adjectives. The meaning of present and past participles is different.

RULE 1 The present participial adjective (*-ing*) refers to an action in progress, an action that occurs regularly, or an action that can occur any time. The past participial adjective (*-ed*) refers to an action that is complete.

> **Growing** children (children under 18 who are in the process of growing) need a lot of help from their parents.
>
> **Grown** children (children over 18 who have finished growing) can help their parents.
>
> The police caught the **escaping** prisoner as he climbed over the fence. (The prisoner was in the process of escaping.)
>
> The police caught the **escaped** prisoner, who had been hiding in the woods for several weeks. (The prisoner had completed his escape.)
>
> I keep my **writing** supplies (the pen and paper that I use every time I write) in this drawer.
>
> I turn in all my **written** work (the work that I have finished writing) to my teacher on time.

RULE 2 Pairs of participial adjectives like *bored/boring* or *interested/ interesting* can describe people's reactions to things and the effect of things on people. The present participial adjective (*-ing*) modifies something (or someone) that affects someone.

The video game was	amazing boring disappointing exciting fascinating uninteresting	for the boys.

The past participial adjective (*-ed*) modifies the people who are affected by that thing (or person).

The boys were	amazed by bored with disappointed by/with excited about/by fascinated by/with uninterested in	the video game.

Check your dictionary to find out which preposition follows a participial adjective.

EXERCISE 4

As you read the paragraph, find and correct the __seven__ errors in participial adjectives. See the example below.

       dining
The ~~dined~~ room was empty.
       polished
The ~~polishing~~ silverware was shining in the candlelight.

¹At 5:00 P.M. the restaurant kitchen was quiet. ²The chefs and their helpers were taking a break as they waited for the orders of the first diners. ³Everything was ready for a busy night. ⁴Hundreds of washing plates were ready on the shelves. ⁵Clean carving knives, served spoons, and fried pans hung from the wall. ⁶A mountain of slicing bread sat near the door, ready for hungry customers. ⁷Freshly iced cakes and appealing fruit tarts waited on a side table. ⁸Chopping vegetables and carefully trimmed pieces of meat and fish were chilling in the refrigerator. ⁹A warming oven was keeping bowls of cooked rice and mashing potatoes hot and ready to serve. ¹⁰A large

pot of steaming soup sat over a low fire on the stove, and its appetized smell mixed with the aroma of freshly ground coffee. [11]The staff appreciated these few quiet moments before the first customers arrived because they would not rest again for six hours.

■ 3. Adverb Clauses

Adverb clauses are dependent clauses that are joined to sentences by subordinating conjunctions. You can use **adverb clauses** to show relationships between ideas. The subordinating conjunction you choose tells what kind of relationship an adverb clause has to a sentence.

Relationship	Subordinating Conjunctions
comparison	as*, just as
concession	although, even though, though
condition	if, in case, unless
contrast	whereas, while
purpose	so that
reason	as*, because, now that**, since*
result	so/such . . . that
time	after, as*, as long as, as soon as, before, by the time, every time, once, since*, the first/next/last time, until, when, whenever, while

*The subordinators **since** and **as** have more than one meaning. When you use one of these subordinators, you have to make sure that the meaning you want to express is clear.

Enrico has been good at math **since** he was in elementary school. (time)

Enrico is majoring in math **since** he likes numbers. (reason)

Enrico's interest in math increased **as** he was taking algebra in high school. (time)

Enrico got straight As in algebra **as** he found it easy. (reason)

Mathematics requires practice with different kinds of problems, **as** playing a musical instrument requires practice with different types of music. (comparison)

**The subordinator *now that* combines two meanings: *now* and *because*.

Enrico has been able to study advanced math **now that** he is in college. (time and reason)

3a. Adverb Clauses and Verb Tense

Sentences with adverb clauses have at least two verbs, one in the main part of the sentence and one in the adverb clause. The tenses of those verbs must make sense together. To choose the correct tense for a verb in a sentence with an adverbial clause, you must consider

1. the meaning of each verb in the sentence
2. the time relationship between the clauses in the sentence
3. the two rules that follow

RULE 1 In sentences about the future, make sure that the verb in the adverb clause is always in the simple present or present perfect tense.

> When we **graduate**, we will have a party.
> As soon as the party **has finished**, we will return home.

RULE 2 Use the subordinating conjunctions *since* and *by the time* only with certain verb tenses.

PRESENT PERFECT OR PRESENT PERFECT PROGRESSIVE   SIMPLE PAST
He **has lived/has been living** in this house *since* he **moved** into town.

PRESENT PERFECT   SIMPLE PRESENT
The sun **has** usually **set** *by the time* we **arrive**.

FUTURE PERFECT   SIMPLE PRESENT
The sun **will have set** *by the time* we **arrive**.

PAST PERFECT   SIMPLE PAST
The sun **had set** *by the time* we **arrived**.

EXERCISE 5

As you read the paragraph, underline the ten adverb clauses, and find and correct the ten verb tense errors. The first one has been done for you.

                                    have

¹I love to visit New York City. ²Every time I travel there, I ~~had~~ new experiences and come away with new impressions. ³The first time I went, I climb to the top of the Statue of Liberty. ⁴When I have reached the top of the spiral staircase and I was looking out over New York Harbor, I thought about the many immigrants from all over the world in New York. ⁵People immigrate to the city since Dutch colonists settled the area in 1625. ⁶Before the Dutch came, Native Americans have been living in the area. ⁷It is astonishing to think that the colonists were paying the Native American tribe only $24 for the island of Manhattan. ⁸Now trillions of dollars change

hands at the New York Stock Exchange every day. [9]On my last trip, I visited the United Nations. [10]As I was touring the U.N., I have been listening to the knowledgeable guide explain how the U.N. works. [11]By the time the tour has finished, I had learned quite a lot. [12]When I left the U.N., I had dinner in a Czech restaurant. [13]New York seems to have as many kinds of ethnic restaurants as there are countries at the U.N. [14]I have tried Puerto Rican, Cuban, Korean, and Indonesian food, and the next time I am going, I plan to eat in Chinatown. [15]I am sure that I will keep visiting New York as long as I will be able to. [16]There will always be more to see!

3b. Reducing Adverb Clauses

Some adverb clauses of time and reason can be reduced to participial phrases, as shown below. Reducing adverb clauses allows you to write more concisely, that is, to put more information in fewer words, as in this example.

> *Having*
> ~~Because Sara had~~ brought her lunch to school, ~~she~~ *Sara* looked for a table to sit down and eat.

3b.1. Reducing Time Clauses

To reduce adverbial time clauses, follow these rules.

RULE 1 You can only reduce an adverb clause when the subject of the adverb clause and the subject of the main clause are the same.

> While Sara ate/was eating her lunch, she read the newspaper.
>
> *While eating* her lunch, Sara read the newspaper.
>
> *Eating* her lunch, Sara read the newspaper.

RULE 2 When you reduce an adverb clause at the beginning of a sentence, you often need to change the subject of the main clause from a pronoun to a noun.

> *Sara*
> *While reading* the newspaper, ~~she~~ ate her lunch.

RULE 3 An *-ing* participial phrase in a sentence indicates actions that are happening at the same time (*Reading* the newspaper, Sara ate her lunch.). To indicate that the action expressed in the phrase occurred at an earlier time, use ***after* + (verb + *-ing*)** or ***having* + (verb + *-ed*)**.

> After Sara had finished lunch, she started to do her homework.
>
> *After finishing* lunch, Sara started to do her homework.
>
> *Having finished* lunch, Sara started to do her homework.

RULE 4 You can reduce time clauses with *after, before, since,* and *while* to participial phrases, but only *after* and *while* can be deleted from reduced adverb clauses.

> *Before starting* her essay, Sara read her textbook.

> *(While) reading* her textbook, Sara took notes.

3b.2. Reducing Reason Clauses

Reduced adverb clauses of reason do not contain *because*. Because reduced adverb clauses that begin with **verb + *-ing*** or ***having + (verb + -ed)*** can express either a time relationship or a reason, you must make sure the meaning of a participial phrase is clear. If reducing an adverb clause will make the meaning of a sentence unclear, do not reduce it.

> Because Sara needed to write an essay, she started brainstorming.
> *Needing* to write an essay, Sara started brainstorming.

> Because Sara had thought about her topic beforehand, she found it easy to brainstorm.
> *Having thought* about her topic beforehand, Sara found it easy to brainstorm.

> Because Sara made lists in order to brainstorm for all of her assignments, she began to write down her ideas for this assignment one after the other. (In this case, the adverb clause should not be reduced because reducing it would produce a confusing sentence.)

EXERCISE 6

Find the eight adverb clauses in the passage that may be reduced to adverb phrases. Reduce them, changing the subject of the sentence to a noun or noun phrase when necessary. The first one has been done for you.

¹Jose Martí was a political activist as well as a lawyer, journalist, teacher, and poet who was born in Cuba in 1853, when Cuba was under Spanish rule. ²Martí opposed the occupation of Cuba, so he spent much of his life outside his native country.

³As a teenager, Martí published a pamphlet protesting the Spanish occupation, for which the Spanish authorities sentenced him to prison for six years. ⁴After his release, he was deported to Spain. ⁵~~While Martí was~~ **While living** ~~living~~ in Spain, **Martí** ~~he~~ studied law and literature at the University of Zaragoza.

⁶In 1875, Martí went to Mexico City, where he lived and published a journal for two years. ⁷Then he moved to Guatemala, where he taught literature for a short time. ⁸Because he wanted to practice law in Cuba, Martí returned to his native country in 1878. ⁹However, the Spanish

authorities did not allow Martí to be a lawyer but instead arrested him for political conspiracy and again deported him to Spain.

[10]After Martí left Spain, he went to Venezuela. [11]He had planned to settle in Venezuela permanently. [12]However, because he found himself in conflict with the Venezuelan government, Martí had to move again.

[13]After Martí had left Venezuela, he moved to New York, where he stayed from 1881 to 1895. [14]While Martí was living in New York, he published a book of poetry called *Ismaelillo* and wrote articles for the Buenos Aires newspaper, *La Nación*. [15]In 1893, Martí organized Cuban exiles in the United States against the Spanish occupation of Cuba. [16]Because the U.S. government supported his efforts against Spain, it appointed Martí to various consular posts. [17]However, Martí was opposed to not only Spanish but also U.S. interests in Cuba. [18]He wanted to see his country independent. [19]Martí resigned from the consular positions and began to organize a revolt against Spanish rule in Cuba.

[20]In 1895, Martí returned to Cuba to lead the insurrection. [21]There, while Martí was fighting against Spanish occupation, he was killed. [22]Martí is remembered both as a national hero in Cuba and as a journalist and poet.

3c. Conditional Sentences

As a writer, you sometimes need to discuss things that are possible. Conditional sentences allow you to do that. Most conditional sentences contain the subordinating conjunction *if*. Conditional sentences are classified according to time (present, future, or past) and according to whether they represent a **real** situation or an **unreal** situation.

Real Conditional Sentences

PRESENT
If (when) I **have** extra money at the end of every month, I always **deposit** it in the bank.

FUTURE
If I **have** extra money at the end of next month, I **will deposit** it in the bank.

PAST
Five years ago, if (when) I **had** extra money at the end of a month, I always **deposited** it in the bank.

Note that in the main clause of real future conditional sentences, you can also use *be going to* (*I am going to deposit*) and various modal verbs (*I might/may/can/should deposit*).

Unreal Conditional Sentences

PRESENT
If I **owned** a car now, I **would travel**. (I don't own a car.)

PAST
Five years ago, if **I had owned** a car, I **would have traveled**. (I didn't own a car.)

Note that in the main clause of present and past unreal conditional sentences, you can also use these modals: *might* (*I might travel/might have traveled*) and *could* (*I could travel/could have traveled*).

EXERCISE 7

As you read the passage, find the <u>eight</u> errors in conditional sentences and correct them. The first one has been done for you.

[1]Weather has a major effect on people, so accurate weather prediction can save lives. [2]For example, if residents are warned in advance of an approaching typhoon or hurricane, they ~~could~~ *can* evacuate to a safe place, or if fishermen knew a storm is coming, they can delay going out to sea.

[3]Forty or fifty years ago, the only way to predict weather was to use statistics. [4]For example, if it rained the first week of March ten times over a forty-year period, one can say that there is a 25 percent chance of rain the first week of March. [5]If one averaged all the recorded temperatures for one day, say September 2, over a thirty-year period, one will be able to predict the September 2 temperature for this year quite accurately.

[6]Since 1960, when the first weather satellite was sent into space, weather prediction has become even more accurate. [7]Without satellite images, weather forecasters could not predict weather affected by atmospheric events over the ocean. [8]For example, the people of the Hawaiian Islands would have had no warning of Hurricane Iwa in 1982 if there are no satellite images. [9]Satellites now send data twice a day to a number of weather centers located around the world. [10]Forecasters can make certain predictions just by looking at the pictures. [11]For instance, if they see an area with a piece of clear sky surrounded by clouds in the morning, they knew that thunderstorms may hit that area later in the day. [12]In addition,

computers can analyze satellite images along with information about air pressure, temperature, and wind speed to create simulations that can predict weather weeks—even months—into the future.

[13]Weather prediction is an example of successful international cooperation. [14]If forecasters on one side of the globe see that potentially dangerous weather events are going to affect people on the other side of the globe, they would have issued advisories to protect those people right away. [15]If everyone followed this model of cooperation and shared other kinds of information as openly as weather information is shared, many people would benefit.

■ 4. Adverbs

Adverbs add various kinds of information to sentences. Some adverbs modify entire sentences, a few adverbs modify adjectives, and many adverbs modify verbs.

Kinds of Adverbs				
Modifying Sentences	**Modifying Adjectives or Other Adverbs**	**Modifying Verbs**		
Sentence Transitions	**Degree**	**Place**	**Manner**	**Time**
fortunately however generally nevertheless	very, quite, rather, especially	here next door	carefully happily	yesterday usually

4a. Adverb Placement

English has several rules that govern where you can put adverbs in a sentence.

RULE 1 The various types of adverbs have different positions in a sentence. The chart below shows the usual placement of most adverbs and adverb phrases.

Placement of Adverbs and Adverb Phrases			
Beginning of a Sentence	**Middle of a Sentence**		**End of a Sentence**
Sentence Transitions	**Frequency Adverbs (*always, often, never*, etc.)**	**Other Mid-sentence Adverbs (*already, also, just, probably, recently, still*, etc.)**	**Place + Manner + Time**
Generally, the spring months are warm.	The boys are *usually* in school.	She has *already* taken the test.	We set the gifts *here carefully yesterday.*
However, this spring was cool.	The boys *never* come to school on time.	Her test has *probably* been corrected.	The children came *into the room happily this morning.*

RULE 2 **Middle-of-sentence adverbs** are one-word adverbs. They should be placed (1) after the *be* verb (The boys are **usually** in school.), (2) after the first auxiliary verb (Her test has **probably** been corrected.), and (3) before simple present or simple past tense verbs (The boys **usually** come/came to school on time.).

RULE 3 End-of-sentence adverbs must be in the order **place + manner + time**.

PLACE   MANNER   TIME
The singer walked off the stage confidently at the end of his performance.

RULE 4 Do not put an adverb between a verb and its direct object.

                           carefully
We set ~~carefully~~ the gifts here.

RULE 5 **Adverbs of degree** are placed directly before the words they modify.

Although the food was **especially** salty, the diners complimented the cook **very** politely.

Exercise 8

As you read the paragraph, find the <u>nine</u> misplaced adverbs and adverb phrases. Move them to the correct positions. The first one has been done for you.

[1]Three quarters of a century after Charlie Chaplin made his silent films, ~~still~~ he is *still* remembered fondly because he created a character that was both funny and sympathetic. [2]Chaplin's character was a poor little tramp, a bum who tried to look like a gentleman in clothes that fit poorly him. [3]The tramp was not a real gentleman, but he maintained his dignity always while he struggled to survive in difficult situations. [4]In *Gold Rush* (1925), the tramp has gone to Alaska. [5]In the cold, snowy wilderness, he finds shelter in a cabin with a stranger. [6]Both men are starving. [7]The stranger considers eating the tramp, so the tramp tries to run away, but the wind is blowing so hard that the poor fellow cannot escape. [8]To relieve their hunger, the tramp cooks his own shoe for dinner. [9]He carves it as though it were roast turkey and eats delicately it with great enjoyment. [10]He goes later into town and sees at a dancehall a beautiful girl. [11]She smiles in his direction and he smiles back. [12]Then he discovers that she at someone else is smiling. [13]Though Chaplin's character faced again and again danger and humiliation, he endured. [14]He overcame difficulty always with optimism and dignity.

4b. Subject-Verb Inversion Following Certain Adverbs at the Beginning of a Sentence

Sometimes subjects and verbs are inverted; that is, the *be* verb or an auxiliary verb comes before the subject of a sentence. By inverting subjects and verbs, you can avoid repetitive sentence beginnings and add variety to your sentences.

RULE 1 When a sentence begins with an adverb or adverb phrase of place, the subject and verb can be inverted.

> **In the corner of the room** *was* a comfortable armchair.

RULE 2 When a sentence begins with a negative adverb such as *never*, *seldom*, or *not only* or an adverb or adverb phrase of place, you must invert the subject and verb.

> **Hardly ever** *does* the bus *come* on time.

> **Not only** *did* Father *sing* well, but both my parents played the violin.

RULE 3 When a sentence begins with *only* and an adverb, you must invert the subject and verb.

> **Only recently** *has* he *spoken* in class.

■ 5. Articles

English has two **articles**, *a* and *the*. Sometimes no article (Ø) is used. When you use articles correctly in your writing, you are telling your readers which nouns represent new information and which nouns represent old information. You are also telling them whether or not singular nouns are countable.

Use the **indefinite article** *a* before singular count nouns that are indefinite or represent new information. Use *an* before words that begin with a vowel sound, as in *an overcoat* or *an hour*.

> I am looking for **a** raincoat and **an** umbrella.

Use the **definite article** *the* before singular count nouns, plural nouns, and uncountable nouns that represent old or known information.

> **The** television, **the** dishes, and **the** furniture you gave us are wonderful.

Use **no article (Ø)** before plural nouns and uncountable nouns that are not definite.

> Ø Homeless people need Ø money, Ø food, and Ø clothing as well as Ø housing.

5a. Definite Nouns

If something is *definite*, it is known to the speaker or writer as well as the listener or reader. A noun can become definite in the following five ways.

1. The noun is followed by a clause or phrase which makes it definite.

   the house you can see in the distance
   the mayor of our town

2. The noun represents something that is unique.

   the sun
   the moon
   the tallest student in the class

3. The noun represents something that the speaker/writer and the listener/reader are familiar with.

> **the** library
> **the** post office

4. The noun has been mentioned in the conversation or text earlier.

> I saw a car. **The** car was traveling too fast.

5. The noun is associated with the topic of the conversation or text.

> I saw a building. **The** roof was bright green.

5b. General Statements

General statements are not definite, so they are usually made with plural count nouns or uncountable nouns.

> **Computers** give people access to knowledge.
>
> **Knowledge** improves people's lives.

Exception: General statements about animals, human inventions, and the organs of the body can be made with *the* and a singular noun, as in the following examples.

> **The** horse provided transportation for people before **the** automobile was invented. (= Horses provided transportation for people before automobiles were invented.)
> **The** diaphragm and **the** lungs make it possible for us to breathe.

5c. Expressions of Quantity

Expressions of quantity are usually indefinite (*a* cup of Ø sugar, *some* Ø salt), but the material to be measured may be definite (a cup of *the* sugar in the cabinet, some of *the* salt on the table).

EXERCISE 9

As you read the paragraph, find and correct the <u>fifteen</u> errors in article usage. The first one has been done for you.

¹You know that the coins in your pocket and the bills in your wallet have ~~the~~ value. ²But why are they valuable? ³Metal your coins are made of and paper your bills are printed on are not worth much themselves. ⁴The money is valued because people in societies all over world have agreed to give it value. ⁵If you give someone handful of the dollars, yen, pesos, rubles, dinars, or euros, you expect to get something in return. ⁶Long ago, people used the things like beads or the seashells as money. ⁷Then they discovered a gold or

silver and used it as currency. [8]Bag of gold bullion or gold coins represented wealth of the owner. [9]Today person's wealth is represented by numbers that are stored in the computers. [10]Imagine! [11]Without the electricity, you would not be able to find out how much money you own.

5d. Special Uses of *the* and Ø

Many uses of *the* and Ø do not have rules, and you just need to memorize them. Many of these uses are shown in the following chart.

the	Ø
Time	
in *the* morning, *the* afternoon, *the* evening	at night
the 1980s, *the* nineties	
the nineteenth century, *the* twentieth century	
the past, *the* present, *the* future	
Numbers	
the first, *the* second, *the* third (ordinal numbers)	Chapter 1, section 2, page three (cardinal numbers)
Location	
the front, *the* middle, the back	
Some Geographic Names	
(mountain ranges) *the* Ural Mountains	(single mountains) Mount Fuji
(oceans, seas) *the* Pacific Ocean, *the* Mediterranean Sea	(lakes) Lake Geneva
(rivers) *the* Yangtze River	
(deserts) *the* Gobi Desert	
Groups of People	
(nationalities or ethnic groups) *the* Chinese, (*the*) Iranians	(ethnic, racial, or religious groups) Hispanics, whites, Buddhists

■ 6. Comparatives and Superlatives

English has various ways to express **comparative** and **superlative** relationships using adjectives, adverbs, and expressions of quantity.

COMPARATIVE WITH AN ADJECTIVE

Networking is hard**er** to learn **than** web-page development.

Web-page development is easi**er** to learn **than** networking.

Networking is **not as** easy to learn **as** web-page development.

COMPARATIVE WITH AN ADVERB

Today's software operates **more** efficiently **than** the software of the past.

The software of the past did **not** operate **as** efficiently **as** today's software does.

The software of the past operated **less** efficiently **than** today's software.

Note in the above examples that one-syllable adjectives and adverbs and two-syllable adjectives that end in *-y* form the comparative with *-er*. All other adjectives and adverbs form the comparative with **more**. In addition, note that some adjectives and adverbs, such as *bad, good,* and *far,* have irregular comparative and superlative forms. To find irregular comparative and superlative forms of adjectives and adverbs, check your dictionary.

COMPARATIVE WITH AN EXPRESSION OF QUANTITY

There is **more/less** activity on campus in the morning **than** in the afternoon. (There is **not as much** . . . **as** . . .)

There are **more/fewer** people on campus in the morning **than** in the afternoon. (There are **not as many** . . . **as** . . .)

Use *less* and *not as much* before uncountable nouns. Use *fewer* and *not as many* before countable nouns.

SUPERLATIVE WITH AN ADJECTIVE

Of all the buildings on campus, the science center is **the most used**.
The science center is **the most used** building on campus.

SUPERLATIVE WITH AN ADVERB

Of all the courses, computer science classes are the ones that students choose **most frequently**.

Computer science classes are the ones that students choose **most frequently** of all the classes.

SUPERLATIVE WITH AN EXPRESSION OF QUANTITY

Of all the instructors, Dr. Tong demands the **most/least** effort from his students.

Note that one-syllable adjectives and adverbs and two-syllable adjectives that end in *-y* form the superlative with *-est*. All other adjectives and adverbs form the superlative with **most**. Note also that **the** precedes superlative adjectives and expressions of quantity but not superlative adverbs.

6a. Modifying Comparative Statements

The meaning of comparative statements can be changed slightly by adding these adverbs: *a lot, a few, a little, many, much, quite a bit, quite a few,* or *quite a lot.*

> **BEFORE A COMPARATIVE ADJECTIVE**
> The automobile repair program is **a little/quite a bit/quite a lot/much/a lot** more challenging than Saleem thought.

> **BEFORE A COMPARATIVE ADVERB**
> Saleem is working **a little/quite a bit/quite a lot/much/a lot** harder this semester than he did last semester.

> **BEFORE A COMPARATIVE EXPRESSION OF QUANTITY**
> Saleem has done **a little/quite a bit/much/a lot** more studying this semester than last.

> Saleem has taken **a few/quite a few/quite a lot/many/a lot** more tests this semester than last semester.

6b. Ellipsis in Comparative Statements

In comparative statements, you should omit repeated words after *than*. This is called using **ellipsis**. Using ellipsis means omitting all but the essential information in order to make your writing concise. (See Ellipsis, page 257.)

> Saleem's grades are higher this semester than ~~they were~~ last ~~semester~~.

> Students in the automobile repair program today study harder than ~~students~~ ^they^ ~~in the automobile repair program studied~~ ^did^ ten years ago.

■ 7. Coordination

Coordination is the linking of words, phrases, or clauses that are equally important with coordinating or correlative conjunctions. You can use coordination to connect ideas and avoid unnecessary repetition.

7a. Coordinating Conjunctions

English has seven **coordinating conjunctions**:

and   for   or   yet

but   nor   so

All of them can join independent clauses.

>   INDEPENDENT CLAUSE   INDEPENDENT CLAUSE
> Here the weather is hot, **or** we have tropical storms.

>   INDEPENDENT CLAUSE   INDEPENDENT CLAUSE
> We do not have enough jobs, **nor** is there enough food.

>   INDEPENDENT CLAUSE   INDEPENDENT CLAUSE
> People move to the city to find jobs, **for** the factories are in the urban centers.

You must invert the subject and verb after the negative coordinating conjunction *nor*. That means that you must place a form of the *be* verb or an auxiliary verb (*does, has, will,* etc.) before the subject.

> We do not have enough jobs, nor **do** we have enough food.

In addition to joining independent clauses, the coordinating conjunctions *and, or, but,* and *yet* can also link words, phrases, and dependent clauses within sentences.

> The *courthouse, library,* **and** *museum* are beautiful buildings. (nouns)
>
> *To reward* **or** *to punish* children's behavior is to teach them the difference between right and wrong. (infinitives)
>
> The apartment is *small* **but/yet** *comfortable*. (adjectives)
>
> Boris hopes to *marry soon, have several children,* **and** *enjoy family life.* (verb phrases)
>
> My mother says *that it is economical to buy a used car* **but** (*that*) *it involves risk.* (noun clauses)
>
> A politician *who can communicate ideas simply, who understands people's fears,* **and** *who can give them hope* gains popularity. (adjective clauses)

EXERCISE 10

This passage does not have coordinating conjunctions. On another piece of paper, rewrite the passage using coordinating conjunctions to combine sentences and link words, phrases, and clauses. Omit unnecessary repetition. Check your finished paragraph for subject-verb agreement. (See Subject-Verb Agreement, page 274.) The first paragraph has been done for you.

[1]Choosing a career is a very important step. [2]You will spend a good part of your life working. [3]The career you choose can determine who your friends are. [4]It can determine where you live. [5]It can determine how much money you make.

Choosing a career is a very important step, for you will spend a good part of your life working. The career you choose can determine who your friends are, where you live, and how much money you make.

[6]People differ in their abilities. [7]They differ in their interests. [8]They differ in their temperaments. [9]A job may be perfect for one person. [10]It may be a nightmare for someone else. [11]For instance, Patricia is very good at working with abstract ideas. [12]Gina is very good at working with abstract ideas. [13]Patricia likes to solve problems. [14]Gina likes to solve problems. [15]They are

both considering computer programming as a career. [16]Only one of them, Gina, is able to work quietly alone for long periods of time. [17]Only Gina should consider going into programming. [18]Consider two other people, Alexi and Etien. [19]Alexi is thinking about becoming a graphic designer. [20]Etien is thinking about becoming a graphic designer. [21]One of these men should not choose graphic design as a career. [22]Alexi is creative. [23]Etien is creative. [24]Alexi is very patient. [25]Etien is not very patient. [26]Etien does not like to do precise work. [27]Etien does not have the patience to redo flawed projects. [28]Etien has artistic talent. [29]He would not make a good graphic designer.

[30]A career can make you happy. [31]A career can make you unhappy. [32]Before choosing a career, get to know yourself well. [33]Learn what kind of jobs are available. [34]Ask your relatives for advice. [35]Ask your teachers for advice. [36]Ask your friends for advice. [37]Making the right career choice can have a big influence on your future well-being.

7b. Parallel Structure

When two or more words, phrases, or dependent clauses are linked by a conjunction (*and, or, but,* or *yet*), make sure the items are in the same grammatical form. This is called **parallel structure**.

In the following example, *sunny* is an adjective, and *wind* is a noun. To make these words parallel, change *wind* to an adjective.

> **windy**
> The day was sunny but ~~wind~~.

In the next example, *drove to the city* and *visited our relatives* are verb phrases, and *to the movie theater* is a prepositional phrase. To make these phrases parallel, put a verb before *to the movie theater.*

> **went**
> We drove to the city, visited our relatives, and ^ to the movie theater.

In the following example, *to get health information* and *to check the prices of products* are infinitive phrases, and *online games* is a noun phrase. To make these phrases parallel, put an infinitive before *online games*.

> I usually use the Internet to get health information, to check the prices of
> **to play**
> products, or ^ online games.

In this final example, *who is able to speak effectively* is a dependent clause, and *a good listener* is a noun phrase. To make these sentence parts parallel, change the noun phrase to a dependent clause.

> For the position of manager, we need someone who is able to speak effectively
> **who is**
> yet also a good listener.
> ^

EXERCISE 11

As you read this paragraph, find and correct the <u>eleven</u> errors in parallel structure. The first one has been done for you.

[1]Adaptation is a characteristic of an individual plant or animal that allows it to survive and ~~reproducing~~ **reproduce** in its environment. [2]Adaptation allows a plant or animal to get the water and nutrients it needs to survive, avoid being eaten, adjustment to climatic conditions, and reproduce. [3]For example, most plants produce tens of thousands of seeds because so few seeds will actually germinate and growth. [4]Some pine trees are adapted to reproduce only when there is a forest fire. [5]The heat of the flames causes the pine cones to open and scattering seeds. [6]Animals show various adaptations as well. [7]Many animals have camouflage—the ability to blend into their environment so that they are not seen by predators. [8]Small animals can call out or running away fast when they are threatened, while larger predatory animals have keen senses of smell, hearing, and vision in order to locate prey. [9]In regions where the winters are harsh, animals grow thicker fur in the fall to prepare for cold weather and then loss of that extra hair in the spring. [10]In the heat of the desert, reptiles maintain a constant body temperature by moving back and forth between sunny and shade. [11]Mammals in the desert are inactive in the heat of the day and activity at night. [12]For the purpose of mating, male and female animals and birds look different. [13]Male animals are often larger, and the colorful feathers of male birds. [14]Adaptation is so important that unless a plant or animal is successfully adapted, it will have little chance of survival and reproducing.

7c. Correlative Conjunctions

Correlative conjunctions work in pairs to join items in sentences.

both . . . and   neither . . . nor

either . . . or   not only . . . but

Correlative conjunctions give you a way to draw attention to parallel items. Notice in the following examples that some correlatives can be replaced by coordinating conjunctions, but using correlative conjunctions adds emphasis.

> Rafael can play **both** the saxophone **and** the piano. (Rafael can play the saxophone *and* the piano.)

> **Either** Sylvain **or** Marie will lead the group. (Sylvain *or* Marie will lead the group.)

> The furniture was **neither** attractive **nor** well made. (The furniture was not attractive, *and* it was not well made, either./The furniture was not attractive, *nor* was it well made.)

> Ali **not only** speaks three languages **but also** has a master's degree in history. (Ali speaks three languages, *and*, in addition to that, he has a master's degree in history.)

The first three pairs of correlative conjunctions (*both . . . and, either . . . or, neither . . . nor*) emphasize both items in the correlative phrase equally. However, *not only . . . but also* puts greater emphasis on the second item in the correlative phrase. Look at these examples.

> He excels in **both** sports **and** academic work. (In this example, *sports* and *academic work* are equally important.)

> He excels in **not only** sports **but also** academic work. (In this example, *academic work* is more important than *sports*.)

In sentences with *not only . . . but, as well* and *too* may replace *also*.

> He excels in **not only** sports but academic work **as well**.

> He excels in **not only** sports but academic work **too**.

The items in correlative phrases must follow the rule of **parallel structure**. In the following example, *work in his father's company* is a verb phrase and *college* is a noun. To make these sentence parts parallel, place a verb before *college*.

> *attend*
> After high school, Jose will either work in his father's company or ^college.

In the following example, *the basic subjects such as math and reading* is a noun phrase, and *they need art and music* is a clause. To make these sentence parts parallel, omit the subject and verb.

> Students need not only the basic subjects such as math and reading but ~~they need~~ art and music as well.

■ 8. Ellipsis

Repeated words and phrases in a sentence can distract us from new information, so it is usually best to omit them. Omitting repeated words and phrases is called **ellipsis**. Notice in the following examples that auxiliary verbs are repeated but other parts of the verb phrase are not. (Words in parentheses may or may not be omitted.)

ELLIPSIS WITH COORDINATING CONJUNCTIONS
Tomiko will major in architecture, and Hanh **will** ~~major in architecture~~ too.

ELLIPSIS WITH SUBORDINATING CONJUNCTIONS
Alex is studying engineering, (just) as his father ~~studied engineering~~ **did**.

ELLIPSIS WITH COMPARATIVE STATEMENTS
The engineering program has been in existence longer than (the) materials science (program) **has** ~~been in existence~~.

■ 9. Gerunds and Infinitives

Two verb forms, the **gerund** (-*ing*) form and the **infinitive** (*to* + simple form), act as nouns in sentences.

A gerund can be the subject of a verb, the direct object of a verb, or the object of a preposition.

Jogging is good exercise.

He enjoys **jogging**.

This path is a good place for **jogging**.

An infinitive can be the subject of a verb or the direct object of a verb.

To exercise is important.

He needs **to exercise**.

Infinitives are only used in the subject position to make general statements.

9a. Gerunds and Infinitives after Verbs

Some verbs, such as *enjoy*, can have a gerund as a direct object, and other verbs, such as *need*, can have an infinitive as a direct object. A number of verbs, such as *like*, can have either a gerund or an infinitive as a direct object, but sometimes the meaning changes, as with the verb *stop*.

I **stopped buying** milk at the corner grocery store. (I no longer buy milk there.)

I **stopped to buy** milk at the corner grocery store. (I bought milk there while I was going somewhere else.)

To find out if you can use a gerund, an infinitive, or either one after a certain verb, consult your dictionary.

9b. Expanding a Gerund or Infinitive Phrase

You can expand gerund phrases to include more information in your sentences. A gerund or infinitive phrase may include a noun object (Making *cookies* is fun.), a prepositional phrase (I plan to swim *in the ocean*.), or an adverb (She decided to exercise *more often*.). Negative infinitives are common (We promised *not to forget*.), but negative gerunds are rare (Instead of *I enjoy **not** working*, use *I enjoy relaxing*.).

9c. Gerund and Infinitive Forms: Active, Passive, Simple, and Past

This chart shows all possible forms of gerunds and infinitives.

		Active Forms	**Passive Forms**
Gerunds	**Simple Form**	I love **driving**.	I love **being driven**.
	Past Form	I regret **having spent** all my money.	I appreciate **having been given** a gift.
Infinitives	**Simple Form**	I expect **to attend** college.	I expect **to be admitted** to that college.
	Past Form	I expected **to have received** the letter by now.	I expected **to have been sent** the money by now.

■ 10. Noun Clauses

A **noun clause** allows you to place a statement and or a question inside a sentence. A noun clause occupies a position in a sentence that is usually occupied by a noun. It can be the subject of a sentence, the direct object of a verb, or the object of a preposition.

> **That Juan is friendly** is easy to see. (subject)

> Everyone knows **that Juan is friendly**. (direct object)

> Juan differs from his sister in **that he is friendly**. (object of a preposition)

Many noun clauses are the direct objects of verbs such as *know, believe, think,* or *say*. When a noun clause is the object of the verb, you can omit *that*.

> Everyone knows **Juan is friendly**.

That can join a noun clause to a sentence. A question word (*who, which,* etc.), an *-ever* word (*whoever, whichever*), or *whether* or *if* can also connect a noun clause to a sentence. Some clauses are introduced by a phrase like *the fact that* or *the idea that*.

> **That** some people steal is upsetting.
>
> **Who** stole the purse is **what** we want to know.
>
> **Whoever** took it should be punished.
>
> The police will find out **whether/if** the purse was taken by a neighbor.
>
> I am disturbed by **the idea that** someone would steal something from me.

10a. Reported Speech

You can use noun clauses to report statements and questions.

Reported Statements

When you change a quoted statement to a noun clause (reported speech), you may need to make two changes. Consider the following:

1. The point of view (pronoun) may change.

   > He says, "I am right." → He says that **he** is right.
   >
   > He says, "You are right." → He says that **I am/we are** right.

2. Reported speech is introduced with a reporting verb such as *say* or *write*. If the reporting verb is past tense (*said* or *wrote*), the verb tense in the reported speech usually changes.

   > She says, "The store sells coffee." → She **says** that the store **sells** coffee.
   >
   > She said, "The store sells coffee." → She **said** that the store **sold** coffee.

However, if you want to emphasize that the situation is continuing, you can use the present tense in the reported speech.

> She said, "The store sells coffee." → She **said** that the store **sells** coffee.

The following chart shows how verbs change after a past tense reporting verb like *said* or *wrote*.

Quoted Speech	Reported Speech
She said, "I exercise . . . ."	*She said she exercises/exercised . . . .
She said, "I am exercising . . . ."	She said she *was* exercising . . . .
She said, "I have exercised . . . ."	She said she *had* exercised . . . .
She said, "I exercised . . . ."	She said she *had* exercised . . . .
She said, "I was exercising . . . ."	She said she *had been* exercising . . . .
She said, "I had exercised . . . ."	**She said she had exercised . . . .

(continued)

Quoted Speech	Reported Speech
She said, "I was going to exercise . . . ."	She said she *had been* going to exercise . . . .
She said, "I will exercise . . . ."	She said she *would* exercise . . . .
She said, "I am going to exercise . . . ."	She said she *was* going to exercise . . . .
She said, "I can exercise . . . ."	She said she *could* exercise . . . .
She said, "I have to exercise . . . ."	She said she *had* to exercise . . . .
She said, "I may exercise . . . ."	She said she *might* exercise . . . .
She said, "I must exercise . . . ."	**She said she must exercise . . . .
She said, "I should exercise . . . ."	**She said she should exercise . . . .
She said, "I might exercise . . . ."	**She said she might exercise . . . .
She said, "I would exercise . . . ."	**She said she would exercise . . . .

*Statements in the simple present tense often do not change in reported speech because they refer to the past, present, and future.

**Statements in the past perfect tense (*had* + past participle) and verbs containing the modals *must, should, might,* and *would* do not change in reported speech.

Reported Questions

A noun clause can also report a question. Reported questions do not contain auxiliary verbs such as *do,* and so reported questions have the same word order and the same verb form as statements, subject + verb.

He asked me, "Where do you work?"

He asked me where I worked.

Introduce reported *yes/no* questions with *if, whether,* or *whether or not.*

He asked me, "Have you worked there very long?"

He asked me **if/whether/whether or not** I had worked there very long.

Reported Texts

When you report a dialogue or a series of statements using past tense reporting verbs, shift the tenses throughout the text. However, when you see a sentence in the text that describes a continuing or permanent situation, you may leave the verb in that sentence in the present tense. Sometimes either present or past tense is possible. Look at the boldface verbs in the dialogue and the reported dialogue that follows.

Dialogue

Sandra asked José, "**Did** you **find** the movie theater?"

José answered, "Yes, I **found** it easily, and I **saw** the movie called 'Up.' I **enjoyed** it. The animation **is** beautiful and the story **is** both funny and touching."

Sandra replied, "Really? **I may see** it, too, then."

Reported Dialogue

Sandra **asked** José if he **had found** the movie theater. José **said** he **had found** it easily and **had seen** the movie called "Up." He **added** that he **had enjoyed** it. He **mentioned** that the animation **is/was** beautiful and the story **is/was** both funny and touching. Sandra **said** she **might see** it, too.

EXERCISE 12

Read the dialogues and the reports of the dialogues that follow. As you read each report, find and correct the five errors in it. The first one has been done for you.

Dialogue 1

Julio: Is Haiti's Carnival like Carnival in Brazil?
Claude: It's similar, but not exactly the same. Both Haitian Carnival and Brazilian Carnival have music and dancing in the streets. The music at a Haitian Carnival celebration is called *ra-ra* rock. It's a mixture of traditional Haitian rhythms and techno-rock. People wear traditional Haitian costumes. Some of them paint their faces or wear masks. They enjoy all kinds of rich foods, like fried bananas.
Julio: Are you going to go back to Haiti sometime?
Claude: I've been saving money, and if possible, I will go next year for Carnival.

Report of Dialogue 1

¹Julio asked Claude if Haiti's Carnival is like Carnival in Brazil. ²Claude replied that it ~~was~~ is similar, but not exactly the same. ³He said both have music and dancing in the streets. ⁴He said the music at a Haitian Carnival celebration was called *ra-ra* rock, and it is a mixture of traditional Haitian rhythms and techno-rock. ⁵He added that people wore traditional costumes, and that some of them paint their faces or wear masks. ⁶Julio asked Claude if was he going to go back to Haiti sometime, and Claude replied that he had been saving money and, if possible, he will go next year for Carnival.

Dialogue 2

Giselle: Are you reading a novel?

Marie: I am reading an autobiography by Maya Angelou called <u>I Know Why the Caged Bird Sings</u>. The story is about Angelou's youth, which was difficult. Still, the book is uplifting. Although Angelou experienced a number of painful incidents in her early years, she became a confident person. In spite of racism, which was common in the 1940s, Angelou found work as a streetcar driver at age fifteen. It's a story that shows that people can overcome adversity.

Giselle: I am going to read that book because I enjoy coming-of-age stories and I like stories with a positive message.

Report of Dialogue 2

[1]Giselle asked Marie if she was reading a novel. [2]Marie said that she is reading an autobiography by Maya Angelou called <u>I Know Why the Caged Bird Sings</u>. [3]She went on to say that the story is about Angelou's youth, which was difficult, but the book is still uplifting. [4]Marie explained that although Angelou experienced a number of painful incidents in her early years, she becomes a confident person. [5]Marie added that, in spite of racism, which had been common in the 1940s, Angelou had found work as a streetcar driver at age fifteen. [6]Marie finished by saying that <u>I Know Why the Caged Bird Sings</u> is a story that shows that people could overcome adversity. [7]Giselle responded that she is going to read that book because she enjoys coming-of-age stories and liked stories with a positive message.

■ 11. Nouns

Nouns identify persons, places, objects, or ideas.

11a. Irregular Nouns

Some nouns have irregular plural forms.

> child, children
> man, men
> woman, women

Some nouns have special endings in both the singular and the plural.

> crisis, crises
> medium, media
> phenomenon, phenomena

Some nouns have only a plural form.

> belongings
> clothes
> manners

When you are unsure about the form of a noun, check your dictionary.

11b. Countable and Uncountable Nouns

Countable nouns can be made plural: *one statistic, two statistics*. Uncountable nouns are always singular. Generally speaking, English has three types of uncountable nouns:

> **MASS ITEMS**
> air, aluminum, oxygen, sand, water
>
> **GENERAL TERMS THAT REPRESENT CATEGORIES OF THINGS**
> equipment, furniture, jewelry, mail, transportation
>
> **ABSTRACT IDEAS**
> education, freedom, honesty, strength, wealth

Many nouns are both countable and uncountable. The choice of form depends on the meaning of the noun in a particular sentence.

> I ordered **two coffees** in the restaurant. **Coffee is** getting expensive.

When you are unsure about whether a noun is countable, uncountable, or both, check your dictionary.

11b.1. Expressions of Quantity with Countable and Uncountable Nouns

Some expressions of quantity are used only with uncountable nouns. Some are used only with countable nouns. Others are used with both.

> **USED WITH UNCOUNTABLE NOUNS**
> **a little** humor
> **quite a bit of** traffic
> not **much** time
>
> **USED WITH COUNTABLE NOUNS**
> **a** story
> **a few** joke**s**
> **several** idea**s**
> **quite a few** vehicle**s**
> not **many** minute**s**
>
> **USED WITH BOTH COUNTABLE AND UNCOUNTABLE NOUNS**
> **some** plant**s**, **some** vegetation
> **a lot of/a great deal of** fact**s**, **a lot of/a great deal of** information

You can use all of the expressions above—except the indefinite article *a*—with *of the* if the noun is definite (some *of the* plants, some *of the* vegetation).

■ 12. Prepositions

Prepositions are words that come before nouns, pronouns, and gerunds. Most prepositions refer to time (*at* ten o'clock, *in* the morning) or place (*by* the library, *on* the street). A few prepositions express logical relationships.

> **Because of/Due to/As a result of** the weather, the party was held indoors. (reason)

> **In spite of/Despite** the late hour, the guests did not seem ready to leave. (surprising result)

> **Like** the children, the adults enjoyed themselves. (similarity)

> **Unlike** the adults, the children did not get up and dance. (difference or contrast)

> The guests ate some food, **such as** sandwiches and chips. (example)

> **According to** my uncle, everyone had a good time. (citation)

Some prepositions (*as a result of, according to*, etc.) are more than one word.

A preposition always has a noun or pronoun object. A preposition, together with its object and any modifiers of that object, is called a **prepositional phrase**. Prepositional phrases can occur anywhere in a sentence and can modify nouns, verbs, or complete sentences. You can use prepositional phrases to add information to your sentences and make your writing more precise.

When you are not sure about the meaning or use of a preposition, look it up in your dictionary. If you are not sure which preposition should follow a particular verb, adjective, or noun, look up the verb, adjective, or noun in your dictionary.

■ 13. Pronouns

Pronouns replace nouns and noun phrases. You can use pronouns to avoid repetition and to create links between sentences. English has four kinds of pronouns (subject, object, reflexive, and possessive) and possessive adjectives, which are similar to pronouns.

Subject Pronouns	Object Pronouns	Reflexive Pronouns	Possessive Pronouns	Possessive Adjectives
I	me	myself	mine	my
you	you	yourself, yourselves	yours	your
he	him	himself	his	his
she	her	herself	hers	her
it	it	itself	its	its
we	us	ourselves	ours	our
they	them	themselves	theirs	their

13a. Pronoun Agreement

Pronouns not only replace nouns and noun phrases but also refer back to them. That means pronouns make your writing cohesive (full of well-connected ideas). A pronoun usually refers to a noun in the same sentence or the preceding sentence.

> I took some pictures of the governor's old house. (It) is a two-story wooden structure.

Pronouns must agree in person and number with the nouns they refer to.

>   **They**   **them**
> I showed the photographs to Henri and Paul. ~~He~~ enjoyed ~~it~~.

They refers to *Henri and Paul*, and so must be plural. *Them*, which refers to *photographs*, must also be plural.

EXERCISE 13
As you read this paragraph, find and correct the <u>eight</u> errors in pronoun agreement. The first one has been done for you.

¹Ann Landers published a popular newspaper column in the United States that helped people solve ~~his~~ **their** problems with relationships, health, and etiquette. ²In the column, Landers printed people's letters and her responses to it. ³Landers's replies were honest, sympathetic, and practical. ⁴For

example, a married woman wrote saying that she and her parents could not enjoy their monthly visits because her husband did not get along with her parents. ⁵Landers advised the woman to leave their husband home and "make everyone happy." ⁶When a single woman wrote that, upon returning from vacation, she had found that her steady boyfriend was dating someone else, Landers advised them to "do some looking around herself." ⁷Because readers felt Landers' advice made sense, he trusted her. ⁸Her column was so popular that they continued for forty-six years, 1,000 newspapers carried them, and many readers even asked her local newspapers to continue printing it after Landers's death.

13b. Pronoun Reference

Every pronoun must refer to something. The first and second person pronouns (*I*, *we*, *you*) refer to the writer and reader or the community of readers and writers. The third person pronouns (*he, she, it, they*) refer back to a noun or noun phrase mentioned earlier in the text. Two errors can occur with the third person pronouns.

ERROR 1 A pronoun refers back to more than one noun.

INCORRECT: Paula told Karina the story. Then **she** told it to me.

Who does *she* refer to? It is not clear whether it refers to Paula or Karina.

CORRECT: Paula told Karina the story. Then ~~she~~ Karina told it to me.

ERROR 2 A pronoun does not refer back clearly to any one noun in the text.

INCORRECT: The school has a new rule. **They** say that students who are tardy must go directly to the office.

Who does the pronoun *they* refer back to? The pronoun *they* has no referent, or noun to refer back to.

CORRECT: The school has a new rule. ~~They say~~ It says that students who are late must go directly to the office.

INCORRECT: Many violent crimes were committed in this city last year. The residents are concerned about **it**.

What does the pronoun *it* refer back to? To correct this problem, change *it* to a noun.

CORRECT: Many violent crimes were committed in this city last year. The residents are concerned about ~~it~~ this situation.

In some cases, you can use the pronoun *it* as the subject of a sentence without a noun to refer back to.

> *It* is cloudy today.

> *It* is important to study for tests.

> *It* is a well-known fact that eating too much salt is unhealthy.

EXERCISE 14
As you read this paragraph, underline all the pronouns and possessive adjectives. Then find and correct the <u>five</u> pronoun reference problems. The first three sentences have been done for you.

[1]Louis Braille's development of a writing system for blind people was the result of a series of events—some of them unfortunate—in <u>his</u> life. [2]At age four, Louis picked up a sharp tool called an awl that belonged to <u>his</u> father. [3]~~He~~ Louis injured one of <u>his</u> eyes with the awl. [4]The eye became seriously infected. [5]Then the infection spread to the other eye, and he lost sight in both eyes. [6]In 1819, Louis's family sent him to a school for the blind, where the students were taught to read by running their fingers over embossed letters. [7]It was very difficult. [8]In 1821, a soldier visited the school and showed them a military code. [9]It was called "night writing," and it consisted of a rather complicated arrangement of raised dots. [10]He was 12 years old, and he was extremely interested in the code. [11]He studied it and managed to simplify it, creating a system that would allow blind students to not only read but also write. [12]Unfortunately, few people, even among the teachers at the school, recognized the value of his system. [13]One teacher even prohibited them from using it. [14]Nonetheless, Louis and the other students continued to use the code in secret. [15]Years later, as an adult, Louis Braille became a teacher at the school where he had been a student. [16]He taught his students how to read and write using the system he had developed, which came to be known as Braille.

13c. Pronouns that Play Special Roles in Cohesion

One and *another* and *this* and *these* play an important role in **cohesion**. These pronouns, which also function as adjectives, can help you draw readers' attention to your important ideas and create links between the key points in your paragraphs and essays.

13c.1. *One, Another, the Other*

To present items or ideas in a series, use the indefinite pronouns **one**, **another**, **some**, and **others**. If a series has a final item or items, use the definite pronouns **the other** or **the others**. This chart shows the pronouns and their corresponding adjectives.

	First in a Series	Following in the Series	Last in the Series
Singular Pronouns (and Adjectives)	First, here is **one** (*one* coin).	Next, here is **another** (*another* coin).	Finally, this is **the other** (*the other* coin).
Plural Pronouns (and Adjectives)	First, here are **some** (*some* coins).	Next, here are **others** (*other* coins).	Finally, these are **the others** (*the other* coins).

Note that the pronouns *others* and *the others* have a plural form, but the adjectives *other* and *the other* do not.

EXERCISE 15

As you read this paragraph, find and correct the <u>five</u> errors in the use of another, other, the other, others, *and* the others. *The first one has been done for you.*

¹A friend of mine collects musical instruments from all over the world. ²In his collection, he has three stringed, three wind, and seven percussion instruments. ³The stringed instruments are varied. ⁴Two of them are lutes. ⁵One is a large lute from Syria with delicate inlaid decorations on its face.
The other
⁶~~Another~~ lute is a Chinese san xian, which has a long slender neck and only three strings. ⁷The third stringed instrument is a triangular balalaika from Russia. ⁸Like the san xian, it has only three strings, but unlike a lute, it has a flat back like a guitar. ⁹The wind instruments are also interesting. ¹⁰My friend has a set of panpipes from the Andes in Peru which makes a series of sweet, high sounds. ¹¹The others wind instruments are two didgeridoos made by the Aborigines of Australia which produce haunting vibrating

sounds. [12]One digeridoo is about a meter and a half long, and other is about a meter in length. [13]The seven percussion instruments are my favorites. [14]Three are carved wooden drums from Africa that were made by hollowing out sections of tree trunks. [15]The other is a steel pan from Jamaica which was created by pounding the top of a steel drum until it had the shape of a shallow bowl. [16]Finally, other are three leather drums made by Native Americans. [17]My friend's collection illustrates the wonderful variety of instrument forms in the world and the range of sounds that people can make with them.

13c.2. *This, That, These, Those*

To refer back to items or ideas that were mentioned previously in a text, use *this*, *that*, *these*, and *those*. These words are both adjectives and pronouns.

> ADJ.
> The teacher selected three students as reporters. **Those** students had to write down the main points presented by both sides in the debate.

> ADJ.
> The computer is fast, reliable, and moderately priced. **These** features have made it very popular.

The pronoun *this* often refers to an idea that has been expressed in a complete clause or sentence.

> PRON.
> We are cutting down the rain forests. **This** will lead to global climate change.

■ 14. Sentences

To write correct, effective sentences, you need to be able to identify sentence parts and their functions.

14a. Parts of Speech

The parts of speech are identified in the following sections of Appendix IA.

Adjectives—section 2	Nouns—section 11
Adverbs—section 4	Prepositions—section 12
Articles—section 5	Pronouns—section 13
Conjunctions—sections 3, 7	Verbs—section 15

*Identify the part of speech of each of the underlined words in these sentences as noun (**n.**), verb (**v.**), adjective (**adj.**), adverb (**adv.**), pronoun (**pron.**), preposition (**prep.**), or conjunction (**conj.**). The first one has been done for you.*

(n.)
[1]When <u>children</u> have normal contact <u>with</u> adults, they learn language in a fairly predictable way. [2]Most babies say their <u>first</u> word, usually *Mama* or *Da-da*, before they are one year old. [3]At this time, <u>they</u> also respond appropriately to basic questions. [4]If <u>someone</u> asks, *Where's the ball?* they will look for the ball. [5]<u>When</u> they reach eighteen months, they may begin to make two-word sentences <u>like</u> *Book here* or *Want milk*. [6]They can <u>usually</u> answer simple questions, too. [7]After children are two years old, they are <u>eager</u> to have <u>longer</u> conversations, although they frequently respond to questions with *No*. [8]Until children reach age three, they don't use past tense verbs. [9]<u>However</u>, three-year-olds can talk <u>about</u> where they went and what they did today. [10]If someone tells them a story, they can remember <u>and</u> repeat it. [11]Year by year, children's language <u>becomes</u> increasingly complex while they grow.

14b. Sentence Parts

Every sentence has a subject and a verb. Without both, you do not have a sentence.

Subjects

The subject is usually before the verb. The subject tells who or what the sentence is about. If the verb is an action verb, the subject also tells who or what performs the action.

Verbs

The verb describes an action or a condition. The verb of a sentence answers questions about the subject, such as *What did the subject do?* or *What is the state or condition of the subject?*

Transitive and Intransitive Verbs

Some action verbs require a direct object (*she said* **her name**), but others do not (*she spoke*). A dictionary can tell you whether a verb is **transitive** (requires a direct object) or **intransitive** (does not require a direct object) or whether it can be either.

Linking Verbs

English has two groups of verbs: **action verbs** such as *make* and *walk* and **linking verbs** such as *be, become, seem, appear, sound,* and *feel*. Action verbs are either transitive (*we made the dinner*) or intransitive (*we walked*), but linking verbs follow another pattern. Linking verbs are followed by nouns or adjectives that say something about the subject. These noun or adjective modifiers are called **complements**.

NOUN
COMPLEMENT
She is a translator.

ADJECTIVE
COMPLEMENT
She seems intelligent.

Sentences

The following examples show the basic sentence parts.

VERB
Listen. (The subject, *you*, is understood.)

SUBJECT   VERB
The music is playing.

SUBJECT VERB   DIR. OBJ.
Margarita teaches jazz band.

SUBJECT VERB   DIR. OBJ.   INDIR. OBJ.
Margarita teaches jazz band to high school students.

SUBJECT   VERB   COMPLEMENT   SUBJECT VERB COMPLEMENT
The concert will be very interesting. The music will be modern jazz.

EXERCISE 17
In this paragraph, put <u>one line</u> under the subject(s) and <u>two lines</u> under the verb(s) in each sentence. The first one has been done for you.

[1]<u>Stephane Grappelli</u> <u><u>was</u></u> a jazz violinist. [2]Born in Paris in 1908, Grapelli lost his mother at three years old and spent his childhood in orphanages. [3]At age 12, he and his father were reunited, and his father bought him his first violin. [4]First, Grappelli studied classical violin, but he preferred jazz. [5]He liked making up his own music as he played rather than playing from someone else's score. [6]The sounds of the street musicians of Paris and of the jazz musicians from the United States, especially the jazz violinist Joe Venuti, appealed to him. [7]In 1933, Grappelli helped to form the Quintet of the Hot Club of Paris. [8]The Quintet made dozens of recordings, and Grappelli's career as a jazz musician lasted over 60 years. [9]During his long career, Grappelli recorded music with many famous artists.

14c. Phrase or Clause

A **phrase** is a group of two or more words that does not contain both a subject and a verb. English has various kinds of phrases: adjective phrases, adverb phrases, noun phrases, prepositional phrases, and verb phrases.

> an unexpected telephone call (noun phrase)
> at 9:00 in the morning (prepositional phrase)
> was waiting to board the plane (verb phrase)

A **clause** is a group of words that contains a subject and a verb. A clause can be **independent** (a complete sentence) or **dependent** (not a complete sentence). English has three kinds of dependent clauses: **adjective clauses** (see page 229), **adverb clauses** (see page 239), and **noun clauses** (see page 258).

14d. Sentence Types

Three types of English sentences are simple, compound, and complex. **Simple sentences** have **one independent clause** and no dependent clauses.

> Euclid invented geometry.

A simple sentence may have a compound subject and/or a compound verb.

> Alexander Fleming, Ernst Chain, and Howard Florey discovered, purified, and produced penicillin.

Compound sentences have **two or more independent clauses** and no dependent clauses.

> INDEPENDENT CLAUSE   INDEPENDENT CLAUSE
> Henry Ford did not invent the automobile, but he developed the assembly line.

Complex sentences have **one or more independent clauses** and **one or more dependent clauses**.

> INDEPENDENT CLAUSE
> Alexander Graham Bell is given credit for the invention of the telephone,
>
> DEPENDENT CLAUSE
> although Elisha Gray and Thomas Edison were also working on the telephone at the same time.

14e. Logical Connectors

Logical connectors show meaningful relationships (cause and effect, contrast, time, etc.) between sentence parts. English has four types of logical connectors.

- **Coordinating conjunctions** (*and*, *but*, *for*, *nor*, *or*, *so*, and *yet*) connect two or more independent clauses in compound sentences. (See Coordination, page 252.)
- **Subordinating conjunctions** (*after*, *because*, *while*, etc.) connect a subordinate clause to a main (independent) clause in a sentence. (See Adverb Clauses, page 239.)

- **The adverbs known as transitions** (*for example*, *however*, *therefore*, etc.) show logical relationships but do <u>not</u> connect clauses as coordinating and subordinating conjunctions do. (See Adverbs, page 245.)
- **Prepositions** (*because of*, *in spite of*, *such as*, etc.) show logical relationships within clauses. (See Prepositions, page 264.)

Meanings	Coordinating Conjunctions	Subordinating Conjunctions	Transitions	Prepositions
addition	and	—	also furthermore in addition moreover	in addition to
cause and effect (See also page 82 in Chapter 3.)	for so	as because since	consequently	as a result of because of due to
contrast (See also pages 122 and 147 in Chapter 4.)	but	whereas while	by comparison however in contrast on the other hand	unlike
similarity (See also pages 122 and 146 in Chapter 4.)	—	(just) as	likewise similarly	like
surprising result*	but yet	although even though though	however nevertheless nonetheless	despite in spite of
time sequence	—	after as soon as before by the time once	afterward next then	—

*Surprising result refers to a special kind of contrast—the contrast between what you expect to happen and the result that actually occurs.

I didn't study, **but/yet** I did well on the test. (I expected to do poorly.)

Although/Even though/Though I didn't study, I did well on the test.

I didn't study. **However/Nevertheless/Nonetheless**, I did well on the test.

Despite/In spite of my failure to study, I did well on the test.

14f. Subject-Verb Agreement

A subject and verb must agree in number. Singular subjects require singular verbs, and plural subjects require plural verbs.

> The student ask**s** questions.

> The student**s** ask questions.

RULE 1 If a sentence begins with **There**, the *be* verb always agrees in number with the noun that follows it.

> There **is** a **reception** in the hotel.

When a series of nouns follows the *be* verb, the verb agrees with the first noun in the series.

> There **are photographers**, a newspaper reporter, and officials at the reception.

> There **is** a **newspaper reporter**, photographers, and officials at the reception.

RULE 2 Phrases or clauses that come between the subject and verb do not affect subject-verb agreement.

> One **guest** at the reception for the employees of the consulate **is** a reporter.

> The **reporter**, as well as her husband and two daughters, **was** invited by a consular official.

RULE 3 A gerund subject is singular.

> News **reporting is** an exciting career.

RULE 4 When compound subjects are joined by the correlative conjunctions *either . . . or . . ., neither . . . nor . . .*, and *not only . . . but (also) . . .*, the verb agrees with the part of the subject that is closest to it.

> Neither the radio stations nor the television **station is** expected to be here.

> Not only the governor but also several **members** of his cabinet **are** attending the reception.

When compound subjects are joined by the correlative conjunctions *both . . . and . . .*, the verb is always plural.

> Both the **press** and the **guests are** going to enjoy themselves.

RULE 5 Some pronouns and adjectives are always singular.

> **One** of the cabinet members **is** late.

> **Every** member/**Every** one of the members **is** expected to attend the reception.

> **Everyone/Everybody is** expected to be there.

> **Each** person/**Each** of the people **has** been invited.

> Do you think **anyone/someone is** going to make a speech?

> **No one has** spoken yet.

EXERCISE 18

As you read this passage, find and correct <u>fourteen</u> subject-verb agreement errors. The first one has been done for you.

[1]Every person *needs* ~~need~~ a certain amount of sleep every night, but individuals vary in the actual amount they requires. [2]Some adults can get by on six hours, while others needs about nine. [3]Sleep research indicate that the amount of sleep that an individual requires for good physical health cannot be changed.

[4]Not only the body but also the brain benefit from a good night's sleep. [5]Using an electroencephalograph to measure brain waves, scientists have studied the sleeping brain. [6]They have found that sleep consist of two stages, REM and non-REM sleep. [7]During REM (rapid eye movement) sleep, there is intense brain activity, and dreaming are more likely to occur than during non-REM sleep. [8]Scientists believe that in REM sleep, the moving eyes follows the activity of the brain. [9]They also think that REM sleep play an important role in consolidating memories. [10]Perhaps that is why the person who stay up late the night before a test do not perform as well as the person who gets a good night's sleep.

[11]Anyone who have trouble sleeping should maintain a regular sleep schedule. [12]Getting enough physical exercise also help people sleep well. [13]Sleep is vital for health and well-being, so everyone need to make sure to get his or her share.

14g. Sentence Problems

Run-on sentences and fragments are sentence structure errors.

Run-on Sentences

A run-on sentence is a pair of sentences (two independent clauses) that are written as one sentence.

INCORRECT: Mario wants to buy a house in the future he is working at two jobs.

Adding a comma between the two sentences does not correct the problem.

INCORRECT: Mario wants to buy a house in the future, he is working at two jobs.

Three Ways to Correct Run-on Sentences

1. Use a period and a capital letter to mark the sentence boundary.

   Mario wants to buy a house in the future. ~~he~~ ^H is working at two jobs.

2. Combine the sentences using a coordinating or a subordinating conjunction.

   Mario wants to buy a house in the future, *so* he is working at two jobs.

   Because Mario wants to buy a house in the future, he is working at two jobs.

3. Use a semicolon to mark the sentence boundary.

   Mario wants to buy a house in the future; he is working at two jobs.

You can add a transition to make the logical relationship clear.

   Mario wants to buy a house in the future; *therefore*, he is working at two jobs.

EXERCISE 19

As you read this passage, find and correct __eight__ run-on sentences, using all three correction strategies. The first one has been done for you.

[1]Body language is the silent communication of gestures, facial expressions, eye behavior, and posture. [2]^Bbody language communicates information about people's thoughts, feelings, identities, and relationships. [3]Some body-language signals are learned these signals vary from culture to culture. [4]Waving good-bye, nodding the head in agreement, and bowing to show respect are examples of culture-specific signals. [5]Other body-language signals are universal. [6]Smiling with happiness, tightening the fists with anger, and stiffening the shoulders in fear are examples of universal signals, people everywhere use these signals, often unconsciously.

[7]When people are unaware of their body language, they may unintentionally send the wrong message for example, at a job interview, a nervous interviewee may unknowingly send signals that will hurt her chances of getting hired. [8]Due to stress, the interviewee may appear stone-faced, not smiling even when she greets the interviewer. [9]This could send the message that she cannot relate to people socially or that she may not fit in at the company. [10]She may fidget, tapping her fingers or touching her jewelry,

this could send the message that she is not really interested in the job. [11]She may look at the floor she may fail to make sufficient eye contact with the interviewer. [12]In the business culture of the United States, this could send the message that the interviewee does not respect the interviewer it might even be interpreted as a sign of dishonesty.

[13]Anyone can become more aware of nonverbal communication by studying other people in conversation in particular, one should observe how people adapt their body language to specific situations, such as the job interview. [14]By learning about body language, people can improve their communication with others.

Fragments

A fragment is an incomplete sentence. There are four kinds of fragments.

1. A dependent clause

   INCORRECT: When the boss was in the office.

2. A participial phrase (an *-ing* or *-ed* phrase)

   INCORRECT: Running into the office at 9:15.

3. An infinitive phrase (*to* + verb)

   INCORRECT: To attend the meeting.

4. A noun or verb with attached phrases or dependent clauses

   INCORRECT: The responsible person who had come early, made coffee, and turned on all the machines.

Three Ways to Correct Fragments

1. Change the fragment to an independent clause.

   T
   ~~When t~~he boss was in the office.

2. Combine the fragment with another sentence.

   S
   When the boss was in the office., She was usually in a meeting.

3. Add an independent clause to the fragment.

   The boss had come early that day to attend the meeting.

   Running into the office at 9:15, *I thanked Marco*.

   Marco was the responsible person who had come early, made coffee, and turned on all the machines.

Exercise 20

As you read this paragraph, find and correct the __eight__ fragments, using all three correction strategies. The first one has been done for you.

¹Scientists have developed computers. ~~T~~*t*hat can match the best chess players in the world. ²Garry Kasparov, who was the top-ranked chess player in the world for nineteen years. ³In 1997, in a six-game match. Kasparov was narrowly defeated by "Deep Blue," IBM's chess-playing computer. ⁴Kasparov remarked after the match that the challenge for a human playing a computer is that the computer never gets tired. ⁵Five and a half years after his tournament with Deep Blue. Kasparov faced "Deep Junior." ⁶Had been programmed by Israeli scientists. ⁷This match ended in a tie, 3 to 3. ⁸Deep Junior, while not as fast as Deep Blue, played more like a human being. ⁹At times giving up pieces to gain an advantage in position on the board. ¹⁰The most recently developed chess-playing computer is "Deep Fritz." ¹¹Programmed by German scientists. Deep Fritz is said to be superior to both Deep Blue and Deep Junior. ¹²Undoubtedly, in the future even better chess-playing computers.

■ 15. Verbs

To express your ideas clearly in English, you need to understand English verbs. Using English verbs requires knowing tenses, active and passive forms, modal verbs, and phrasal verbs.

15a. Verb Tenses

The twelve English verb tenses fall into three time frames—past, present, and future. The third person singular form of the regular verb *clean* is shown in active voice and passive voice in the following chart. Note that the passive is not used in every one of the twelve tenses.

	Tense	Active Voice	Passive Voice
Present Time Frame	simple present	cleans	is cleaned
	present progressive	is cleaning	is being cleaned
	present perfect	has cleaned	has been cleaned
	present perfect progressive	has been cleaning	—
Past Time Frame	simple past	cleaned	was cleaned
	past progressive	was cleaning	was being cleaned
	past perfect	had cleaned	had been cleaned
	past perfect progressive	had been cleaning	—
Future Time Frame	simple future	will/is going to clean	will/is going to be cleaned
	future progressive	will be cleaning	—
	future perfect	will have cleaned	will have been cleaned
	future perfect progressive	will have been cleaning	—

Remember that English has many irregular verbs. Use a dictionary or a handbook to find out if a verb is irregular and to learn its past tense and past participle.

This passage contains active verbs in the past, present, and future time frames. Find and correct <u>three</u> verb tense errors in each paragraph. When corrected, the passage should contain all the verb tenses. The first error has been corrected for you.

[1]My house stands on a small hill, about a quarter mile from my nearest neighbor's house. [2]It ~~was~~ ^{is} a small wood-frame structure, and it has withstood some very powerful storms. [3]I take very good care of my house. [4]I have painted it outside and inside every three years since I move in. [5]Right now I replace the front porch, which has become rotten with age.

[6]My grandfather built this house fifty years ago. [7]At the time he built it, he and my grandmother had only one child, but they were planning to have a large family. [8]My grandmother give birth to my father, her second child, after they were moving into the house. [9]In subsequent years, she and my grandfather have had five more children, and they raised them all in this house.

[10]By the time summer is coming this year, my wife and I will have been living in this house ten years. [11]In the next few weeks, we will be planting our vegetable garden. [12]We will already finish preparing the soil several days earlier. [13]If we will be lucky, we will harvest a lot of fruits and vegetables this summer.

15b. Modal Verbs

Modals are auxiliaries (helping verbs) that allow you to add various meanings, such as possibility, probability, or necessity, to verbs. Some modals, such as *may* and *can*, have more than one meaning. Most modals have a present form and a past form, and many have progressive forms as well. In some cases, there are differences in meaning between the present and the past forms.

Modal	Present and Future Form and Meaning(s)	Past Form and Meaning(s)
may	**POSSIBILITY** Ping **may attend/may be attending** college now. Ping **may attend** college next year.	**PAST POSSIBILITY** Ping's older sister **may have attended/may have been attending** college in 2002.
	PERMISSION Students **may use** a dictionary during the test.	
	REQUEST **May** I **see** your ticket?	
might	**POSSIBILITY** Ping **might attend/might be attending** college now. Ping **might attend** college next year.	**PAST POSSIBILITY** Ping's older sister **might have attended/might have been attending** college in 2002.
must	**PROBABILITY OR INFERENCE (NEAR 100% CERTAINTY)** The woman is wearing a white coat. She **must be** a doctor. She **must be working** now.	**PAST PROBABILITY (NEAR 100% CERTAINTY)** Louisa is a doctor. She **must have studied/must have been studying** very hard in school.
	STRONG NECESSITY Your application is due today, so you **must turn** it **in**.	Note: Use *had* to for past necessity.
have to, have got to	**NECESSITY** She **has to/has got to** turn in the application today.	**PAST NECESSITY** She **had to** turn in the application yesterday. Note: **Have got to** has no past form.
had better	**STRONG RECOMMENDATION** You **had better take** your medicine so that you will get well.	Note: Use *should have* + past participle for the past.

(continued)

Modal	Present and Future Form and Meaning(s)	Past Form and Meaning(s)
should, ought to	**RECOMMENDATION OR ADVISABILITY** You **should do/should be doing/ought to do/ought to be doing** your homework now.	**PAST ADVISABILITY** You **should have done/ should have been doing** your homework yesterday, but you didn't/weren't, so you will lose points.
	EXPECTATION There are dark gray clouds overhead, so it **should start/ ought to start** to rain any minute.	**PAST EXPECTATION** The letter **should have arrived** yesterday, but it didn't. Note: **Ought to** is not common in the past.
be supposed to	**EXPECTATION** The teacher **is supposed to be** in class now.	**PAST EXPECTATION** The teacher **was supposed to be** in class ten minutes ago.
be able to	**ABILITY** My daughter **is able to read now**.	**PAST ABILITY** My daughter **was able to read** at age five.
can	**ABILITY** My daughter **can read** now.	**PAST ABILITY** My daughter **could read** at age five. Note: Use *could* only for past abilities that lasted for a period of time. For a short-term ability in the past, use *was able* to (I was not the fastest runner in the race, but on that day I *was able* to beat the other runners.).
	POSSIBILITY IN GENERAL STATEMENTS It **can rain** here in June.	
	PERMISSION Students **can use** a dictionary during the test.	
	REQUEST **Can** I **see** your ticket?	

Modal	Present and Future Form and Meaning(s)	Past Form and Meaning(s)
could	**POSSIBILITY** If the neighbors' house is dark, they **could be sleeping**. The letter I am waiting for **could arrive** tomorrow. **REQUEST** **Could** I **see** your ticket? **SUGGESTION** You **could fly** to New York if you don't have time to go by train.	**PAST POSSIBILITY** If the neighbors' house was dark, they **could have been sleeping**. Note: In the past negative, *could* expresses near certainty. The *letter could not have arrived yesterday* = It is (almost) impossible that the letter arrived yesterday.
would	**REQUEST** **Would** you **show** me your ticket? I **would like** a drink of water. **UNREAL CONDITIONAL** I **would buy** the car if I had money.	**PAST UNREAL CONDITIONAL** I **would have bought** the car if I had had money.

15c. Verb Form Problems

Verbs have three parts: the **base** (*clean*), the **present participle** (-*ing* form, *cleaning*), and the **past participle** (-*ed* form, *cleaned*). These three parts combine with endings (-*s* and -*ed*) and auxiliaries (*is, has,* etc.) to make all possible verbs.

Base Form

Use the **base form** in the simple present and simple future tenses (*clean, will clean, is/are going to clean*), in present modal verbs (*may clean*), and in the infinitive (*to clean*).

Present Participle

Use the **present participle** or **-*ing* form** in the progressive tenses in the active voice (*is cleaning, has been cleaning, was cleaning, had been cleaning, will be cleaning, will have been cleaning*) and in progressive modal verbs (*may be cleaning*).

Past Participle

Use the **-*ed* form** in the perfect tenses in the active voice (*has cleaned, had cleaned, will have cleaned*), in all tenses in the passive voice (*is cleaned,* etc.), and in past modal verbs (*may have cleaned*) and passive modals (*may have been cleaned*).

Some Common Verb Form Errors

Error 1 The base form is not used in a modal verb.

rain
It might ~~rains~~ tonight.

Error 2 The base form is not used in an infinitive.

marry
This is the woman he chose to ~~married~~.

Error 3 The present participle is not used in a progressive tense.

enjoying
Meanwhile, they were ~~enjoy~~ themselves at the party.

Error 4 The past participle is not used in a perfect tense.

developed
They have ~~develop~~ a new plan.

Error 5 The past participle is not used in the passive voice.

saved
A great deal of money was ~~save~~.

Exercise 22

As you read this passage, find and correct <u>ten</u> verb form errors which reflect the five problems listed above. The first one has been done for you.

may erupt
[1]A volcano ~~may erupts~~ about every 100 years. [2]In between eruptions, a volcano may appear quiet, but actually it is changes constantly. [3]Inside, there is always great pressure as liquid rock, called *magma*, moves upward from deep inside the Earth. [4]This upward pressure causes the volcano to expands outward and upward. [5]As the volcano grows, loose rock falls down its sides.

[6]Before May 1980, Mount St. Helens in Washington State had been quiet for over 100 years. [7]It had been calling "the Fuji of America" because its symmetrical cone resembled the famous volcano in Japan. [8]Its massive eruption on Sunday, May 20, 1980, changed that shape. [9]Mount St. Helens lost 3.7 billion cubic yards of rock. [10]Volcanic ash was send fifteen miles into the air, and very hot winds blew in all directions. [11]Two hundred thirty square miles of forest were flatten. [12]Seventy percent of the snow and ice on the mountain melted, causing an enormous landslide of mud, volcanic ash, rocks, and trees to speeding down the mountain at 500 miles per hour. [13]In the eruption, fifty-seven people lost their lives, some as far away as thirteen miles from the mountain. [14]Most of them were scientists, loggers, and journalists.

[15]On August 27, 1982, an area of 110,000 acres around the volcano was designated as the Mount St. Helens National Volcanic Monument. [16]Over the years since, visitors to the monument have observe the regrowth of plants and the return of wildlife to the area. [17]Scientists know that, deep within the mountain, changes are continually occur, but no one knows when Mount St. Helens might erupted again.

15d. Phrasal Verbs and Particles

Some verbs combine with prepositions to create new meanings. These prepositions are called **particles**, and the verb + preposition combination is called a **phrasal verb**. Here are some examples.

> I **ran into** a friend. (met)
>
> We **called off** the picnic because of the rain. (canceled)

Some phrasal verbs can be separated by their objects.

> I **looked up** a word. → I **looked** a word **up**.
>
> I **turned in** my homework. → I **turned** my homework **in**.

Other phrasal verbs cannot be separated.

> She **looks after** her younger sister.
>
> The party **turned out** well.

To find out which particles can combine with a verb and what new meanings are created by those combinations, look the verb up in a dictionary.

■ 16. Word Choice

English, like other languages, has a rich and varied vocabulary. Some words are appropriate in formal situations, and some are appropriate in informal situations. Compare the following sentences.

> That **gentleman** spoke with the **police officer**.
>
> That **dude** spoke with the **cop**.

The choice of formal words (*gentleman* and *police officer*) or informal words (*dude* and *cop*) greatly affects the meaning of a sentence, so you must consider formality and informality when you choose words. Academic and business writing are formal, so you should not use informal language in these types of writing.

A good dictionary can tell you whether a word is formal, informal, or **slang** (an informal word used by a specific group of people, usually young people).

■ 17. Word Families

English has many **word families**, or groups of related words, such as the following.

love

lovable

loveless

unlovable

A word family shares a common **root** (in the example above, *love*) to which **prefixes** (such as *un-*) and **suffixes** (such as *-able* and *-less*) are added. A prefix, which attaches to the beginning of a word, adds meaning. A suffix, which attaches to the end of a word, tells what part of speech the word is. Word-family members with different suffixes are called **word forms**.

Knowing prefixes and suffixes is important to you as a writer. Prefixes and suffixes expand your vocabulary and help you choose the right word forms for your sentences.

17a. Prefixes

The following chart lists some common **prefixes** and their meanings. Some prefixes have more than one meaning.

Prefixes	Meanings	Examples
anti-	against	antiwar
com-, con-, co-	with	company, connect, co-pay
contra-	against	contradict
de-	from	deduct
dis-	not, apart	dislike, disconnect
ex-	out from, former	exhale, ex-president
extra-	outside, beyond	extraordinary
il-, im-, ir-	not	illogical, impossible, irrelevant
in-	not, into	insecure, inhale
inter-	between	international
intra-	within	intramural
mal-	bad, badly	malfunction
mis-	not, wrongly	misunderstand
post-	after	postpone

Prefixes	Meanings	Examples
pre-	before	preview
pro-	forward	progress
re-	again	review
super-	over, above, extra	supervision
trans-	across, over, through	transfer
un-	not	unable
uni-	one, undivided	unified

17b. Suffixes

The following chart lists some common noun, verb, adjective, and adverb **suffixes**.

Noun Suffixes	**-ance, -ence**	appearance, independence
	-er, -ar, -or	worker, burglar, actor
	-ment	employment
	-ness	happiness
	-ship	friendship
	-sion, -tion	invasion, recommendation
	-y, -ity	harmony, electricity
Verb Suffixes	**-ate**	investigate
	-en	brighten
	-ify	beautify
	-ize	modernize
Adjective Suffixes	**-able, -ible**	usable, responsible
	-al	musical
	-ful	delightful
	-ive	defensive
	-less	humorless
	-ious, -ous	serious, generous
Adverb Suffix	**-ly**	responsibly

Appendix IB: Punctuation and Capitalization

■ 1. Apostrophe

The **apostrophe** has two uses: possessives and contractions.

1a. Possessives

With singular nouns, show possession with the **apostrophe + s**.

> a student**'s** composition
> Aiko**'s** laptop computer
> Klaus**'s** notebook

With plural nouns, show possession with the apostrophe alone.

> all the students**'** compositions
> the Parks**'** house

(Note that to refer to two or more members of a family or to a husband and wife, place *the* before the last name, and add *-s* to the last name. For example, *Mr. and Mrs. Park* are referred to as *the Parks*.)

When two or more nouns are joined by *and*, the last noun in the series shows possession.

> Mr. and Mrs. Park**'s** house
> Juana, Leyla, and Fatima**'s** group assignment

In general, do *not* use the apostrophe + s to show that a thing possesses another thing. Use a noun modifier or a prepositional phrase instead.

> the house's windows → *the house windows* or *the windows of the house*
> the classroom's computer → *the classroom computer* or *the computer in the classroom*

1b. Contractions

In informal letters and written dialogue, you can contract (shorten) the words *am, has, have, had, is, not, will*, and *would* by omitting letters and using the apostrophe to show the omission. Here are some common contractions.

I am → I'm	we have → we've	did not → didn't
she is → she's	you had → you'd	will not → won't
he has → he's	they would → they'd	

Note that contractions are usually *not* used in formal writing such as college papers, letters of application, or business letters and memos.

■ 2. Capital Letters

Use **capital letters** in the following nine situations.

1. The first word in a sentence or a quotation

   He said, "**D**inner is ready."

2. Proper names of people, places, and things

   Gustave **E**iffel designed the **E**iffel **T**ower in **P**aris.

3. The names of organizations and people's official titles when used with their names

   The speech was given by **S**ecretary-**G**eneral of the **U**nited **N**ations **B**an **K**i-moon to the **I**nternational **A**tomic **E**nergy **A**gency.

   Do *not* capitalize unless proper names are used.

   The ~~P~~rincipal of our ~~H~~igh ~~S~~chool asked us to support the ~~S~~occer ~~C~~oach.
   (corrections above: p, h, s, s, c)

4. The names of companies and their products

   Microsoft developed a computer operating system called **W**indows.

5. Days of the week, months, and holidays

   Sunday **S**eptember 16 will be **I**ndependence **D**ay.

   Do *not* capitalize the names of the seasons.

   Fashions change every ~~S~~pring, ~~S~~ummer, ~~F~~all, and ~~W~~inter.
   (corrections above: s, s, f, w)

6. Countries, nationalities, races, and languages

   The **K**urds in **I**raq, **I**ran, **S**yria, **T**urkey, and other countries speak **K**urdish.

7. The names of school classes

   I took **S**ociology 101, **S**peech 150, and **M**ath 155.

   Do *not* capitalize the names of school subjects.

   I learned a lot about ~~S~~ociology, ~~P~~ublic ~~S~~peaking, and ~~C~~alculus.
   (corrections above: s, p, s, c)

8. The titles of books, magazines, essays, short stories, movies, television programs, songs, etc.

   In my English class, we studied Gothic works: We read Edgar Allen Poe's short story "**T**he **T**ell-**T**ale **H**eart" and Bram Stoker's novel *Dracula*, and we watched the movie *Frankenstein* and an episode of the TV series *Mystery*.

9. The names of relatives only if they are not preceded by a possessive adjective such as *my*

   This photograph, which was taken by **G**randpa, shows **G**randma with my mother and her sister.

Exercise 1

As you read this paragraph, supply the <u>twenty-five</u> missing capital letters. The first one has been done for you.

O

[1]on october 29, 1923, a military leader named Mustafa Kemal ended the ottoman Empire that had ruled Turkey for 600 years and established the republic of turkey. [2]During his fifteen-year presidency, Mustafa Kemal Ataturk, as he was called, introduced major political, legal, and social reforms in Turkey. [3]He separated political and religious leadership and introduced democracy. [4]He abolished religious laws and oversaw the writing of new legal codes based on european models which gave women equal rights. [5]Ataturk even changed the calendar and the language. [6]Roman letters replaced arabic script, and turkish words replaced borrowed arabic, persian, and french vocabulary. [7]education played a major role in implementing ataturk's reforms and in bringing about his modernization of turkey. [8]Ataturk unified the educational system and promoted the teaching of science so that turkish students would have the necessary skills to contribute to the country's economy. [9]In *ataturk: The biography of the founder of modern turkey*, turkish writer andrew mango states that Ataturk was "a statesman of supreme realism." [10]The turkish people call him Ataturk, that is, Father of the turks, because the Turkish parliament voted to give him that title in 1938.

■ 3. Colon

The colon has the following uses:

1. To introduce an explanation of the statement that precedes the colon

   For an adult, learning a second language is difficult: The adult learner has to learn numerous rules of grammar, multiple meanings of thousands of words, and complex social rules that affect use of the language in different situations.

2. To introduce a list that explains the noun or noun phrase that precedes the colon

   When I travel, I always carry the following items: a small pillow, a lightweight umbrella, and a tiny first aid kit.

To prepare to write an essay, follow these essential steps**:** Brainstorm, determine the main point you want to make, select two or three supporting points, and make an outline.

Do *not* use a colon after a verb or a preposition.

INCORRECT: My goals include: getting a bachelor's degree and finding an administrative position in the airline industry.

CORRECT: My goals include getting a bachelor's degree and finding an administrative position in the airline industry.

INCORRECT: In my personal library, I have several classics such as: *Moby-Dick* by Herman Melville, *Dream of the Red Chamber* by Tsao Hsueh-Chin, and *One Hundred Years of Solitude* by Gabriel García Márquez.

CORRECT: In my personal library, I have several classics: *Moby-Dick* by Herman Melville, *Dream of the Red Chamber* by Tsao Hsueh-Chin, and *One Hundred Years of Solitude* by Gabriel García Márquez.

■ 4. Comma

Use a **comma** in the following seven situations.

1. To separate items in a list (see Parallel Structure, page 254)

   The development of written language**,** the printing press**,** and the computer greatly increased human knowledge.

2. To separate independent clauses in compound sentences (see Coordination, page 252, and Sentence Types, page 272)

   Colleges and universities encourage the development of knowledge**,** and libraries encourage the sharing of knowledge.

3. After a dependent clause at the beginning of a sentence or before a dependent clause of comparison, contrast, or surprising result at the end of a sentence (see Adverb Clauses, page 239, and Sentence Types, page 272)

   Until public libraries were created**,** only the wealthy had access to books.

4. After a long prepositional phrase or a participial phrase (reduced adverb clause) at the beginning of a sentence

   With nearly 128 million items on approximately 530 miles of bookshelves**,** the Library of Congress is the biggest library in the world.

   Adding 10,000 new items to its collections every day**,** the Library of Congress has an enormous task to catalogue its holdings.

5. Before and after a non-restrictive adjective clause or reduced adjective clause (see Adjective Clauses, page 229)

   The Library of Alexandria**,** (which was) the most important library in the ancient world**,** was destroyed by fire.

6. Before and after a word or phrase that interrupts the flow of a sentence

    The Egyptian government, with the help of UNESCO, plans to build a new library on the site of the ancient Alexandrian library.

7. Before or after a quotation (see Quotation Marks, page 294)

    Thomas Carlyle said, "The greatest university of all is a collection of books."

EXERCISE 2

As you read this paragraph, supply the <u>nine</u> missing commas. The first one has been done for you.

¹Between about A.D. 250 and 900, the Maya of southern Mexico and Central America developed astronomy, mathematics three calendars, and a writing system. ²The Maya writing system consisted of about 800 symbols. ³These symbols stood for sounds, words, or entire sentences. ⁴After the Maya ruins were discovered in the nineteenth century scholars spent 100 years trying to decipher the writing system and now most of it can be read and understood. ⁵While very few Maya books have survived a good number of texts on buildings, stone monuments, small ornaments and ceramic vessels have been found. ⁶These texts or inscriptions have some interesting features. ⁷Inscriptions on stone monuments contain many dates referring to events in the lives of Maya leaders. ⁸The Maya who seem to have been keenly interested in time and dates took pains to record the dates of their leaders' births, marriages, and battles in great detail. ⁹Maya writing on small objects has another interesting feature: The text often names the object it is on, and it may even state the purpose of the object. ¹⁰For example, the text on cups often contains the word *cup* and sometimes says *chocolate*, indicating that the Maya used cups for a chocolate drink. ¹¹Another aspect of all Maya writing is that it accompanies pictures. ¹²Sometimes a picture of a person shows words near the mouth, indicating speech. ¹³For example, a painting on an eighth-century vase shows a scribe teaching mathematics and saying "Seven, eight, nine, twelve, thirteen, eleven." ¹⁴Maya writing can teach us a lot about who the Maya were and what kind of civilization they developed 1,100 to 1,750 years ago.

■ 5. Dash

The **dash** is an informal punctuation mark that is used for emphasis in place of the colon or the comma in these two situations.

1. Use a dash to introduce a list that explains the noun phrase before the dash.

   The store sells some unusual gadgets—backscratchers, foot warmers, and caps that have small umbrellas attached to them.

2. Use a dash before and after an interrupting phrase or clause.

   At the end of the movie—and this was my favorite part—a huge dinosaur-like monster destroyed the enemy's city.

Because the dash is informal, avoid using it in academic writing.

■ 6. Parentheses

Use **parentheses** to enclose supporting information that is less important than the rest of the information in a sentence.

The longest suspension bridge in the world is the Akashi Kayo Bridge in Japan (6,570 feet), and the second longest is the Storebaelt Bridge in Denmark (5,328 feet).

Whenever possible, avoid using parentheses and place supporting information directly into sentences.

■ 7. Period

The **period** is perhaps your most important punctuation mark. When you use a period at the end of a group of words, you send a signal to readers: You tell them that this group of words is a sentence, that is, a complete thought (see Sentence Types, page 272, and Logical Connectors, page 272).

Every sentence needs a period.

Periods are also used in some abbreviations.

Dr.   Mrs.   A.M.

Mr.   Ms.   P.M.

Many abbreviations (names referred to by their initials) do not include periods.

AIDS   IBM   the UK

the BBC   the UN   GM

Note that the abbreviations of states in the United States do not include periods.

Raleigh, NC   Los Angeles, CA

■ 8. Quotation Marks

Quotation marks have three uses: to show the actual words that someone said or wrote (direct speech); to show that there is something unusual about a word or phrase; to identify a title of a short story, essay, article, poem, or any other part of a book.

8a. Direct Speech

To show the actual words of a speaker or writer, follow these rules.

RULE 1 If a quotation is less than one sentence, don't place a comma before it or start it with a capital letter.

> My mother always said her parents were "as different as night and day."

RULE 2 Place a comma before a quoted sentence, and begin the sentence with a capital letter. If the end of the quotation is the end of the sentence, place a period *inside* the quotation marks.

> My grandmother always said, "Into every life a little rain must fall."

RULE 3 When a sentence continues beyond a quotation, place a comma *inside* the quotation marks.

> "Always look on the bright side," my grandfather would reply.

RULE 4 When a reporting phrase like *he said* interrupts a quoted sentence, place a comma at the end of the first part of the quoted sentence and at the end of the reporting phrase.

> "I don't know why," Grandma would say, "the children have to make so much noise."

RULE 5 When showing a quotation that is more than one sentence long, do not close the quotation marks until the end of the person's speech.

> Grandpa would reply, "They are having a good time. Let them be. Let's go out on the back porch."

RULE 6 When writing dialogue, start a new paragraph every time the speaker changes.

> "I'm afraid they'll break something or get hurt," Grandma fretted.
> "No, they won't," Grandpa said as he ushered her out the back door.

RULE 7 If a quotation is not introduced with a phrase like *Menander said* but with a full sentence, place a colon before the quotation.

> Menander, a playwright of ancient Greece, made the following statement: "The character of a man is known from his conversations."

8b. Quotation Marks that Signal Special Uses of Words

Use quotation marks to indicate that there is something special or unusual about a word or phrase, as in these four cases.

1. A word is being defined

   "Collaboration" means the act of working with others to achieve what you all want.

2. A foreign word is used

   The Cantonese word "ho-ho" means great happiness and good fortune.

3. A new word that has been invented to describe a new situation or a familiar word that is being used in a new way

   The company has developed a robotic window washer that they have decided to call a "washatron."

   In the "language" of driving, a turn signal is your request to other drivers that they allow you time to change lanes or turn.

4. A word that is not appropriate in a certain context, such as an idiom or a slang word or phrase that is used in an academic paper

   A political party is an institution that makes its own rules. Winning is everything, and parties will "fight tooth and nail" for electoral victories.

   When two individuals sign a legal contract, they are bound by the terms of the contract, and they cannot "weasel out" without facing legal consequences.

8c. Quotation Marks in Titles

Use quotation marks around the name of a short text that is part of a longer work, such as a story, essay, article, or poem. Underline the name of a book, newspaper, or magazine (or use italics if you are writing on a computer).

■ 9. Semicolon

A **semicolon** can replace a period between two sentences that you want the reader to see as closely connected.

   The instructor described his plan for the course; the students listened attentively.

You can use a semicolon in place of a period with transitions.

   My friend thought that a course in computer animation would be fun and easy; however, he soon discovered that animation programs are very complex.

Appendix II: Peer Review

Peer Review Form

■ **CHAPTER 1—*Role Models***　　　　　　　　　　　　　　　**EXPOSITORY PARAGRAPH**

WRITER: _____　　　　　　READER: _____

Read a classmate's paragraph and answer each of these questions.

1. Does the paragraph have three levels?　　　　　　　　　　　❏ yes　❏ no

2. Is the main idea stated in the topic sentence?　　　　　　　❏ yes　❏ no

   Write the controlling idea of the topic sentence. _____

   _____

3. Does the paragraph contain supporting points that are clearly presented
   in sentences?　　　　　　　　　　　　　　　　　　　　　　❏ yes　❏ no

4. Did the writer use examples, explanation, or quotations to develop the
   supporting points?　　　　　　　　　　　　　　　　　　　❏ yes　❏ no

   Are the examples and explanation specific enough?　　　　　❏ yes　❏ no

   If you would like more detailed examples, write questions to guide the writer.

   _____

   _____

5. Did the writer use transitions when necessary to mark the supporting points
   and examples?　　　　　　　　　　　　　　　　　　　　　❏ yes　❏ no

   If yes, write down two transitions the writer used.

   _____

6. Does the paragraph contain sentences with subordinating conjunctions?　❏ yes　❏ no

   If yes, write down two subordinating conjunctions the writer used. _____

   _____

7. Does the paragraph have a concluding sentence?　　　　　　❏ yes　❏ no

Peer Review Form

WRITER: _____   READER: _____

Read a classmate's essay and answer each of these questions.

1. What is the writer's thesis? Write the first three words. _____

    Does the thesis statement make clear that the writer will analyze the topic by logical division?   ❏ yes   ❏ no

    Does the thesis reveal the basis of division (time, place, aspects, etc.)?   ❏ yes   ❏ no

    What is the basis of division? _____

2. Do the thesis statement and the topic sentences of the body paragraphs clearly name the parts of the topic?   ❏ yes   ❏ no

    If not, explain. _____

    _____

3. Does the essay have cohesion?   ❏ yes   ❏ no

    If yes, what repeated words, synonyms, or transition words did the writer use to link the thesis statement to the topic sentences of the body paragraphs?

    _____

4. Do any of the body paragraphs need more development (examples or explanation)?   ❏ yes   ❏ no

    If yes, which one(s)? _____

    Write any questions you have that will help the writer expand the body paragraphs.

    _____

    _____

    _____

5. Did the writer use adjective clauses to include additional information in his or her sentences?   ❏ yes   ❏ no

    If not, can you suggest which sentence(s) the writer could add an adjective clause to? Write the first three words of that sentence or those sentences.

    _____

    _____

Peer Review Form

WRITER: _____   READER: _____

Read a classmate's essay and answer each of these questions.

1. What is the writer's thesis? _____

   _____

   _____

   Does the thesis make clear whether the essay will focus on causes or effects? ❑ yes ❑ no

2. What introduction strategy or strategies (background, general statement, anecdote) did the writer use?

   _____

   Do you think this strategy or these strategies are effective in this essay? ❑ yes ❑ no

   Why or why not? _____

   _____

3. Do the topic sentences of the body paragraphs clearly state the supporting points? ❑ yes ❑ no

4. Are the supporting points organized according to time order or order of importance? ❑ yes ❑ no

   If not, do you think the writer should use time order or order of importance? ❑ yes ❑ no

   If yes, explain. _____

   _____

5. Did the writer use transitions in the topic sentences of the body paragraphs to show you how the essay is organized? ❑ yes ❑ no

   Did the writer use other cohesive devices (repeated words, word forms, and synonyms) to link the thesis statement to the major supporting points? ❑ yes ❑ no

■ **CHAPTER 3—*Full Pockets, Empty Pockets***　　　　　**CAUSE-AND-EFFECT ESSAY**

6. Are the body paragraphs sufficiently developed?　　　　❑ yes　❑ no

If not, write some questions that will help the writer expand the body paragraphs.

_____

_____

Are there any problems with unity in the body paragraphs?　　❑ yes　❑ no

7. What strategy or strategies (summary, suggestion, prediction, opinion) did the writer use in the conclusion?

_____

Does the conclusion give you the sense that the essay is complete?　❑ yes　❑ no

Why or why not? _____

_____

8. Did the writer use the vocabulary and structures of cause and effect well?　❑ yes　❑ no

Which sentence(s), in your view, show the best use of cause-and-effect signals? _____

_____

_____

Peer Review Form

■ **CHAPTER 4—*Marriage and Family***   **COMPARISON/CONTRAST ESSAY**

WRITER: _____   READER: _____

Read a classmate's essay and answer each of these questions.

1. What two things is the writer comparing? _____

    _____

2. Does the paper discuss differences only, similarities only, or both similarities and differences?

    _____

    If it addresses both, which did the writer emphasize, and how do you know? _____

    _____

3. What pattern of organization does the essay have (side-by-side or point-by point)?

    _____

4. Are the points of comparison named in the thesis statement?   ❑ yes ❑ no

    What are the points of comparison? _____

    _____

5. Does the essay have balanced development? That is, are the two things being compared equally well developed, and are the points of comparison equally well developed?   ❑ yes ❑ no

    If you would like to see more development in some part of the essay, write some questions to guide the writer.

    _____

    _____

■ **CHAPTER 4—*Marriage and Family***   **COMPARISON/CONTRAST ESSAY**

6. Does the essay have good cohesion overall?   ❑ yes   ❑ no

Check off (✔) the strategies the writer used to link the thesis statement to the topic sentences of the body paragraphs.

_____ repeated words   _____ transitions

_____ word forms   _____ similar sentence beginnings

_____ synonyms   _____ correlative conjunctions (*not only . . . but also*)

7. What point of view did the writer use in most of the essay?

_____ first person singular   _____ first person plural

_____ second person

_____ third person singular   _____ third person plural

Did the writer change pronoun point of view only when necessary?   ❑ yes   ❑ no

8. Did the writer use comparison/contrast signals effectively?   ❑ yes   ❑ no

Peer Review Form

WRITER: _____   READER: _____

Read a classmate's essay and answer each of these questions.

1. Does the introduction engage your interest in the topic?   ❏ yes   ❏ no

   Would you have used a different introduction strategy (general statement, background, anecdote, definition, quotation, turnabout)? _____

   _____

2. Does the introduction define and limit the topic?   ❏ yes   ❏ no

   If not, what would you like it to define, or how would you like the topic to be limited?

   _____

3. How many supporting arguments did the writer include? _____

   Did the writer use transitions to link the supporting arguments and provide cohesion?   ❏ yes   ❏ no

4. Are the supporting arguments developed in a balanced way?   ❏ yes   ❏ no

   Check (✔) the development strategies the writer used.

   _____ the ideas of authorities   _____ examples

   _____ facts   _____ cause-and-effect reasoning

   _____ explanation   _____ comparison

   In your opinion, which body paragraph contains the most persuasive or the best-developed supporting argument?

   _____

5. Did the writer include an opposing point of view?   ❏ yes   ❏ no

   If yes, in what part of the essay does the opposing view appear? _____

   Did the writer respond to the opposing view effectively?   ❏ yes   ❏ no

   If you would have responded to the opposing view differently, explain. _____

   _____

6. Did the writer use any conditional statements in the essay?   ❏ yes ❏ no

If yes, do you think the use of conditional statements is effective?   ❏ yes ❏ no

Did the writer use any qualifiers in the essay?   ❏ yes ❏ no

If yes, do you think the use of qualifiers is effective?   ❏ yes ❏ no

Explain. _____

_____

7. Is the conclusion of the essay effective?   ❏ yes ❏ no

If yes, what elements make it effective?

_____ restatement of the thesis   _____ a prediction about the future

_____ a summary of the main points   _____ a warning about possible future consequences

_____ a suggestion   _____ other (explain) _____

Index

topic sentence, 12, 14, 26–29
transitions, 34–36
expository writing, 12

facts, for development of body paragraphs, 96
final draft, 42, 71–72, 111, 150, 187
focusing, 19. *See also* brainstorming
for example, 35
for instance, 35
fragments, 277–78

general statements, 91, 249
gerunds, 257–58, 274

hyphens, with noun modifiers, 236

implicit opinions, 158
indefinite article, 248, 249
indent, 24
independent clauses, 272
indirect object, 219
infinitives, 257–58
information gap, 223
in or *in terms of*, controlling ideas introduced by, 131–32
in-text citations, 214–15
introductions for essays, 63–64
  argumentative essay, 172–73
  cause-and-effect essay, 90–94
  comparison/contrast essay, 129–31

like, 35
list, transitions signaling, 34–35
logical connectors, 272–73. *See also* conjunctions; prepositions; transitions
logical division, 49–50
  vocabulary for, 58

main point, 12. *See also* thesis statement; topic sentence
  identifying, 220
  paraphrasing, 222–23
MLA (Modern language association) citations styles, 214
  end-of-text, 216
  in-text, 215
modal verbs, 180–81, 280–83
  in conditional statements, 184
  as qualifiers, 185–86

nonrestrictive clause, 231
not only... but also, 136
noun clauses, 258–62
noun modifiers, 67, 236
noun phrases, expanding, 66–68
nouns, 27, 262–63
  adjectives used as, 79

cause-and-effect, 105
countable and uncountable, 249, 263
definite, 248–49
irregular, 262
possessive, 288
noun suffixes, 9, 287

objects
  direct, 229, 257, 258, 270
  indirect, 219
  object pronouns, 265
  of prepositions, 230, 257, 258, 264
of which, 232
opinion. *See also* argumentative essay
  concluding with, 100
  implicit, 158
opposing view, 164, 176–79
outline
  for cause-and-effect essay, 87
  for comparison/contrast essays, 126–27
  expanding a paragraph to an essay and, 55
  for expository paragraph, 15–19, 21
  three levels of development, 21, 52, 87
outside sources, 174, 190
  citing, 191, 214–19

paragraph. *See also* body paragraphs in essay; expository paragraph
  development, 13–14, 21, 32–34, 52
  form, 24–25
  levels and outlining, 52
  summary, 223
  support, 12–14, 29
    major supporting points, 12–13, 26–29
    specific support, 13–14, 32–34
  three levels, 12, 52
  topic sentence, 12, 14, 26–29
parallel lists for comparison/contrast essays, 124
parallel structure, 254–55, 256
  after *in* or *in terms of*, 132
  in thesis statements, 60
paraphrasing, 198–213
  identifying source, 205
  integrating source material in body paragraphs, 211–13
  partial, 209–11
  plagiarism distinguished from, 204–5
  strategies, 199–204
  in summary, 222–23
  word changes to avoid, 204
parentheses, 293
partial paraphrase, 209–11
participial adjectives, 80–81, 237–39
participles, 80, 283, 284
particles, 285

parts of speech, 269–70
passive voice, 279
past participle, 80, 283, 284
peer review forms, 296–303
period, 293
persuasive argument, 157
phrasal verbs, 285
phrase, 272
    adjective, 30, 234
    adverb, 246
    gerund and infinitive, 258
    noun, 66–68
    prepositional, 67, 264
    synonymous, 147
place, as basis of division, 49–50
plagiarism, 174, 190
    paraphrasing distinguished from, 204–5
point-by-point organization, 122–23, 126
pointing words, 138
point of view, 140–43
    analyzing topic to decide, 162–63
    change in, 141
    consistent, 140–43
    opposing, 164, 176–79
points of comparison, 118, 121, 125, 126
possessives, 138, 265, 288
prediction, concluding with, 100
prefixes, 286–87
prepositional phrases, 67, 264
prepositions, 264, 273
    multiword, 109
    objects of, 230, 257, 258, 264
    particles, in phrasal verbs, 285
present participle, 80, 283, 284
prewriting, 19
    brainstorming cluster for, 86
    brainstorming list for, 19, 84, 85
        parallel lists, 124
    focusing, 19
pronouns, 265–69
    agreement, 265–66
    always singular, 274
    cohesion and, 138, 268–69
    object, 265
    point of view, 140–43
    possessive, 265
    reference, 266–67
    reflexive, 265
    relative, 68–71, 229–33
    subject, 265
punctuation, 288–95
purpose, 50

qualifiers, 185–87
quantity, expressions of, 249–50
    comparatives and superlatives, 251–52
    with countable and uncountable nouns, 263
quantity words, 138
quotation marks, 294–95
    direct speech, 294
    signaling special uses of words, 295
    in titles, 295
quotations, 14, 33, 190–98
    brackets in, 193
    combining paraphrases and, 209–11
    ellipsis in, 192
    punctuation for, 191
    within quotations, 195–96
    responding to, 196–98

reason clauses, 109
    reducing adverbial, 242
refutation, signaling, 176–79
related words, paragraph cohesion and, 138
relative pronoun, 68–71, 229–33
reported speech, 259–62
reporting verbs, 219
research paper, 190–219
    citing sources in, 191, 214–19
    paraphrasing in, 198–213
    quotations in, 190–98
    summarizing in, 220–27
restrictive clause, 231
revising, 54
    argumentative essay, 172–87
    cause-and-effect essay, 89–108
    comparison/contrast essay, 129–49
    expository paragraph, 25–41
run-on sentences, 275–77

semicolon, 107, 295
sensory information, 96
sentences, 269–78. *See also* topic sentence(s)
    combining, 38–41, 201, 272, 273
    complements, 271
    complex, 272
    compound, 272
    concluding, 37
    conditional, 182–85, 243–45
    fragments, 277–78
    parts, 270–71
    run-ons, 275–77
    simple, 272
    subjects, 270
    subject-verb agreement in, 274–75
    types, 272
    verbs, 270–71